Dad, I wish
I was normal

Dad, I wish I was normal

A diary of obsession

Richard Vos

JARRAH ❦ PRESS

National Library of Australia Cataloguing-in-Publication entry

A catalogue record for this book is available from the National Library of Australia

NATIONAL LIBRARY OF AUSTRALIA

ISBN
978-0-6482788-0-1 (paperback)
978-0-6482788-1-8 (hardback)
978-0-6482788-2-5 (ebook)

Permission
The author is grateful for permission to include the following previously copyrighted material:
Excerpt from a Wall Street Journal article, *Modern Witch Hunt – Child Abuse Charges* written by Richard Gardner and published on February 22, 1993. Reprinted with permission of The Wall Street Journal, Copyright ©1993 Dow Jones & Company, Inc. All Rights Reserved Worldwide. License number 4293860637540
Excerpt from *Outbreak! The Encyclopedia of Extraordinary Social Behavior*, written by Hilary Evans and Robert Bartholomew, published by Anomalist Books. Copyright © 2009. Reprinted by permission of the publisher.

Printed & Channel Distribution
Lightning Source | Ingram (USA/UK/EUROPE/AUS)
Cover design: Pickawoowoo Publishing Group. Laila Savolainen
Interior typeset: Pickawoowoo Publishing Group

Publisher
Jarrah Press
www.jarrahpress.com

For Elizabeth and Jennifer

For them that quail to bring men out of ignorance, as I have quailed, and as you quail now when you know in all your black hearts that this be fraud — God damns our kind especially, and we will burn, we will burn together!

Arthur Miller, *The Crucible*

If you haven't the strength to impose your own terms upon life, then you must accept the terms it offers you.

TS Eliot

Contents

Author's Note x

Acknowledgements...xi

Main Characters..xii

Prologue...1

Introduction 3

Part One, USA: July 13, 1992 – July 20, 1993 .... **9**

Chapter 1. Ten Days to Ritual Abuse 11

Chapter 2. Paul Roland and the Abyss..21

Chapter 3. Waiting on Schwartz 31

Chapter 4. Some Family History 40

Chapter 5. On Thin Ice..44

Chapter 6. Schwartz Talks Again..51

Chapter 7. Abigail and Dale 54

Chapter 8. Mikee and Alan 58

Chapter 9. Questioning...61

Chapter 10. Multiple Personality Disorder......................................67

Chapter 11. Goodbye, Tom Dohne 75

Chapter 12. Hello, Penny Blake 82

Chapter 13. I Want an Expert 85

Chapter 14. Satanic Ritual Abuse 90

Chapter 15. The Behaviour War 101

Chapter 16. Barbara Tillman and the Ritual Abuse Swamp.............107

Chapter 17. Albuquerque...114

Chapter 18. Back to Tillman and the Swamp 118

Chapter 19. Elizabeth Sees Tillman 127

Chapter 20. Out in The Cold 133

Chapter 21. Madness and Depression 137

Chapter 22. Calm and Codependency 148

Chapter 23. Veronica Oliver-Bell..152

Chapter 24. The Veronica Tapes – Part One............................162

Chapter 25. Tillman's perspective 171

Chapter 26. The Veronica Tapes – Part Two............................175

Chapter 27. The Tulsa Justice Center and the American Endgame....192

Part Two, Australia: July 22, 1993 – August 12, 2010..................201

Chapter 28. The Obsession Travels 203

Chapter 29. The Lull Before School 215

Chapter 30. School Starts..218

Chapter 31. Would I Be Normal if It Wasn't for The Monsters?.......220

Chapter 32. Epilepsy 225

Chapter 33. The Move to Margaret River 230

Chapter 34. Retirement 235

Chapter 35. The Obsession Returns 238

Chapter 36. Cape Town...248

Chapter 37. Back into the Fray 252

Chapter 38. India...258

Chapter 39. On Borrowed Time..263

Chapter 40. Divorce and Departure 267

Chapter 41. Last Contact and Loss 276

Epilogue...285

Postscript: Jenny's Short Story 290

Further Reading..298

Apendices 300

Author Biography 322

Author's Note

This is my story about the tragedy that struck my family, and especially my daughter Elizabeth. The story is drawn from diaries, journals, therapists' and medical reports, audiotapes and my memories. It is my version of events, told as truthfully and as accurately as the data sources and my memories allow. It is a cautionary tale of the tragic consequences of hysteria and obsession. It is also a tale of weakness in the face of fraud.

Acknowledgements

I was inspired to write my story after reading Meredith Maran's memoir, *My Lie, A True Story of False Memory*. Maran wrote her book to explain how she came to falsely accuse her father of sexual abuse, and to make amends. Her story is a moving account of her personal journey, and an excellent synopsis of the recovered memory hysteria that destroyed so many lives and so many families in the 1980s and 1990s. Thank you, Meredith.

My heartfelt thanks to those who read drafts of my story and offered valuable suggestions. My ever supportive and loving partner, Elaine Symons. My amazing sister, Suzanne Vos. My good friends Paul Downes, Marilyn Hopkins, David Mason-Jones, Deborah Pallet, Keith Rasmussen and Lesly Smith. David Mason-Jones also edited an early version of the manuscript, helping me on my way to fewer exclamation marks. Eddie Albrecht provided excellent copyedit advice and wonderfully supportive comments. And, finally, a huge thank you to Tony Ryan, whose structural and copyedit suggestions helped reduce a two hundred thousand word document by half, and guided the telling of my story to its completion. When I thought I'd told my story as best I could, Tony, you urged me to use my voice and do better. Your advice was invaluable.

A big thank you to the team at Pickawoowoo Publishing Group for helping bring this book to life.

Main Characters

Some of the people who populate this story are given their real names, including my family and relatives, as well as some of the therapists and doctors who crowd its pages. The names of others have been changed to protect their privacy, especially friends, teachers, babysitters, acquaintances and staff at day care centres.

The main characters are listed below in groups, beginning first with my family and relatives, and then the country in which they enter the story. The characters are listed alphabetically by first name, or surname if no first name is used.

My family and relatives:

Richard Vos: father of Elizabeth and Jennifer

Niki Vos: mother of Elizabeth and Jennifer

Elizabeth Vos: daughter of Richard and Niki

Jennifer Vos: daughter of Richard and Niki

Dell: mother of Richard Vos

Gerard: father of Richard Vos

Suzanne: sister of Richard Vos

Charlie: father of Niki Vos

Faye: mother of Niki Vos

Carmen: sister of Niki Vos

Chuck: brother of Niki Vos

Uncle Billy: brother of Niki's father, Charlie

Wilson, Carmen's son, cousin to Elizabeth and Jennifer

Yvonne: Uncle Billy's wife

People who enter the story in the USA:

Abigail and Dale: adult babysitters, Bartlesville

Barbara Tillman: social worker and therapist, Bartlesville

The Bruces: parents of sexual abuse victim, Peter Bruce, Bartlesville

David King: attorney, Bartlesville

Ethan: son of Rachel and John, Bartlesville

Faye Hegburg: social worker and therapist, Bartlesville

Jake: Rick's therapist in Albuquerque

John: husband of Rachel, father of Ethan, Bartlesville

Judy Richman: social worker, Tulsa Justice Center

Kacey: teenage babysitter, Bartlesville

Dr Kramer: psychiatrist, Tulsa

Dr Linda Doyle: Elizabeth's paediatrician, Bartlesville

Linda Foster: social worker, Department of Human Services, Bartlesville

Miss Mabel: director, Children's Home Day Care, Bartlesville

Mike Miller: police officer, Bartlesville

Mikee and Alan: older boys at Children's Home Day Care, Bartlesville

Paul Roland: attorney and church deacon, Bartlesville

Dr Paul Schwartz: clinical psychologist and therapist, Tulsa

Penny Blake: employee, child advocacy program, Bartlesville

Peter Bruce: sexual abuse victim, Bartlesville

Rachel: Niki's friend, mother of Ethan, wife of John, Bartlesville

Rick: Niki's friend, victim of satanic ritual abuse, Albuquerque

Sandra: Niki's friend, works at Call Rape, Tulsa

Dr Tom Dohne: clinical psychologist and family therapist, Bartlesville

Veronica Oliver-Bell: social worker and therapist, Tulsa

People who enter the story in Australia:

Dr Geoff Dixon: child and adolescent psychiatrist, Princess Margaret Hospital, Perth

Helen Davidson: occupational therapist, Princess Margaret Hospital, Perth

Jodie: clinical psychologist and therapist, Margaret River

Liz Riley: psychologist and therapist, Perth

Michele: occupational therapist, Margaret River

Dr Silberstein: neurologist, Perth

Prologue

Wednesday March 19, 1997

Elizabeth and I walk toward the hospital for another medical test. Just seven years old, she has a courageous spirit and keeps up an adult pace, focused ahead, holding tight to my right hand with her left. Then she slows, turns and looks up at me. 'Dad, I wish I was normal,' she says, with sad, pleading eyes.

'You are normal, sweetheart. You're a great, normal kid,' I reply, trying to sound positive.

At that moment my heart breaks. My precious daughter thinks she's not normal. I have not protected her enough. I have not done enough. I have completely failed Elizabeth. This is the worst moment of my life.

* * *

It took five years to reach that moment. In July of 1992, my wife Niki told me she believed that Elizabeth, at two years of age, had been forced to participate in torture, pornography, satanic ritual abuse and other perverse cult activities. She suspected babysitters, day care centre employees, and sometimes me.

Medical examinations showed no evidence of mistreatment, and a parade of therapists couldn't diagnose sexual abuse, but Niki remained utterly convinced it had happened. What was going on? To cope with the craziness I began a diary. My diary records what happened, but I don't know why it happened. What colliding eddies in the swirling currents of Niki's life made her obsessed with the belief our two-year-old daughter had suffered ritual abuse?

The therapists engaged to diagnose Elizabeth's abuse became more concerned with Niki's obsession and her constant questioning of

Elizabeth: 'Who are the naughty people?' 'Who are the monsters?' 'What did they do to you?' This questioning went on for years, locking Elizabeth inside Niki's fixation and eroding the love in our marriage, lighting a fuse that smouldered for fifteen years until our family finally exploded in March 2007.

Three years after the explosion, and nearly eighteen years after Niki's delusion began, Elizabeth, at twenty years of age, stunned me with news of a bizarre mental health diagnosis. When I tried to explain what I saw happen to her as a child, that her mother's obsession had brainwashed and disabled her, she told me goodbye.

This is my diary of an obsession built around a fantasy, a story of hysteria, a lost grip on reality, and weakness in the face of fraud.

Introduction

In the 1980s and early-to-mid-1990s, America seemed to go quite mad. Entire communities believed their children were being raped and tortured by sex rings and Satanists. An epidemic of accusations involving pornography, sexual abuse and satanic ritual abuse swept across the country.

The epidemic began when hundreds of adults were accused of the abuse of children in day care centres. The media storm accompanying these accusations led to widespread panic, and the abuse of children in day care became a national fixation. Of the hundreds of childcare workers and parents who were prosecuted, nearly half were convicted. These felons were punished with long terms of imprisonment – often consecutive life terms. Proof of guilt rested on the children's statements and testimonies. No physical evidence was found to corroborate the accusations: no blood, no semen, no injuries, no satanic covens, no pornographic pictures, no satanic paraphernalia. Nothing.

As the day care panic spread, Americans were stunned by a second set of accusations, which layered neatly onto the first. Psychotherapists claimed repressed memories of childhood abuse were the underlying cause of many, if not most, of the mental, emotional, behavioural and relationship problems experienced by women. A frenzy of recovered memory therapy revealed vast hidden reservoirs of incest and abuse in women who'd previously had no such memories. Diagnoses of repressed memories were often embellished with diagnoses of 'multiple personality disorder' and 'satanic ritual abuse'. Researchers estimate several million women in recovered memory therapy accused family members and friends of abusing them when they were children. Some of the accused were prosecuted and imprisoned. Again, no evidence corroborated the accusations. Proof of guilt rested on recovered memories.

Together, the day care and recovered memory abuse accusations sent a tsunami of abuse hysteria through the media, through psychotherapy, through the criminal justice system and through American neighbour-hoods. I lived in one of those neighbourhoods. My family, and especially my daughter Elizabeth, was picked up and tumbled around in the froth and surge of this tsunami.

In the decades that followed, almost all of those convicted and impris-oned were exonerated and freed. The accusations were proven false, and the convictions a miscarriage of justice. How did this happen?

History yields examples of social hysteria setting the stage for injus-tice. In 1692, in Salem, Massachusetts, more than two hundred people were accused of practising witchcraft on children. Those who confessed (usually under torture) were freed. Those who would not confess were prosecuted: nineteen were hanged (fourteen of them women), one man was pressed to death by stones, and four died in prison. No physical evi-dence corroborated the charges. The convictions rested on the testimony of children, who claimed the accused had exercised supernatural power over them. This power was demonstrated in court by 'spectral evidence', whereby the accused person's spirit – which the children claimed to see – left their body to inflict pain and fits on the children. Their screams and faints in court settled the matter.

In the child abuse trials of the 1980s and 1990s, it was also the tes-timony of the children, including memories recovered from childhood, that settled the matter.

Numerous appalling cases of physical and sexual abuse of children in homes and institutions are well documented. This terrible and agonis-ingly sad reality is not in question. The abuse of children is an abhorrent act, and accused suspects, even before guilt is proven, are generally despised. This visceral response to alleged evildoers was certainly appar-ent in America in the 1980s and 1990s.

Leading the charge against the evildoers were parents, police and prosecutors, who abandoned the presumption of innocence. Their coer-cive questioning of children elicited a kaleidoscope of incredible and often implausible accusations. If children at first denied anything bad had happened to them, investigators persisted with suggestive, leading and even bullying questions until the right answers were provided. These fabricated statements were then used in criminal prosecutions.

Charging alongside the parents, police and prosecutors was a phalanx of psychiatrists, psychotherapists and social workers, who, through their own coercive, suggestive and leading questioning, also elicited falsehoods from children. And not just children – adult women in therapy recovered false memories of horrific childhood abuse.

Right behind these charging parents, police, prosecutors, psychotherapists and social workers was the galloping media, eager to leap onto the bandwagon of abuse hysteria hurtling across the American cultural landscape. Books, radio programs, television news and talk shows, newspaper and magazine articles, and even popular movies, shouted a warning to the shocked, gullible and salaciously entertained American public: 'Child sexual abuse and satanic cults are all around you!'

As the saying goes, a lie travels halfway around the world before the truth gets its boots on. Fortunately, with scepticism and a search for evidence, the truth can catch up with a lie.

Following the executions in Salem, the Massachusetts state legislature informed Salem's magistrates that a prosecution based on 'spectral evidence' could not be refuted because it could not be proved. The governor of Massachusetts dismissed the court, and several children admitted that their accusations had been false. Five years later the jurors in the trials signed a statement of repentance, declaring they had brought upon themselves, 'the guilt of innocent blood', apologised for acting on 'spectral evidence' and admitted, 'we justly fear we were sadly deluded and mistaken'.

A similar awakening to injustice occurred in the decades following the epidemic of bizarre child abuse accusations in the 1980s and 1990s. One of the judges involved in overturning some of the prior convictions, Isaac Borenstein, stated the following in 1998:

> Overzealous and inadequately trained investigators, perhaps unaware of the grave dangers of using improper interviewing and investigative techniques, questioned these children and parents in a climate of panic, if not hysteria, creating a highly prejudicial and irreparable set of mistakes. These grave errors led to the testimony of the children being forever tainted.

Before Judge Borenstein, and others like him, could make such profound rulings, it required the dogged efforts of lawyers and investigative journalists to prove the convictions rested on tainted evidence. Standing alongside the lawyers and journalists were memory scientists, who – sometimes in the face of personal attacks and lawsuits – testified in court on the dangers of coercive, leading and suggestive questioning of both children and adults, and the creation of false memories. 'Recovered memory therapy', 'satanic ritual abuse' and rampant 'multiple personality disorder' were eventually debunked as hysterical fads and hoaxes, and the rules of criminal investigation were rewritten to prevent tainted testimony arising from the improper questioning of children.

These welcome outcomes provided little comfort to all the people whose lives had been destroyed, whose families had been shattered, and whose freedom had been stolen. The casualties – the total number of people impacted by this hysteria – are estimated by researchers to be in the millions. They include the childcare workers, parents, relatives and family friends who were falsely imprisoned, or, if not convicted, ruinously slandered. They include the children and adults who falsely believed they were victims of childhood abuse. And they include the members of families torn apart by the abuse accusations. Many still suffer from their injuries.

This era of abuse hysteria is widely considered the most disgraceful episode in the history of American psychotherapy. Numerous books, studies and investigative articles document this debacle from legal, personal, psychiatric and sociological perspectives.

When I read these accounts of implausible accusations and flawed prosecutions, I despair that such an outbreak of irrational hysteria was allowed to permeate society and destroy so many lives. And I feel cheated, in a self-righteous way, because this hysteria and injustice has not been showcased – at least, not with the same enthusiasm with which the media broadcast the false abuse accusations – as an example of what happens when reason and truth are sacrificed on the altar of hysteria and delusion. An aggrieved part of me wants to share in the reparations of a loud societal mea culpa, because my family also was destroyed by this hysteria.

I was not falsely accused of child abuse, but I so easily could have been. Year after year, as my daughters grew up, I witnessed episodes of hysteria in my own home. I said and did nothing. I naively assumed the crazy behaviour would, one day, end. And I was too scared to speak out for fear of losing my children. So why do I wonder that irrational forces prevailed in society when they prevailed in my own home? And why should I expect society to loudly protest this injustice and reconcile with itself, and reconcile with me, when I've never uttered a single protest of my own? And what right do I have to expect others to speak out when I listen to my own mealy-mouthed excuses to remain silent?

For years after losing my family to the same hysterical forces in play in the 1980s and 1990s, I choked on silent screams of grief and frustration. This felt unsustainable. To find relief I had to muster the courage to raise my voice in protest at the frauds and hoaxes that percolate through society creating falsehoods, and flow through the murky backwaters of wacky therapy, dispensing refuted diagnoses. I had to scream out loud and tell my story.

Part One

USA:
July 13, 1992 – July 20, 1993

one

Ten Days To Ritual Abuse

Monday July 13, 1992

Today seems like just another day. I'm a forty-two-year-old geologist working at Phillips Petroleum Company's corporate headquarters in the small, quiet Midwestern town of Bartlesville, Oklahoma. Born and raised in Perth, Australia, I have till now lived a truly magical life of adventure and learning. My first eighteen years were spent in the surf and bushland of south-west Australia. For the next twenty-four years I travelled the world – studying and teaching geology, exploring for oil and touring through parts of Europe, Africa, America, China and India.

Today, as on so many other days, my wife Niki visits her friend Rachel with our two daughters, Elizabeth and Jennifer. Niki is a full-time mother and housewife – loving, kind and devoted. Elizabeth just turned three in May and Jenny is ten months old, born in September last year. Rachel has a four-year-old son, Ethan.

When I arrive home from work Niki tells me she's very worried about Elizabeth. 'She was playing doctor with Ethan and stormed back to me saying, "Ethan isn't my friend anymore. I don't like him. I want to go home."'

Niki says she asked how Ethan hurt her, and Elizabeth said he poked her in the tummy and touched her tee-tee.

'Richard,' Niki exclaims, 'she was very upset!'

I check to see if Elizabeth's okay. She's happy, watching a Disney video. When I try to talk to her, she's annoyed by my interruption. 'Elizabeth seems cranky at you,' Niki says, 'and I'm really worried about that too.'

It doesn't bother me. Elizabeth's not afraid to express her displeasure with anyone. She has a robust sense of her status as our miracle baby. With only one faulty ovary, Niki told me children weren't likely. Well, the ovary agreed to a pregnancy on our honeymoon in South Africa. We joked that this miracle conception resulted from our appetite for Indian curries.

Niki and I married in August 1988, four months after meeting, when she was thirty-eight years old. Side by side, we were an image of opposites: my tall, lean, athletic frame beside her short, round figure; my quiet, analytical introversion next to her eccentric, assertive nature; my life built on a foundation of science next to her passion for the mystical. But we loved each other. I loved her artistic talent and intuitive imaginings. Niki loved my scholarly, patient and dependable personality.

Before marriage, my dream was to work as a geologist in America until about forty-five years of age and then return home to Perth. Now, my dream has become our dream. And we have two beautiful daughters. Our family's future looks nothing but bright, prosperous and happy.

Tuesday July 14, 1992

This morning Niki calls me at work, still worried about Elizabeth.

'Richard, I think her strong reaction to Ethan yesterday is because of sexual abuse. My mother and my sister, and even my mother's housekeeper, think Elizabeth has a sexual aura and is provocative and flirty.'

Sexual abuse? Why has Niki leapt to this drastic conclusion? Surely there's a benign explanation for Elizabeth's upset with Ethan, and Niki's mother and sister have highly dramatic personalities. But what grandmother or auntie looks at a three-year-old and sees a sexual aura? What is Elizabeth doing that's provocative and flirty?

Niki then says she called her friend Sandra who works at Call Rape in Tulsa, an hour's drive south of Bartlesville.

'Sandra said I should contact Dr Schwartz, a psychologist who specialises in child sexual abuse. Richard, I've made an urgent appointment for this Friday. And I took Elizabeth to Dr Doyle. Linda said she hasn't been penetrated.'

Elizabeth is scheduled for sexual abuse therapy, starting this Friday? And she's been examined for sexual penetration by her paediatrician? What's going on?

When I arrive home from work, Niki barely greets me and Elizabeth doesn't want to play. Dinner is quickly served and Elizabeth clings to Niki, demanding to sit on her lap. A moment after settling, she looks at me scornfully and says, 'I don't like you.' 'I don't like you' is her refrain to anyone who causes her displeasure.

Speaking slowly and deliberately, like they've rehearsed their lines, Niki tells Elizabeth, 'Now, you tell Daddy why you don't like him.'

'Because he touched my tee-tee.'

I'm stunned. When those words sink in, I ask, 'Niki, do you think I've sexually abused Elizabeth?' I can't believe she thinks that.

'I'm giving equal weight to all possibilities,' she replies. 'As a retired counsellor, I know what people do to children.'

I can't believe I'm having this conversation. 'Niki, I know I have not abused Elizabeth. And I know you have not abused Elizabeth.'

Niki stuns me again. 'Richard, I include myself as a possible abuse perpetrator. We can do things and not remember it.'

That's absurd. 'Niki, I know I have not abused Elizabeth.'

After dinner, I play with Elizabeth; we have our usual run-around chase and I read her a story. But most of the evening's a blur. Eventually I go to my bedroom. For months Niki has slept with the girls in a separate room, to comfort Elizabeth with her constant ear infections, to more easily night-feed baby Jenny and to help us both sleep.

I can't sleep. What the hell is this about? I know children are abused, but I know I haven't abused Elizabeth. Has Niki questioned her? Asked her, 'Did Daddy touch your tee-tee?' Why else would she say that? I get up and write down the evening's back-and-forth dialogue. Writing is my reaction to stress. Niki also gets up and comes to the study, and I tell her, 'Niki, I feel like I was set up. Listen to my notes of what was said tonight and you tell me if they're accurate.'

'I'm sorry,' Niki says. 'I was klutzy the way the issue was raised.'

Niki insists I tear up my notes. But I don't tear up my memory, and I keep making notes.

Wednesday July 15, 1992

This morning, Niki calls me at work, excited and friendly, and in a conspiratorial tone tells me, 'Richard, Elizabeth is revealing about Mikee and Alan. She said, "Mikee and Alan are naughty boys, and Alan hurt me with his gun."'

I'm not the abuse perpetrator. It was Mikee and Alan, older boys who attended Children's Home Day Care with Elizabeth once or twice a week, early this year.

Revealing? Does this therapy-speak mean Elizabeth has harboured dark secrets about Mikee and Alan for six months, and now, suddenly, wants to reveal their bad behaviour? Or is she responding to questioning? Niki believes Elizabeth's been sexually abused, and is on a mission to find out what happened and who did it. But has Elizabeth been abused? Or is this a witch-hunt?

Thursday July 16, 1992

This evening Niki's exhausted, anxious and agitated, like she's upset by bad news. After we bathe the girls for the night, she shares her news with me. Facing each other in the bathroom, Niki tells me that today she used her counselling skills and allowed Elizabeth to direct their play with nude Barbie dolls.

'Richard, it was awful,' Niki says, distressed. 'I was horrified by her sexual energy. She sucked on my fingers, wanted to French-kiss, wanted me to tickle her tee-tee, wanted me to lie on her. Then she climbed all over me, threw her legs around my neck and brought her crotch near my mouth. Then she pulled a tape measure in and out and sucked on the tape.' Niki says she thinks Elizabeth's performed oral sex, licked men's penises and participated in other sex acts.

I'm dazed. These are horrendous conclusions. 'Niki,' I try to reason, 'Elizabeth plays dancing and kissing Barbie dolls with me. She copies the dancing and kissing in the Walt Disney videos. And she climbs over me, and it doesn't feel sexual. And French-kissing is the term you taught her for the mouth-to-mouth kissing in all the videos. Niki, it's your term.'

I also tell Niki that if Elizabeth's performed oral sex on men, surely she would act differently around me. She's seen me step out of the shower naked, but hasn't said anything about touching someone's anatomy, like mine.

'Well,' Niki replies, adamant, distraught, 'I believe Elizabeth's been tricked by game-playing into performing oral sex.' Niki goes on, eyes locked onto mine, conveying utter conviction in her beliefs, 'And I asked Elizabeth, "Who likes to French-kiss?" and she said, "Miss Mabel".'

Miss Mabel is the director of Children's Home Day Care.

I've lost my bearings. I need a signpost back to the real world. I know I'm in our bathroom, in our home, in our real world. But what just happened – what Niki just said – is off the planet.

Friday July 17, 1992

Today we drive south to Tulsa to meet Dr Schwartz. On the way, Niki tells me that this morning Elizabeth saw a neighbour and said, 'She's a bad lady called Miss Mabel who puts apples with worms into my mouth.'

Does Niki believe this? 'Niki,' I say, 'I've watched the videos *Snow White* and *Sleeping Beauty* with Elizabeth. I said the witch put poisoned apples into the children's mouths because the witch is a bad lady. That's probably where her comment comes from.'

Niki ignores my explanation. 'Well, Elizabeth's building sand piles in our backyard and she's putting holes into the sand and she's putting holes into playdough. And she's touching baby Jenny's bottom in the bath in a sexual way.'

Holes in sand and holes in playdough? Does Niki think the holes represent vaginas? I don't ask.

Our conversations have become mini debates. Niki describes concerning behaviour by Elizabeth, which she believes indicates sexual abuse, and I respond with an alternate explanation, hoping to calm her. We're reading from different reality scripts. I sense I'm watching an unravelling ball of string roll away from me, toward craziness. As hard as I try to wind the loose thread back around logic and reason, it slips off again.

Paul Schwartz is middle-aged and fit, with a serious demeanour. He greets us in his bright, modern low-rise office.

Niki tells Schwartz, 'I believe Elizabeth may have been sexually abused at Children's Home Day Care.'

Schwartz replies in a confident, concise, no-nonsense manner: 'It's difficult with three-year-olds to find out what really happened. I'll see Elizabeth for three sessions and then put my cards on the table. If I think sexual abuse occurred, I'll have to report your case to the Department of Human Services.'

Saturday July 18, 1992

By late this morning, Niki's anxiety has spiked. 'Richard, Elizabeth's been putting a finger into my nose and then a finger into her nose and making more holes in playdough. And she looked at a hole and shouted, "The monsters are coming! The monsters are coming!" She's expressing a fear of monsters. She's regressing. Richard, Elizabeth is a child in crisis.'

I look over at Elizabeth, slouched on the couch, watching a Disney video. My mind screams, Niki, this is crazy! But I don't scream that. I control my anxiety and calmly say, 'Niki, Elizabeth looks pretty happy to me.'

'That's because I managed to stabilise her!' Niki shouts, angry at my lame response.

I can't empathise. The only crisis I see is in Niki. But I'm not sure what to safely say, so I stand mute, frozen by Niki's anger.

Silence isn't safe either. 'Richard, I feel totally unsupported and abandoned by you!' Niki shouts. 'I think you're in denial about Elizabeth's sexual abuse, probably because you're in denial about your own sexual abuse.'

I've been slapped. What does 'in denial' mean? I'm in denial about Elizabeth's sexual abuse, for which we have no evidence. I'm in denial about my own abuse, which I can't remember. I don't understand these accusations, so just offer explanations for Elizabeth's monster talk.

'Niki, I've played monster games with Elizabeth since she could walk. She shouts, "The monsters are coming! The monsters are coming! Let's run!" And we run off together, laughing and holding hands, to get away from the monsters. Then we do it all over again in the other direction. We play monster games in the backyard and inside the house. Niki, you've watched us playing this game.'

I also remember when Elizabeth and I played monster games on the beach in South Africa, last May. We pretended the waves were monsters; they crashed and chased us up the foreshore. We held hands, laughed, and ran back and forth in front of the waves – the monsters. Sometimes I carried her right down to where the waves broke, before running back up the foreshore. Elizabeth's salt and sand encrusted arms were wrapped tight around my sunburnt neck, and she screamed with joy, 'Do it again, Dad! Do it again, Dad!'

Sunday July 19, 1992

Niki's anxiety is undiminished. This afternoon she tells me, 'I was driving with Elizabeth and she poked her finger into and out of the hole in a drink container. And she only sucked on her gummy worm. She didn't eat it! Then she stuck out her tongue. Richard, I'm sure she's performed oral sex.'

Tonight, Niki writes out a long dot-point list of reasons she thinks Elizabeth's been abused, probably at Children's Home Day Care, early this year. The list includes 'stimulating herself, French-kissing, provocative posing for family photos, sexual aura, nightmares, giant fits, refusing to bathe in the bathtub or take naps, becoming obsessive about certain clothing and games, clinging to Niki, becoming withdrawn and inattentive, hitting her dolls, biting herself and trying to cut herself with kiddie scissors, riding Richard like a horse, refusing to wear clothes, not drinking water or urinating for extremely long periods of time, using bottles and pacifiers – she always refused them in the past.'

Niki's list so far seems, to me, like normal child behaviour that she now interprets through her prism of sexual abuse. Some of them, like Elizabeth trying to cut herself, are news to me.

When I read the remaining items, it hits me that Niki's obsessed with sexual abuse:

- Arranging me in bed in a sexual way, touching my breast to fall asleep, laying on my naked tummy, definitely a compulsive feeling about it.
- Almost all of Elizabeth's play and spontaneous complaining about 'naughty boys' and 'bad kids' has to do with Children's Home …
- When wiping her bottom a few times I broached the topic of, 'No one should ever touch your tee-tee, it's private.' I remember the glazed blank look she would give me in response, like there was something to talk about, but she wasn't going to do the talking.
- When I picked her up one day after school, she was dazed and started walking off in the wrong direction, toward some apartments

instead of to our car. The thought flashed through my mind that the apartments could be set up for pornographic materials using the kids.

Monday July 20, 1992

This drama is just a week old. Each day brings new developments. Tonight it's a doozy. In the summers of 1990 and 1991, when Elizabeth was one and two years old, Niki used a babysitter named Kacey, who was sixteen and seventeen in those years. Niki's brother, Chuck, and his wife also used Kacey to babysit their three young boys.

Tonight Niki tells me, 'Richard, I think Kacey sexually abused Elizabeth. I think she got in bed with her and she touched her genitals and she French-kissed her. And maybe her father sexually abused Elizabeth as well, at their house.'

Here's why introducing Kacey into our drama is a stunning development. A few months back, Kacey accused Chuck of raping her on a night she babysat for him. Chuck has been charged with sexual assault and awaits trial. Lawsuits are flying back and forth between Niki's father and Kacey's father. And the local media are having a field day, running headline stories. And now Niki and her mother think Kacey and her father have sexually abused Elizabeth. Our family life has become a small-town soap opera.

Wednesday July 22, 1992

Niki has started her own journal to record Elizabeth's statements and behaviour, and shares her notes with me. They read like a three-year-old's gibberish made in response to constant questioning. Niki asks Elizabeth about her monsters, how they hurt her, where they hurt her, if they were girl or boy monsters and on and on. Then asks Elizabeth if our bodies have holes. When she says 'yes', Niki asks where one is? When Elizabeth answers her tee-tee, Niki asks if anyone has touched her tee-tee? Elizabeth says Mikee and Alan touched her tee-tee with a knife. Niki also asks if Kacey took her to bed and liked to French-kiss her. Elizabeth told Niki 'yes'. When asked the same question about Miss Mabel, she answered 'no'.

Thursday July 23, 1992

This afternoon Niki calls my office in complete distress. 'Richard, Elizabeth's disintegrating. She had a thorn in her foot and was hysterical, screaming, "Are you going to cut my foot off?" She cried with a terror in her eyes I've never seen before in my life. Then she wanted to make the sign of the cross with my body, by lying across me.'

Niki tells me she called Dr Schwartz for help, but, 'he just blew me off. He just said to maintain a calm home environment. Richard, I'm at the end of my ability to cope.'

I leave for home expecting the worst. I don't know what to do to help Niki. I don't know what to do to end this sudden crisis in my family. I don't understand what's happening.

Niki greets me on the lawn, outside the garage door, happy, excited, smiling. 'Richard, guess what. Brace yourself for this.'

I laugh and ask, 'What?' It's wonderful to see her happy again. Has she uncovered a benign explanation for Elizabeth's behaviour? Is our crisis over?

'Richard, Elizabeth's been ritually sexually abused,' Niki says. 'It all fits! I'm going to church on Sunday to cleanse Elizabeth, and I would encourage you to come too.' Niki tells me she wondered about ritual abuse after Elizabeth made a 'body cross' by lying over her, so she called Paul Roland, her church deacon. 'He's also an attorney and handles child abuse cases. He said ritual abuse happens, even in Bartlesville. Richard, someone has finally listened to me. I'm meeting Roland tomorrow afternoon.'

After this conversation, Niki makes a beeline for the bookstore to purchase *Out of Darkness: Exploring Satanism and Ritual Abuse*. She reads late into the night, pausing occasionally to tell me, 'Richard, this agrees exactly with my observations of Elizabeth's behaviour, including her play with crosses.'

'Niki, Elizabeth asked about the cross on the church near our house,' I say. 'And she plays with your metal cross. And I've been drawing crosses with her.'

Niki hears nothing I say.

Friday July 24, 1992

This morning Niki gives me *Out of Darkness* to take to my office and photocopy from it a checklist titled 'Signs and Symptoms of Ritualistic Abuse in Children'. The checklist contains 106 symptoms and behavioural criteria for children who are supposed to have suffered satanic ritual abuse. Most of the checklist behaviours are bizarre:

> Child destroys toys. Child fears ghosts, monsters, witches, devils, dracula, vampires, evil spirits, etc. Child fears closets or being locked in a closet. Child becomes excessively angry or upset when told what to do … Child hurts self frequently, is accident prone.

And on and on. Surely these are the normal fears and behaviours of two- and three-year-old children?

Other checklist behaviours are beyond bizarre:

> Child talks about ingesting urine or feces, having it put on his/her body or in his/her mouth, being urinated or defecating upon, or having any of these things happen to someone else. Child sings odd, ritualistic songs or chants, sometimes in a language incomprehensible to the parent; sings songs with a sexual, bizarre, or "you better not tell" theme. Child talks about animals, babies, human beings confined, hurt, killed, mutilated, eaten, etc.

And on and on.

I've lived in America for over ten years. I love this free country of wild creativity and endless opportunity. I also appreciate the huge diversity of beliefs, attitudes and behaviours among its more than two-hundred-and-fifty-million people. As I scan this checklist, I sense I've just discovered a new loony American subculture.

Niki believes Elizabeth exhibits 40 of the 106 behaviours in the checklist, and an additional eighteen symptomatic behaviours not even on the list. She now interprets most of Elizabeth's behaviour within the framework of satanic ritual abuse.

I dutifully copy the checklist, then leave for the meeting with church deacon and attorney Paul Roland. I think positive. I hope he's a rational professional who'll help calm Niki's anxiety.

two

Paul Roland And The Abyss

He's not. If I wanted to find someone able to take our family situation from bad to calamitous, I'd look for Paul Roland.

His office is in the basement of an old brown brick building. Middle-aged, tall and lean, Roland has a melodramatic manner. Bent and sorrowful, he shuffles to greet us in his dark and gloomy office, like the world's on his shoulders and he knows it's on our shoulders too.

'Do you have a sore back?' I ask.

'No,' he answers, 'I played a hard game of basketball during my lunch break.'

Niki and I sit in chairs about a metre apart, facing Roland's desk, Niki to my left. I expect to be greeted by an attorney with a professional demeanour. Instead, Roland talks histrionically about the horrors per-petrated on children and his benevolence in defending their rights. He shares stories of animals skinned alive, blood drained over children tied to beds and other depraved acts. Alarm bells go off in my body. We're sitting in front of a fanatic who will inflame our situation.

Niki, on the other hand, bonds with Roland. She's found a professional who'll listen to her concerns about Elizabeth's disturbing behaviour, about Children's Home and Kacey, about Elizabeth's drawings of male and female genitalia.

As Niki vents, Roland nods and voices agreement. 'Elizabeth must have been ritually sexually abused to behave this way.' When I offer alter-native explanations, Roland looks at me, smirks, turns back to face Niki and says, 'He's not convinced about ritual abuse. Niki, I don't think he believes us.'

Roland's smarminess angers me. In my hostility, I begin to wonder whether he's involved in some of the abuse he describes, because he delights in talking about it.

Niki tries to defuse the tension. 'Richard's really a nice person,' she tells Roland, 'but with a PhD in geology, he's a scientific sceptic. Paul, his rational, scientific background makes it hard for him to cope with ritual abuse.'

'Niki, based on your account,' Roland answers, 'we should contact the Department of Human Services and report Elizabeth's been ritually abused at Children's Home. And, you know, there's big money in civil suits in these kinds of cases against day care centres.' Roland dismisses Niki's concerns about Kacey. 'At best, Kacey just set Elizabeth up for ritual abuse at Children's Home.'

Roland is adding stress to our situation. I know nothing about the implications of going to the Department of Human Services. We could make libellous accusations against Children's Home. We should wait until Schwartz has seen Elizabeth.

But Roland insists, 'Going to DHS', as he calls it, 'is the smart thing to do. That way the parents are considered beyond suspicion.'

Finally, Niki turns to face me and says, 'I want to go to DHS, as Paul recommends.'

I know if I object, Niki will go with Roland to the Department of Human Services without me. So he calls, and his first words are, 'We have a child in crisis.'

As he utters those words I'm shocked by a high-pitched scream. It's Niki. She turns to me, crying, weeping. 'That's what I've wanted to hear. That's what I wanted Schwartz to say.'

My mind screams back, Niki, this is crazy! We're in the process of making this a crisis!

But no, I don't scream that.

Roland tells the Department of Human Services, 'We'll be right there.' Then he tries to call a Bartlesville therapist, Barbara Tillman. 'She specialises in children who've been sexually abused,' Roland tells us. But he can't reach her.

At the Department of Human Services office, Niki starts to give a statement to a social worker, Linda Foster. Her attempt lasts for a couple of sentences before she dissolves into incoherent sobbing, so Roland steps in and tells Foster about Elizabeth's disintegration and sexualised drawings.

Foster is caring, and tells a weeping Niki, 'We believe you. We believe you.' This support makes her weep in ever-greater torrents of relief.

I sit mute. I wonder how Foster can say she believes Niki. I ask myself: What do we actually know? What evidence do we actually have? What can we ever really know about what might have happened to Elizabeth at two years of age? How can we make such serious allegations against Children's Home based on the statements of a three-year-old who talks gibberish in response to questioning?

These thoughts remain lifeless, stuck, locked in place, not allowed into the light of day. I tell myself I'm just along for the ride, that it's pointless to contradict what Roland tells Foster, especially as Niki sobs and everyone tells her, 'We believe you.'

But the truth is I don't have the courage to speak out. I don't have the courage to say, 'Niki, I don't believe you. I think this is bullshit.' If I do that, I'll be in massive conflict with Niki. So instead I surrender my right to have input into what's happening. But what I think just happened is we've all gone over the edge into the abyss, into a black hole of hysteria and madness. Worse, I just let myself get pulled over the edge.

After the meeting with Foster, Roland asks Niki, 'Would you like me to drop by your house later this afternoon to lay hands on Elizabeth? I'm amazed at how it promotes healing in abused children.'

My silent gut reaction is – if you touch my daughter, I'll rip your head off.

Niki welcomes the offer. So I return to my office, take care of urgent business, pack my things and head home. I don't want Roland in our house if I'm not there.

My nerves don't need another jolt, but the shocks keep coming. When I walk into our house it looks vandalised. The furniture in the family and living rooms is upside down and strewn around. Cushions and laundry are scattered over the floor. In the middle of this chaos Elizabeth holds balls of wool and an audiocassette she's somehow pulled apart, and gleefully wraps wool and cassette tape around overturned furniture, making a gigantic tangled web.

I'm stunned. When I can move, I bend toward an overturned chair to lift it upright. Halfway through bending, I see Niki. She stands like a statue to my left, in the shadow of a curtain, at the edge of the room: at attention, arms straight by her side, blank stare straight ahead, an obedient audience to the apocalypse.

As I start to lift the chair, she hisses to life, looks at me, and commands, 'Don't touch that chair! You leave that chair exactly where it is. I want Paul to see what Elizabeth's doing. She's making cubbies and traps against the monsters to feel safe.'

I look across at Elizabeth, under a pile of cushions, a smile on her face. She's had fun making her mess. But how did she move this heavy furniture? Who let her rip open the cassette tapes? I'm falling deeper into the abyss.

Roland arrives and sits with Niki, and together they watch Elizabeth crawl under and over and through a pile of jumbled furniture, cushions and laundry. They speak gravely and agree, 'Elizabeth's obviously doing this to feel safe.' Roland places a hand on Elizabeth's head, saying some kind of prayer. I sit, watch, listen and say nothing. I'm no longer in a soap opera; I'm in a horror movie.

And I'm traumatised. I've abandoned myself. I've abandoned Elizabeth. Did I have a choice? Yes, I had a choice. But I didn't speak up. I feel like an actor in a drama with no control over the role they play. And the consequence of this drama could be horrendous.

Saturday July 25, 1992

I don't sleep. This morning I tell Niki, 'I feel very uncomfortable about Paul Roland. Niki, he gives me the creeps. I don't like him and I don't trust him. And I feel very anxious about the way everything's developing. Niki, I need a hug.'

We hug, but Niki's oblivious to my distress, only strengthened in her belief. She wants to spend the day reading *Out of Darkness* and making more notes about Elizabeth's abuse symptoms. She needs the day to study satanic ritual abuse.

To calm my nerves, I take the girls to Birch Lake and walk with Elizabeth along the shoreline with baby Jenny in a backpack, then to Woolaroc

Museum to walk through the exhibits. Elizabeth's happy. She enjoys being out on an excursion. She's amazed by the hanging aeroplane in the museum.

In the car she says, 'Dad, Alan and Mikee hurt me. They pushed me in the tummy.'

'I'm sorry, Elizabeth. That's naughty behaviour,' I reply.

This evening's a blur. Again, I don't sleep. I get up and scan a *Newsweek* magazine. Niki also gets up, feeds baby Jenny, sees me reading my magazine, glares, says nothing and returns to her bed.

Sunday July 26, 1992

This morning the storm breaks. Niki's furious. 'Richard, you read your magazine last night when you could've read *Out of Darkness* to learn about what happened to Elizabeth.'

I'm so tired I don't cushion my words. 'Niki, I skimmed the book on Friday. I read the chapter on signs and symptoms of ritual abuse. Niki, I don't agree with your diagnosis of ritual sexual abuse and I don't want to read it. I know despicable things happen to children, but I don't want to read about them.'

Niki's posture is rigid, combative, her eyes narrowed, lips pursed. I expect her to unleash, but she contains her anger, then leaves with Elizabeth to attend the church service. I play with Jenny and tidy the house. Niki returns late, about two in the afternoon, with red, teary eyes. 'I made a real spectacle of myself at church,' she says. 'I asked the congregation to pray for Elizabeth and wept throughout the service.'

After church she went to her parents' home, to call her mother and sister for support. Niki's parents are now at their ski condo in Colorado.

I need to catch up on office work. Elizabeth wants to come with me, to play on my computer and scribble on paper with coloured pencils. All's well as I work and she scribbles.

After about an hour, Niki calls. 'Is Elizabeth okay?' she asks.

'She's really happy,' I reply, and switch on the speakerphone. When Elizabeth hears Niki's voice she wants to go home, so Niki drives to my office.

'I missed Elizabeth,' she says on arriving.

When I arrive home late afternoon, I walk into our open-plan kitchen and living room to a surreal scene of chaos. Everything's upside down again. Elizabeth crawls out from under a pile of furniture and cushions, and smiles at me. I notice Jenny crawling on the floor around Niki's feet, screaming for her attention. I look up at Niki. She's in a serious, teary conversation on the phone. She ignores me. Not a glance. I walk into the chaos, pick up Jenny and try to comfort her.

Eventually, Niki hangs up the phone, looks defiantly at me, and declares, 'Well, Richard, I've called on all my support. I'm sorry you can't do the same thing.'

I presume Niki means, 'I'm sorry you can't call on support for your beliefs, which oppose my beliefs.' It feels like she's telling me, 'Richard, the battlelines are drawn.' Avoiding conflict has meant it's following me.

I still don't want to argue, so I carry baby Jenny into our backyard. Niki follows, carrying a handful of photos. We watch Elizabeth play in her sandpit. I'm dazed.

Niki whispers, 'Richard, it's occurred to me that a lot of the people who might be sexually abusing Elizabeth, and even those who have contact with these abusers, have first or last names beginning with the letter 'K'. And today Elizabeth used a hand signal for the number three, which is exactly the same as an occult hand signal.' Niki told this to one of her friends who deals in the occult, and, 'the hair stood up on the back of my friend's neck.'

Niki continues in a hushed voice. 'I wonder if child pornographers in Bartlesville – maybe connected to a nationwide pornography ring – are involved in her abuse? Richard, Elizabeth's poses in our family photos are exactly like those of an experienced porno star.'

Niki hands over a collection of photos from our albums. I see Elizabeth playing with balloons, then mimicking the pose of her favourite doll. I see nothing pornographic.

We go back in the house and Elizabeth says, 'Dad, let's play "I'm gonna get ya."'

'Sure, Elizabeth!' I reply, relieved by the thought of doing something normal. She loves me to play chase with her. I'll say, 'I'm gonna get ya,' and chase her. Then she chases me back. We run back and forth through the house, laughing and chasing each other in turn.

Niki vetos our play. 'Richard, I don't want you to play chase with Elizabeth anymore. It makes her go into a sexual frenzy and stick out her tongue, like she has to give oral sex.'

What a sick thought. I'm dumbstruck. Elizabeth's been encouraged, maybe helped, to turn our house upside down and rip open cassette tapes, but she isn't allowed to play chase with me. I slowly scan the bizarre state of our house, and then look back at Niki with an expression that says, Are you serious?

My challenge enrages Niki. Standing erect, arms by her side, she declares, 'Richard, if you're unhappy with the state of the house, I'll take the girls and move into my parents' house.'

It's an easy option. Her wealthy parents have an empty mansion in town, and money's no problem.

Niki has threatened to leave me? And take Elizabeth and Jenny? I would lose Niki and I would lose my children into this craziness? I feel assaulted. I can't speak. I can hardly breathe. My vision darkens and collapses into the frame of Niki's face, which glares, angrily, waiting for my response. All I can do is slowly turn, take three-year-old Elizabeth's hand for courage, and walk with her into our front yard. She climbs on the branches of a pear tree. I sit on the lawn in shock.

Later, alone in my bedroom, I pray on my knees, next to my bed, that this crisis will be resolved somehow. And I consider myself an atheist. I just put it out to the universe that I need help from somewhere. Then I take a pill prescribed for business travel and finally sleep.

Monday July 27, 1992

At the office this morning I ask colleagues who've also used Children's Home Day Care what their experience has been. One father says he thought supervision had lapsed in the last year, and that his son, Mikee, had learned bad language from another boy, Alan. He also says that Mikee can be rough.

Another father has recently transferred to our Egyptian office, but faxes me a report, addressed, at my request, to the Department of Human Services. He compliments Children's Home and says he and his wife 'had the pleasure of personally knowing Mabel and assistant Karly', and that, 'Mabel is a very caring individual who loves kids.' He also says he and his wife 'frequently stayed during the day to help' and that he 'personally dropped by numerous times unannounced' and 'did not ever notice anything abnormal.'

Later this morning Niki calls my office in attack mode, telling me Elizabeth has just revealed my mother 'gave her a big swat and pushed her into the swimming pool to drown her' when they babysat Elizabeth last May, in South Africa. Elizabeth then said she was saved from drowning because my father gave my mother a big swat. 'Richard,' Niki continues, 'I'm concerned about the abuse of Elizabeth by your mother. I suggest you call your parents to find out exactly what happened to her.'

The notion my mother pushed her granddaughter into a swimming pool to drown her is preposterous. Elizabeth has not suddenly 'revealed' about my mother. Niki is questioning Elizabeth about anyone and everyone she thinks might be an abuser. She has placed an accusatory gun into Elizabeth's hand. Elizabeth can either spray accusations at random, or she can aim an accusation at whomever Niki names. 'Did they touch your tee-tee?' 'Did they French-kiss you?' 'Did they try to drown you?'

This is Bartlesville, 1992, but it feels like Salem, 1692.

* * *

Because Niki made a complaint of suspected sexual abuse to the Department of Human Services, we have to meet police officer Mike Miller this afternoon. Linda Foster will also attend. How will this interview play out? Will Niki collapse into incoherent sobbing? Roland won't be there to pick up the script.

Niki prepares a written statement for Officer Miller, summarising her concerns about Kacey and Children's Home. She writes that Elizabeth's abuse symptoms – fits, nightmares, French-kissing, sexual awareness, increased aggression, refusing to take naps, refusing to have her hair washed – all started when Kacey was her babysitter. And while attending Children's Home, Elizabeth suffered nightmares and made comments like, 'The kids put toys in my tee-tee.' Niki says she hopes the police will investigate Kacey and Children's Home. I'm curious to see how Officer Miller reacts to Niki's statement.

I don't find out. Our meeting is cancelled and Officer Miller never receives Niki's statement. Foster and Miller somehow found out that Schwartz is already on the case. They'll wait for his opinion and then decide if further investigation is warranted.

* * *

Niki's a true believer in therapy. She feels therapy is something all couples should do, and 'especially us, because you emotionally withdraw'. So, for about a year, we've been seeing clinical psychologist and family therapist Dr Tom Dohne.

Late this afternoon I arrive on Dohne's doorstep, in despair. I need to unload. I like Tom Dohne. He listens quietly before offering an occasional considered opinion. He looks a bit like Abraham Lincoln without a beard. Middle-aged, tall and lean, Dohne has a dark complexion, deep-set eyes and a penetrating gaze.

I tell Tom what's happened over the past two weeks. I say Niki thinks I'm unsupportive, unfeeling and uncaring about Elizabeth's sexual abuse, that I think Niki's hysterical and overreacting. During my ad-lib summary, the stress breaks through and I cry. Tom listens to my blubbering and says, 'You're all under a lot of stress.'

'Tom,' I plead, 'I don't understand why Niki believes Elizabeth's been ritually sexually abused. This might do untold damage, labelling her as a victim of abuse for the rest of her life. I feel like I'm on a galloping horse that I can't control, that I can't stop. Two weeks ago, I felt in control of my life. Now my life feels crazy, out of control.' I ask Dohne why presumably educated people have written books about satanic cults taking over neighbourhoods, taking over America. 'Tom, it feels like the rest of the world's gone crazy as well.'

Dohne's assessment is concise: 'Richard, the therapy world is full of nut jobs.'

* * *

After Niki spoke yesterday with her mother, Faye flew back from Colorado to help Niki through our crisis. Niki and her mother are very close. We're invited to have dinner with Faye this evening. After leaving

Dohne's office, I drive to Niki's parents' house.

When I arrive, Niki rushes out with the girls to greet me in the drive-way, gushing, 'It's Daddy! It's Daddy!' She's happy, animated, loving. It's wonderful to be greeted so enthusiastically. But I do wonder what the heck's going on; Niki's behaviour feels strange after days of marital tension.

Throughout the evening Niki and her mother openly discuss Elizabeth's abuse. I feel invisible. They agree, 'Elizabeth's obviously been ritually sexually abused.' And, 'Oh, my God! Oh, my God! Elizabeth will need lifelong therapy for her sexual abuse. I know it! I know it!'

I listen in silent incredulity to their assured opinions and adamant conclusions. Do they understand that accusing a babysitter and day care centre staff of abuse is serious? Do they understand that labelling three-year-old Elizabeth an abused victim needing lifelong therapy could have crippling consequences?

But what seems most incredible to me – the invisible audience – is that Niki and her mother are chirpy and excited about their opinions and conclusions. I feel like I'm at a ritual abuse dinner party, as two wealthy women, without any money or work worries, find something to really worry about – the unsubstantiated belief Elizabeth has been ritually sex-ually abused.

But no, I don't say that.

three

Waiting On Schwartz

Wednesday July 29, 1992

Twelve days ago, Niki told Schwartz she was concerned about the possible abuse of Elizabeth. Now she believes Elizabeth was ritually sexually abused, and has pointed a finger of suspicion at Children's Home Day Care and the babysitter Kacey. The police and the Department of Human Services are waiting on Schwartz to render judgement.

Today Niki takes Elizabeth to her first session with Schwartz. She wants to make the case for ritual abuse, and prepares a letter:

> In the past two weeks I have seen my 3-year old Elizabeth, our precious child, disintegrate … I am convinced we have a serious problem on our hands, probably ritual abuse …
>
> Terror: hysterical crying, illogical fits, triggers such as revealing a secret, slight hurt, nightmares, regresses totally to baby state, determined to build safe places and does so compulsively, afraid of monsters …
>
> Secrets: funny secrets, scary secrets, trigger anxiety, terror, becomes distant, blank
>
> Sexuality: awareness as if she was taught, inappropriate sexuality … much touching of self, appears to be the perfect porno star
>
> Violence: play themes include violence: killing people, knives, guns, bad men/monsters, etc.
>
> Pain: extremely low pain threshold; was previously very high, expresses terror of being hurt (again) as if she has been tortured
>
> Occult: some play and talk of possibly occult material

Accompanying this letter is a folder of Elizabeth's supposedly sexualised drawings, as well as six typed pages listing hundreds and hundreds
of Elizabeth's supposed fears, phobias and terrors, which Niki attributes to ritual abuse. Niki believes these symptoms began in 1990, when
Elizabeth was fourteen months old.

Tonight, Niki's furious. 'After he saw Elizabeth, Schwartz didn't want
to talk to me,' she says. 'He didn't want to discuss my list of symptoms,
or even Elizabeth's drawings!'

Monday August 3, 1992

Unbeknown to me, Niki scheduled for this morning a forensic medical
examination of Elizabeth at the Tulsa Justice Center, to search for physical evidence of abuse. Late morning, she calls me at work to tell me,
'Elizabeth refused to go into the examination room. She was terrified by
the doctor and the scary table.' The examination table had an elaborate
set-up with lights, cameras and maybe other paraphernalia.

'Niki,' I say, 'maybe her response was because of her fright with ear
surgery and the scary mask.'

Elizabeth's had chronic ear infections from age one, requiring two
rounds of ear surgery, the last one in February this year, when the doctor
placed a black mask over her face to begin anaesthesia. Elizabeth still has
nightmares about 'the black mask', and about a tube that she says was
pushed down her throat.

'Richard, I'm losing my patience with you,' Niki replies, angry. 'You
always find excuses for Elizabeth's sexual abuse.'

'Niki, I'm entitled to my opinion,' I reply, also angry, but mainly frustrated.
Niki hangs up on me.

I call her back to smooth feathers and ask for the Tulsa Justice
Center's phone number. I call the number and speak with social worker
Judy Richman.

'Elizabeth's reaction was unusual,' Richman tells me, 'not like other sexually abused children, more like someone afraid of hospitals and doctors.
And she threw dolls around shouting, "Kill those naughty children!"'

'Could this be in response to rough play by older boys at day care?'
I ask.

'Maybe,' Richman replies, 'but how do you ever really know with three-year-olds?'

After talking with Richman, I ponder all the other traumas in Elizabeth's young life. When she was two, she waited for me, alone, at the garage door, to arrive home from work. As soon as I walked through the door, Elizabeth, pale and distraught, took hold of my left arm, and, with considerable force, pulled it down until my left ear was near her mouth.

Then she whispered, 'Daddy, Mommy's really sick. She stays in bed and she cries a lot.'

Niki suffered gestational diabetes during her pregnancy with Jennifer. Elizabeth worried her mommy was going to die, just like the mommy in the *Prancer* video she watches over and over.

Elizabeth's a video baby. She watches videos most days, even the scary ones, both hands across her eyes, a couple of fingers cracked open. I tell her they're just made-up stories, but they're very real to her. *Beauty and the Beast* and *FernGully* terrify her.

Elizabeth was also upset when baby Jenny arrived, throwing tantrums when Niki breastfed Jenny. I talked her around by explaining, 'Jenny has no teeth and can only nurse Mummy's milk. You have teeth and can eat hamburgers.' Elizabeth loved the doting attention she received as the only child, and isn't at all happy sharing it with a new sibling.

And now she knows her mother believes naughty people have hurt her. She sees distress in her mother, who wants answers about who the naughty people are and what they did to her, answers that Elizabeth probably doesn't have. She looks anxious when Niki continually questions her. On top of that, she now sees tension between her parents, something she's never seen before.

* * *

This afternoon Niki and I meet David King, a Bartlesville attorney recommended by Niki's father. He's also working on Niki's brother's sexual assault case. Now he's supposed to review Niki's notes on her suspects.

King works for a law firm in a modern high-rise building in downtown Bartlesville. We're ushered into his small office, just big enough for his desk, buried under piles of documents. He looks to be in his early thirties, and stressed. He seems annoyed, like he has more important things to do.

As Niki begins to describe our crisis, he interrupts and asks, 'Why have you already gone to the Department of Human Services and to the police?'

Niki tries to explain, but he interrupts again. 'Roland has acted far too hastily.' King cuts our meeting short. 'Keep things calm and wait for Schwartz's report,' he says.

His precise manner is a relief to me. Niki looks flustered and threatened.

As we're about to leave his office, something unexpected happens. King hands over a pile of photocopied publications by the False Memory Syndrome Foundation. The publications explain how false memories of sexual abuse were created during recovered memory therapy. King tells us, 'This is a controversial topic in the legal world at the moment, and might interest you. The sexual abuse never happened. The patient's memories of sexual abuse were the result of questioning and suggestion by the therapist under recovered memory therapy.'

It's the first I've heard about 'false memory syndrome'. It'll be a controversial topic in our household as well. It contradicts the validity of Niki constantly questioning Elizabeth.

Niki and I walk out of King's office building and stand side by side on the pavement, silent, lost in our own thoughts. Niki looks upset by King's comments. I feel her agitation. She looks exhausted, stuck, like she's searching for the answer to a question or trying to reach a decision. I don't know what to say, so I turn away and stare at late afternoon shadows lying across the road. They look peaceful, content to lie there.

After a minute or so Niki makes up her mind, looks at me with steely determination, and declares, 'Richard, I can't go forward in our marriage feeling so unsupported by you.'

'Yes, I know our marriage is in jeopardy,' I reply.

Nothing more is said. I walk back to my office wondering what will happen next. I also wonder how I can support Niki's beliefs if I don't see Elizabeth as a victim of ritual sexual abuse or a disintegrating child in crisis.

Wednesday August 5, 1992

Today Elizabeth has her second therapy session with Schwartz, and again Niki's furious.

'I want to cancel the sessions with Schwartz,' she tells me this evening. 'He doesn't want to discuss Elizabeth's terrors and phobias. He still won't talk with me about her drawings.'

Niki's mother and sister, and Linda Foster, somehow persuade Niki to continue with Schwartz. But Niki warns me, 'I'm prepared to file away his opinion and start with someone else.'

We then agree that I'll take Elizabeth to her last session.

Monday August 10, 1992

Which happens today. After the session, Schwartz wants to talk to me. He leaves Elizabeth playing with toys and comes into the reception area. He looks worried.

'Mr Vos, I'm very concerned your wife is questioning Elizabeth about sexual abuse. Her counselling background may be leading her to make unnecessary assumptions.'

I wonder how Schwartz knows Niki's questioning Elizabeth.

Then he holds up Elizabeth's drawings, given to him by Niki – scribbled lines and coloured splodges. 'We can see whatever we want to see in young children's drawings.' He doesn't elaborate, but looks frustrated, lost in his thoughts, like he wants to say more but restrains himself. Finally, he just says, 'Elizabeth's a lovely and bright young girl,' and strides back into his office.

I drive home with a deep sense of foreboding. Niki will have a huge negative reaction if Schwartz doesn't diagnose sexual abuse. Unless this issue is resolved, everything in Elizabeth's life could be tied back to 'unresolved issues related to her sexual abuse'. Her future emotional and mental health feel at stake. It feels to me like her entire life is under threat. How did she come into so much danger, so quickly? How can I protect her?

I also grapple with the horrible reality that my marriage is in crisis. Niki needs to feel supported in her belief about sexual abuse. I'm not doing that. I need to feel that, together, we have four feet on the ground, dealing rationally with facts. We're not doing that. And as a couple we have to pull together instead of pull apart. We're not doing that.

We're not doing well at much at all.

Wednesday August 12, 1992

A month has passed since Niki's concerns about sexual abuse erupted, and today we'll hear Schwartz's verdict. As we drive to Tulsa, Niki tells me, 'I won't argue with Schwartz. I'll just listen to what he has to say.'

She doesn't add 'and ignore him', but I catch her drift.

Schwartz tells us he's concerned about Elizabeth's anxiety, but he doesn't see signs of sexual abuse. 'It's difficult with three-year-olds, and various stressors could cause her anxiety: being frightened during ear surgery, Niki's illness during pregnancy, Jenny's arrival and sibling rivalry, or rough play at day care, which Elizabeth has talked about. Getting to the truth is difficult.'

Schwartz thinks little would be gained from more therapy, and cautions us against over-therapising Elizabeth, as she could become conditioned to the topic and give answers to please. 'Questioning a three-year-old about sexual abuse must be handled extremely carefully by the therapist, to avoid suggestion and contamination,' Schwartz says, adding the warning, 'And you should also refrain from questioning Elizabeth. I think there's already been contamination from questioning.'

We thank Schwartz for his assessment. Niki makes no comment. It's all smiles, good wishes and handshakes as we exit, stage left. I think Schwartz has nailed it. As we walk to the car, my head and my heart hope Schwartz's assessment will end Niki's concern. But my gut tells my head and heart – mate, that won't happen.

As soon as we're in the car, Niki says, 'Elizabeth didn't tell Schwartz about her sexual abuse. Richard, she clammed up! Just like she clams up when I question her. And three sessions weren't enough to reach a diagnosis of sexual abuse, let alone a diagnosis of ritual sexual abuse.'

My gut was right.

* * *

When I arrive home from work, Niki's on a roll.

'I called Sandra. She thinks Schwartz only used three sessions because he just wanted to see if there's enough evidence for a lucrative criminal case.'

What is Niki implying? 'At least he didn't believe sexual abuse occurred,' I reply. This fact feels like a lifebuoy in a storm. At least I have that to hang on to.

Niki looks at me as if to say, You dumb, stupid, ignorant man. 'Yes, he did!' she exclaims.

I'm stunned. How could we hold opposite opinions about what Schwartz said? I've lost my toehold on reality. I'm on a cliff face, and what I thought was sure footing is gone. Niki and I have no basis for rational discourse about an issue that is fracturing our marriage and could seriously harm Elizabeth. I have to make a toehold or I'll fall to oblivion. So I sit down, write out our different opinions, and read them aloud to Niki. 'Are they accurate?' I ask.

'So what?' Niki answers. 'As far as I'm concerned, Schwartz's analysis is piddly-poop. I've dealt with hundreds of psychologists who had unfinished business with their mothers.'

Niki has swung a sword. She has cut off rational discussion. A combative tirade erupts in my head: Okay, Niki, this tirade goes, I'm going to write to Schwartz for clarification. And I'm going to write down exactly what you just said. If you want to reduce our discussion of this crisis to childish put-downs, well, then, I intend to hold up a mirror to your behaviour. Niki, your behaviour is totally unacceptable to me.

This silent fighting monologue with myself avoids a fight with Niki. Writing to Schwartz makes our confrontation safe, intellectual, my preferred rules of engagement. If I go face to face and toe to toe with Niki in a verbal stoush, she'll become enraged, and I'll freeze.

Thursday August 13, 1992

Even before hearing Schwartz's assessment, Niki had booked an appointment for today with Faye Hegburg, a Bartlesville social worker in practice with Tom Dohne, to discuss ongoing therapy for Elizabeth. I want to attend. Niki summarises Elizabeth's situation, and I say we have different opinions on the subject. Strangely, there's no tension. Maybe we're exhausted.

Hegburg seems like a calm, friendly and competent person. Middle-aged, although grandmotherly in dress and appearance, she appears confident enough to stand her ground in the face of Niki's strong opinions. She tells us, 'I'm not highly qualified regarding child sexual abuse. Barbara Tillman would be a better therapist.'

Since Tillman was Roland's go-to choice of therapist, I'm not inclined to use her. So we agree Hegburg will work with Elizabeth using 'unstructured play therapy', whatever that is.

Tonight I give Niki a copy of my letter to Schwartz, which seeks clarification of his assessment of Elizabeth. It's not my finest hour as a grown man. In the letter, I repeat Niki's suggestion that he may have unresolved mother issues, that his work is 'piddly-poop', and that he was only interested to treat Elizabeth if he could establish a lucrative criminal case.

Friday August 14, 1992

Late this morning Niki calls me at work. 'Richard, you totally misrepresented me in your letter to Schwartz, and my comments were made in the privacy of our home.'

'Yes,' I agree, 'I divulged your private statements. But, Niki, that's what you said.'

'You painted me as irrational and you as rational,' Niki asserts.

'Niki, you cut off rational discussion.'

'Richard, we are so far apart on this issue, and your perceptions of me are so skewed, that it would be best if I take the girls to Colorado and stay with my mother.'

I'm shocked. 'Niki, please stay here and work with Dohne.'

'Richard, I'm no longer sure Elizabeth is safe around you,' she replies. 'I don't know what you say to her when you're alone with her. I'm taking the girls to Colorado.'

Niki hangs up and flies out.

I put in a call to Dohne – to share my pain and explain what just happened. Dohne's already aware of our situation. I sense he's already talked with Niki. 'A cooling-off period might be best,' he suggests.

'Richard,' he then asks, 'did Niki say anything about you abusing Elizabeth?'

Huh? I suspect Niki raised this question with Dohne, that she asked Dohne if he thought I might be an abuser. I repeat what Niki told me on the phone.

'Richard,' he asks again, more forcefully, 'did Niki say she thought you had abused Elizabeth?'

'No.'

At home, I try to calm my anxiety. First, I meticulously clean every room of the house. Then I sit, motionless, in a quiet, pitch-black room. Niki breaks the silence by calling from Colorado. I ask her to please not break up the family.

'I'm not going to poison Elizabeth against you,' she answers.

I take a sleeping pill.

four

Some Family History

Here I'll stop the diary clock and talk about dysfunction – mine and Niki's. The child abuse hysteria during the 1980s and 1990s was not the only cause of the tragedy that struck my family. Inside the walls of our home were two more factors: Niki's obsession and my weakness.

Tracing the roots of personal dysfunction to find its original seed involves dangerous and speculative digging. But I think it's safe to say that family history plays a role in creating dysfunction; we're all partly the products of our upbringing. So, before restarting the clock, I'll share some family history.

Richard

My parents' lives were stories of trauma, heroism, brilliance, ambition and sheer hard work. With just brains and determination they built productive lives on top of the ashes of the Depression and the Second World War.

My father, Gerard, gave meaning and purpose to his life through scientific research. His life was a journey of passionate curiosity and acclaimed discovery. My mother, Dell, gave meaning and purpose to her life by striving to be better than those around her and equal to those she admired. Her life was a tortured journey of shame, judgement, criticism and conflict. But together they strived mightily and lovingly with the tools they had, to give my sister Suzanne and me the opportunity and aspiration to be successful. They succeeded admirably.

My father was born and raised in the Dutch East Indies. In 1939, at age seventeen, he travelled to Holland to commence naval cadet training. On

May 10, 1940, Germany launched a surprise invasion and aerial bombardment of Holland. Three boatloads of cadets attempted to flee the Den Helder naval base for England. My father was aboard the only boat to survive. He watched his fellow cadets perish under German Stuka attack. For the remainder of the war he fought on navy destroyer's and trained as a medical technologist. He was torpedoed, wounded, lost at sea, rescued, repaired and shipped off again. He talked with me only once about the horrors of his wartime experiences, on the day before he died.

His father died as a Japanese prisoner of war and his mother, two sisters and one younger brother were brutalised in prison camps on Java. Following Japan's surrender, my father recovered the tattered remains of his family and helped repatriate them from Java to Holland.

My father took an Australian bride, my mother, Dell, in 1943, after they met during one of his shore leaves in Perth. After the war, and because of his wartime medical technology training, my father ran the medical technology laboratory at King Edward Memorial Hospital for Women in Perth. He became a passionate medical researcher. He published numerous scientific papers on serology and immunology, discovered a rare blood group, Rh Null, and was awarded the Order of the British Empire for his research. Following Christiaan Barnard's breakthrough heart transplant, the South African medical establishment sought talent to work on rejection immunology. My father accepted the post of head of the Institute for Immunological Research in Durban, South Africa, in 1968.

My mother worked tirelessly as my father's laboratory assistant, as the editor of his publications (his native language was Dutch), and in various secretarial jobs.

I completed an honours degree in geology in South Africa and a doctorate in geology in the USA. After two years as a university lecturer and then two years as a geological consultant, I joined US oil giant Phillips Petroleum (now ConocoPhillips) and rose through the corporate hierarchy.

When my parents worked to common purpose they were formidable. However, when they worked at cross-purposes, they were apocalyptic. So there is a flipside, a dark side, to this glowing account of family success. During the postwar decade, my parents were emotionally and financially traumatised by war and poverty, family loss, and their own personal demons. My sister and I experienced terrifying episodes of rage and violence, between and from our parents. Experiencing this violence, I thought I was going to die. Anger and conflict came to feel like death to me. My survival mechanism became avoidance of conflict at almost all costs.

During my teenage and adult years my parents' emotional and financial situation improved dramatically, and they were loving and wonderfully supportive. But the early damage was done. And so my parents' trauma echoed through the corridors of my life and on into Elizabeth's life, as one source of her tragedy.

Niki

Niki's father, Charlie, also led a stellar life of accomplishment. After graduating in engineering from the University of Arkansas, he went to work for oil giant Phillips Petroleum with his young bride, Faye. Charlie rocketed up the corporate ladder to become an executive vice-president and a member of the board of directors.

'Richard, I loved that company and could have run the whole damn thing,' he once told me. He didn't elaborate because, by then, I knew his extramarital affairs had put an end to his meteoric rise toward chairman of the board. Charlie was brilliant, outspoken, handsome, charming and charismatic. A born leader. He conquered the corporate world and he conquered whatever other tasks he put his mind to. His mind drifted to women – lots of them.

Charlie enjoyed the trappings of American corporate leadership: meeting presidents, making speeches, television appearances and newspaper interviews. He told me one of his fondest memories was cracking a joke with Prince Charles while christening a new oil platform in the North Sea. 'Richard, the Prince was in hysterics.'

Charlie also plunged into philanthropic and political causes. He befriended the actor Robert Redford, who appointed him chairman of the executive committee of the Board of Trustees of the Institute for Resource Management. This institute is a non-profit organisation created by Redford in 1981. He befriended Bill and Hillary Clinton through his Arkansas connections. Hillary called on Charlie to help with Bill's first presidential campaign, and Charlie gave up his reserved seats to the president whenever Clinton showed up at the University of Arkansas basketball arena. 'Thanks, Charlie!'

In retirement, Charlie travelled to the world's remote locations, chasing adventure. He became a passionate photographer and trekker. 'Between trips to London, Paris, China, Tibet, Nepal and India, I chased gorillas in East Africa.' At age sixty-three, in 1990, Charlie became the oldest man in history to climb to Advanced Base Camp (altitude 6,500 metres) on Mount Everest. After that accomplishment he was appointed to President Clinton's advisory council on health and physical fitness. He told me he hoped to be appointed Secretary of Commerce.

Charlie was a celebrity and loved it.

For her own reasons and rewards, Faye remained Charlie's loyal wife. But the price the family paid for his affairs was a sense of abandonment and a loss of trust. There remained a constant undercurrent of distrust in Niki toward her father, along with bizarre comments, accusations and speculation between Niki and her sister, Carmen, about their father's sexual behaviour.

Niki completed a bachelor's degree in art history and a master's degree in art education and counselling. She worked as an alcoholism unit counsellor and then established her own private counselling service, Tools for Living. This work ended when she contracted chronic fatigue syndrome.

Growing up, Niki said she struggled to cope with the psychological and financial enmeshment imposed by her wealthy parents, as well as her father's celebrity, womanising and abandonment. And so another root of family dysfunction grew through the corridors of Niki's life and on into Elizabeth's life as a further source of her tragedy.

five

On Thin Ice

Saturday August 15 – Saturday August 29, 1992

It's a month since our crisis began and Niki has fled with the girls to her parents' Colorado ski condo. She says she left me because my perceptions of her are skewed, because I paint her as irrational and because she fears what I say to Elizabeth when I'm alone with her. I think she left because I challenged her obsession.

How will this play out? Niki's mother and sister agree Elizabeth's been ritually sexually abused. Carmen also thinks I'm unfeeling and uncaring. So, are we headed for divorce and a custody battle? Will Officer Mike Miller arrive on my doorstep with an accusation of sexual abuse? My marriage and my life with my children are on thin ice.

Niki and the girls stay in Colorado for two weeks. We speak by phone most days, and all Niki talks about is Elizabeth's ritual abuse. I grudgingly admire her mindset, her insistence to operate on the basis of only one truth, her truth. But it seems surreal when she talks with me as if I'm an ally, fighting alongside her in the trenches, to win the war against the abusers.

Saturday August 29, 1992

Today Niki and the girls fly in to Tulsa from Colorado. Elizabeth runs up the walkway from the plane and jumps into my arms, hugs my neck and wants me to carry her.

Niki says she thinks the time apart has done us some good, but the atmosphere's tense.

At home, Elizabeth makes a cubby in her room with a pile of pillows, and wants me to play with her. Niki's distressed. 'Elizabeth needs to make a cubby to feel safe,' she says.

'Is Elizabeth anxious?' I ask, because she looks happy to me. I can't figure this out. My question angers Niki. I'm on probation.

Late afternoon, Elizabeth and I walk, hand in hand, through the neighbourhood. She says she missed me. I say how much I missed her. We climb on a boulder at the end of a cul-de-sac.

As we play, I watch her, and see an intelligent, assertive, beautiful child. I love Elizabeth with all my heart. This young life has so much potential. But as I watch, I sense a tragedy spiralling around her, a developing vortex of powerful irrational forces trying to suck her into madness. I laugh and smile along with her on the outside, as she plays. On the inside, my world is black, collapsing into a knot of anxiety and depression.

Tonight, the girls sleep in their room, Niki and I in our room. Elizabeth wakes alone and yells, 'Mommy!'

Niki rushes to her, apologising. 'Sorry! Mommy and Daddy were just talking,' she says, and sleeps with Elizabeth.

Sunday August 30, 1992

This morning I take Elizabeth for another walk in the neighbourhood, with baby Jenny in a backpack. It calms and soothes me. In the afternoon, I leave for a five-day management seminar. Phillips Petroleum managers from around the world will meet at a lakeside resort in Oklahoma.

Monday August 31 – Thursday September 3, 1992

Niki and I talk in the evenings by phone. Early in the week Niki's happy; later in the week she's distressed. 'Elizabeth won't tell me who the naughty people are,' Niki weeps. 'She said, "You figure it out, Mom." Richard, Elizabeth knows more than she lets on.'

Friday September 4, 1992

I return home midafternoon Friday, acutely anxious. Nothing in my life makes sense to me. Elizabeth asks me to play with her. Niki looks exhausted. After dinner, she takes Elizabeth on an errand. When they return, I'm in the backyard, playing with Jenny. Elizabeth runs to join our play, shouting, 'Daddy!'

When we eventually go inside the house, Niki's in torment. 'Elizabeth told me she wants to stay at Nanna's tonight,' she says, 'and for ever and ever, because she feels safe there, but she doesn't feel safe here.'

'Is she anxious about something?' I ask.

Niki doesn't answer. She's struggling with a decision. 'I wish I were all-wise and knew what to do,' she finally says, then asks Elizabeth, 'Do you want to go back to Nanna's?'

Elizabeth looks confused and says nothing, so I tell her, 'You're safe here with Daddy.'

My statement triggers Niki. 'That's it! We're leaving! I promised Elizabeth I'd do whatever she asks, to make her feel safe. We're leaving.'

I help load the girls into Niki's car. I sense that an iota of opposition from me and my world will come crashing down. Reversing out of the garage, Niki looks at me with contempt, or sadness, or anger – I don't know what she feels. Her parting statement is, 'Watch Oprah Winfrey's program on TV tonight – it's pertinent to our situation.'

I watch Oprah's program, 'Scared Silent: Exposing and Ending Child Abuse'. America's on the warpath against child abuse, and I think the cavalry is about to trample me in its stampede to catch the bad guys. Oprah's message is the need to break the silence about child sexual abuse. Eva, twenty-one years old, has had an incestuous relationship with her father for fourteen years. Fifteen-year-old Tanya has been sexually assaulted by her brother.

I call Niki after the program and try to be pleasant. Niki's angry. 'Why are you so chipper, given the circumstances?' she asks.

'Niki, are you at your mother's house to avoid me?'

'No,' Niki replies, curtly, 'but I have to go now. Elizabeth's crying for me to come to bed. I have a hair appointment tomorrow. I'll take the girls.' And she hangs up.

Niki seems intent on staying away from me. So, is this it? Is this the end? I'm surprised when she calls back about eleven-thirty at night, in a completely different mood, friendly and conspiratorial.

'Richard,' she says, 'there are some exciting new developments I haven't told you about. During the week, Elizabeth wanted to watch a TV program about sexual abuse, even when I tried to switch channels. After the program, she said she wanted to learn more about sexuality. So I bought some books about where babies come from, with pictures.'

After a crash course on sexual behaviour and reproductive anatomy, Niki probably hopes Elizabeth will respond to her questions with anatomically correct answers.

Niki goes on, 'After Elizabeth saw the pictures, she told me, "Penises get hard and black, yucky stuff comes out of them."'

A vile taste washes through my mouth. 'Niki, did you question her about penises?'

'I showed her a picture of a penis,' Niki replies. 'She said, "It's a naughty penis." When I asked her if it was a hard penis or a soft penis, she said, "It's a hard penis." Richard, Elizabeth was answering my questions up to then. But then she mentioned the black, yucky stuff without any questioning from me. So she must have been sexually abused.'

Niki has a robust confidence when she talks about her interactions with Elizabeth. During this conversation, however, for once, this once, she has a guilty hesitation in her voice. Surely Niki understands she's contaminating Elizabeth, implanting sexual imagery and vocabulary in her three-year-old mind while she's in therapy to diagnose possible sexual abuse?

After this moment of hesitation, she needs to reassert. 'Richard,' Niki says, accusingly, 'Elizabeth said she's afraid of you. That's why she wants to stay here.'

I've been kicked in the guts. 'Why do you think she said that?' I ask.

'She gets upset when you and I hold hands or sit together,' Niki answers. 'I think it's disturbed behaviour from sexual abuse. She's afraid of men.'

'Niki, maybe it's just manipulative behaviour? She was upset about losing your full attention when baby Jenny arrived.'

Niki disagrees. 'Elizabeth gets upset and angry if I'm not with her, to keep her safe. Richard, from now on you can't spend much time alone with her. And you can't take her far from home. She needs to be somewhere close by, so she can get to me quickly.'

We live in a small town with few attractions. Elizabeth loves our excursions to Tulsa Zoo and other playgrounds. She's cranky when we have to return home. I remind Niki how much Elizabeth enjoys playing with me, at home and on vacations.

Niki agrees. 'That's what makes all this so crazy. But, Richard, children keep secrets. They don't talk about bad things that happen to them. You need to read a book I have on sexual abuse. The abuse when Elizabeth was one and two years old will come out. It's not her choice. Like when she's older and scared by a male schoolteacher. We have to uncover her sexual abuse now so we can understand her fears around men when she's older.'

What a tragedy. Now Niki will tie all of Elizabeth's fears back to child-hood sexual abuse.

'Niki,' I say, 'I don't agree with you taking the girls away from our home. We should stay together. We need to get to the bottom of this.'

'Richard, I promised Elizabeth I'd do whatever she asks to keep her safe.'

Saturday September 5, 1992

I'm surprised when Niki arrives home midmorning. Elizabeth's excited to see me, but Niki says, 'She still wants to stay at Nanna's and still says she's afraid of you. I've left a phone message with Hegburg for advice. We'll camp out at Mother's until this is sorted out.'

'Niki, let's ask Elizabeth why she's afraid of me.'

'Richard, it's unfair to put her on the spot.'

'Niki, we should talk to Elizabeth about her fears,' I plead.

'Richard, you're being egotistical, only thinking about yourself.'

We're standing on the back patio for privacy. Elizabeth comes out to the patio and asks me to go play with her in our front yard, on her climbing tree. So we walk together, hand in hand, by the side of the house. We're alone together, for a few moments.

'Elizabeth, are you afraid of me?' I ask, meekly, humbly.

She's embarrassed. 'I told Mommy not to tell you that,' she says, almost in a whisper. 'I'm afraid of you just a tiny bit.' She holds her thumb and forefinger almost together, to illustrate her point. How bright she is. How sad I feel. I wonder what I've done. I remember times when I've been tired and cranky. And I think about my own father, his huge angry presence towering over me. I was definitely afraid of my father. Is this how she feels?

Niki joins us in the front yard and I convince her to ask Elizabeth why she's afraid of me. 'He punched me twice in the tummy at Tiny Tots,' she replies, like a bored automaton, answering one of a thousand similar abuse-related questions with whatever thought bubble pops into her three-year-old head. I don't know where Tiny Tots is. I've never punched Elizabeth. Niki knows Elizabeth's statement is untrue, and looks relieved.

'Niki, do you really think I'm abusing Elizabeth?' I ask.

'I have enough information to have you investigated, if I wanted to,' Niki replies assertively, almost petulantly. 'Carmen and I made a list.' Niki ticks off their list: 'Elizabeth said you touched her tee-tee when all this started. She told Carmen you taught her how to French-kiss. And when I told her I don't like her sticking her tongue out, she said, "Daddy does!" And when I talked to her about privacy, she said, "My daddy needs to give me more privacy."'

Then Niki adds, 'I did ask if you'd ever hurt her with your penis, and she said no.'

Had Elizabeth said yes, if she thought that was the right answer, I could now stand accused of sexual abuse, with my marriage, my family, my career, my life – all blown apart. Niki is brainwashing Elizabeth about sexual abuse and playing Russian roulette with my life.

But I'm not angry. All I want is for the craziness to end. I cling to the hope we can get our happy family life back. I take Niki's hands in mine to say, 'I'm not abusing Elizabeth,' but as I try to speak, I cry. We then talk about respecting each other's right to hold different opinions, and staying together to solve our problems.

Niki's doubts about me seem to fall away, and, almost without taking a breath, she shares her latest theories about babysitters and day care centres involved in Elizabeth's ritual abuse. She must think I've gone back down the rabbit hole with her, into her fantasy world, and that I'm again an ally in her war against the abusers. I don't get it. Do I need to walk around wearing a placard saying, 'Niki, I don't agree with your theory about ritual abuse!'? Does Niki hear me when I say I hold different opinions?

Niki's mood elevates. She wants to celebrate by driving Elizabeth past all the houses of all the babysitters and all the day care centres she's ever had any contact with, 'to see if she has any kind of reaction'. She returns, excited. 'Richard, Elizabeth had a strong reaction at Abigail and Dale's house.'

Abigail is a middle-aged woman who occasionally babysat Elizabeth. Dale is her husband.

Niki tells me Elizabeth wanted to go inside Abigail's house and play with toys. When Niki asked her what happened inside the house, Elizabeth said, 'Monsters live in there and people take their clothes off, and play naughty games and do naughty touch.' Niki says she's also suspicious about a new shed beside the house. 'Richard, it could be used for ritual abuse.'

Niki's excitement increases. 'This is a breakthrough. Someone has tried to disrupt our bonds with Elizabeth. Tried to replace us with surrogate parents. Tried to program her with negative thoughts about us.'

Sunday September 6, 1992

Niki's mood remains elevated. Today she wants to retrace yesterday's excursion past all the babysitters' houses and all the day care centres. I go along for the ride. Elizabeth has no reaction at any of the babysitters' houses, and Dale mows the lawn in front of his house. When Niki asks Elizabeth if she knows him, she says, 'No.'

The shed door is open – tools, clutter and garden equipment. We drive on.

Then Niki tells me, 'This is Tiny Tots Day Care.'

I ask Elizabeth if this is where I punched her twice in the tummy.

'Yes!' she answers, with a proud smile, 'and you taught me to French-kiss in Tiny Tots as well.'

six

Schwartz Talks Again

Tuesday September 8, 1992

A month has passed since our final meeting with Dr Schwartz and the ensuing debacle. Today Schwartz calls Tom Dohne to clarify with him his assessment of Elizabeth. I assume he's already contacted the Department of Human Services and the police, as sexual abuse investigations of Kacey and Children's Home Day Care have been shelved.

Late this afternoon Niki meets Dohne to hear a replay of Schwartz's assessment. She returns home with red, teary eyes. 'I spent time alone at my parents' house calling my mother and my sister for support,' she says. 'Schwartz's diagnosis was just as I expected. He thought I was hysterical and overreacting. Richard, he didn't uncover Elizabeth's ritual abuse. He didn't hear my concerns. He's the reason our family's in crisis.'

Schwartz later provides a written report (Appendix 1):

Elizabeth presented herself as a rather normal and healthy young girl ... No thought disorder was suspected and her overall reality contact appeared intact ... She generally presented herself as a rather bright, verbal and sociable young girl ...

... the mother continued to be very concerned (and seemingly somewhat obsessed) with the fact that she felt her daughter was being ritually sexually abused and that there was occult activity and possible child pornography also going on.

... I did not find any significant clinical support to confirm that Elizabeth Vos was sexually abused ... Elizabeth had told this examiner ... that she was touched around her genital area by ... Mikee and Alan

… one would not interpret this as being sexual abuse … Realizing this young girl's age … it is very difficult if not impossible to elicit consistent information … I also … felt there was possibly some degree of contamination and continued to prompt the parents to … refrain from asking her questions which this examiner felt was over done by the mother.

Sunday September 13, 1992

A lovely, mild autumn day, perfect for a family picnic. I suggest to Niki we drive north to Independence, Kansas, to a beautiful park and playground Elizabeth and I recently discovered. Niki is suspicious about where I take the girls on our weekend driving adventures, so this is a great opportunity to allay her fears. And Jenny's first birthday was yesterday, so that calls for something special.

Before our excursion, Niki wants to attend her Sunday church service. Elizabeth, after hearing me talk about going to the park, isn't keen on a church service. Niki coaxes her to church, but returns ten minutes later. 'She thought you'd leave without her and threw a huge fit.'

After Niki returns to church, Elizabeth shouts, 'We have to go to the park! Straight away!' When I say we have to wait for Mommy to come home from church, Elizabeth shouts, 'No! We have to leave before Mommy gets home! Mommy hurts me!'

Later, while driving, I tell Niki about Elizabeth's attempt at manipulation.

Niki has a different perspective. 'No-one except Paul Roland appreciates Elizabeth's terror. Her terror could not result from anything other than programming through ritual abuse. Richard, she even distrusts her own mommy. There are dark forces influencing Elizabeth. The devil selects innocent children as his victims.'

Wednesday September 16, 1992

Today Niki updates her list of Elizabeth's ritual abuse symptoms, then delivers it to Hegburg. Tonight, she cries in my arms for hours. Nothing brings her out of her distress.

Thursday September 17, 1992

Today Niki's mood flips. She calls me at work, ecstatic. 'Richard, Mom and I just had an amazing breakthrough. We sat Elizabeth down, with pen and pad, and we asked her for the names of all the naughty people, all the monsters and all the bad people who hurt her, so the police can arrest them. She got very sombre and said, "Newester, Dewester, Miss Mabel, Abigail, Mikee and Alan are the bad people." After that, she was her old happy self again.'

* * *

This afternoon Niki and I have our first parent session with Elizabeth's new therapist, Faye Hegburg. Niki's excited, and asks, 'Faye, can you see evidence of ritual abuse in the list of Elizabeth's symptoms I gave you yesterday?'

'No,' Hegburg replies, 'the known stressors in her life could explain her symptoms.' Faye only wants to discuss the ways in which Niki should interact with Elizabeth. 'Niki, she needs to learn to sleep by herself. And she needs to accept other carers, to build up her confidence. Niki, Elizabeth needs to be able to separate from you.'

Saturday September 19, 1992

This evening we take Elizabeth to an 'Indian Summer Powwow' at the Bartlesville Community Center, with lots of music and dancing by Osage Indians. Niki claps, which, for some reason, annoys Elizabeth. 'Don't clap!' she demands. Niki continues clapping, so Elizabeth ups the ante and shouts, 'Mommy! I need to tell you a secret!' So, of course, Niki stops clapping. Elizabeth whispers the secret into Niki's ear, but with all the surrounding noise, she can't hear what Elizabeth says.

Driving home, she asks Elizabeth to repeat her secret. Elizabeth, in the back seat, answers in a bored monotone, 'Newester, Dewester, Brewester'. These are the names of some of the naughty people Niki's desperate to identify.

'If only someone who understood ritual abuse could work with Elizabeth,' Niki tells me, within earshot of Elizabeth. 'Richard, she's ready to disclose.'

seven

Abigail And Dale

Thursday September 24, 1992

Up to now, 'Mikee', 'Alan' and 'Miss Mabel' have been Elizabeth's go-to names when Niki asks, 'Who are the naughty people?' These naughty people have hit Elizabeth in the eye, the tummy and the tee-tee. They've shot her with guns, French-kissed her, put apples with worms in her mouth, and maybe other ghastly abuse I've forgotten. Niki thinks Kacey is also a perpetrator; however, Elizabeth rarely mentions her name. 'Newester', 'Blewester', 'Brewester' and 'Dewester' are also perpetrators. Niki's desperate to find out who these people are, their real names. Today, a new suspect comes to life.

This morning, Niki calls me at work, elated. 'Richard, there's been a disclosure!' She tells me Elizabeth was sad watching the scene in *Dumbo* where Dumbo's mother is put in jail. Niki told her she'd never leave her, like Dumbo's mother left Dumbo, and that Elizabeth won't be hurt by the naughty people ever again. Then Niki asked Elizabeth if her sadness was 'because we were apart, like Dumbo and his mother, or because a naughty person really did hurt you?'

Niki goes on. 'In an adult voice, Elizabeth said, "There is a naughty person. It's Dale."' Elizabeth told Niki that Dale, the babysitter Abigail's husband, showed her his penis, cut her tummy with his penis, and held Ethan's penis, and Ethan went tee-tee all over him. 'Richard, she laughed when she said that.'

Niki's friend Rachel also used Abigail to babysit her son Ethan. Niki wants to corroborate Elizabeth's disclosure through Ethan. 'Richard, I'm going over to Rachel's now. This is a breakthrough!'

Niki calls back later, even more elated. 'Rachel asked Ethan if Dale cut Elizabeth's tummy with his penis. Ethan was shy, but said, "Yes, and I beat Dale up."'

'We have a perpetrator!' Niki exclaims. 'Richard, I'll expect an apology from you if we find out Dale abused Elizabeth. You abandoned me. You just fought against me all through this. You were the only one who ignored all the obvious signs of sexual abuse. My mother and my sister and Linda Foster and Paul Roland, they all saw the signs of sexual abuse.'

This evening I call Rachel, who says, 'I'm concerned by what Ethan said about Dale, but he was answering our questions, so I can't say for sure what really happened. Ethan also talked about seeing Elizabeth's penis. John might get more out of him. They have a good rapport.'

Rachel is married to John, a geologist and a colleague of mine.

John calls me back. 'Richard,' he says, 'Ethan hasn't been traumatised by whatever went on at Dale and Abigail's, so I'm not going to introduce trauma by questioning him.'

Friday September 25, 1992

This morning Niki asks Paul Roland to please tell Linda Foster about her new abuse suspect. Roland ducks Niki's request, and suggests Faye Hegburg should call Foster.

'Foster probably thinks I'm just a hysterical mother after hearing from Schwartz,' Niki tells me. 'I'm so angry with Schwartz. But, Richard, isn't it wonderful Elizabeth's disclosed. I left an urgent message for Foster to call me.'

By this afternoon, Niki's despondent. Rachel has told Niki she thinks Ethan's statement was tainted by their questioning. And today Ethan told Rachel the things he said yesterday didn't really happen.

'I think it's just all too hard for Rachel,' Niki tells me. 'I understand how traumatic it is for mothers to deal with the sexual abuse of their children.'

Saturday September 26, 1992

Today a new abuse scenario emerges. Niki again asks Elizabeth if Dale hurt her with his penis, and Elizabeth tells us, 'No, no, he just showed me his penis.' Then she adds, 'Dale told me Mommy and Daddy didn't love me, Nanna and Poppa didn't love me, Jenny didn't love me. No-one loved me. And Ethan cut Dale's neck off with his sword. And then Abigail put Dale in the naughty corner.'

Niki turns to me, in tears. 'Richard, this vindicates my suspicion some-one was alienating Elizabeth from me. And when I was most vulnerable – when I was pregnant with Jenny.

Niki believes this gibberish? 'Niki,' I ask, hesitantly, trying to be subtle, 'have you asked Elizabeth about someone saying her mommy and daddy didn't love her?'

Niki agrees she probably has. She doesn't understand why I've asked her that question.

'Well, Niki,' I say cautiously, 'maybe Elizabeth talked about Dale say-ing no-one loved her because you had asked her if someone had said her mummy and daddy didn't love her?'

Niki can't grasp that concept. 'No, Richard,' she insists, 'Elizabeth dis-closed what Dale said to her, that her mommy and daddy didn't love her.'

Sunday September 27, 1992

Today Niki continues interrogating Elizabeth about Dale.

'Did Dale touch your tee-tee?' Niki asks.

Elizabeth looks confused and says nothing.

'Did Dale tell you not to say anything about him touching your tee-tee?'

Elizabeth looks confused and says nothing.

'It's alright,' Niki says, 'we can talk about it some other time, when you're ready.'

Elizabeth looks anxious.

Monday September 28, 1992

Today Foster returns Niki's urgent call. Niki updates her about Dale, and tells her, 'Abigail might provide information about Dale, if she regrets his behaviour and comes clean.'

This evening, with a hint of triumph, Niki tells me, 'Richard, today Elizabeth disclosed that Dale did touch her tee-tee, and that he stuck a plastic rod into her bottom as well, like this one.' Niki holds a large, long plastic rod.

Tuesday September 29, 1992

Today at work, John tells me he drove Ethan past Dale's house and asked if he'd had a good time there. Ethan had said it was okay.

'Richard,' John says, 'we won't assist you in any police investigation of Dale and Abigail.'

Later today, Rachel calls Niki to tell her she's seen a counsellor for advice about Ethan and Dale. The counsellor advised Rachel not to pursue therapy for Ethan. Niki disagrees. 'Ethan should go into therapy!' she exclaims. 'He needs to bring up the abuse he's hiding inside.'

eight

Mikee And Alan

Thursday October 1, 1992

Two days after the Abigail-and-Dale earthquake settles, a new tremor arrives. Niki calls my office, sombre, with the news that Hegburg had used an anatomically correct doll to videotape confirmation of Elizabeth's abuse.

'I just watched the tape,' Niki tells me. 'Elizabeth went into a sexual frenzy. She ripped off the doll's pants and rammed her fingers into the vagina. Faye asked if anyone did this to her, and she said, "Yes, Mikee and Alan".'

Niki unleashes. 'Richard, this is just the first layer. This is just the beginning. Just the tip of the iceberg. Just the smallest part. Just the safest part. I'm sure there's been adult sexual abuse.'

I then call Hegburg and ask what happened.

'Elizabeth said Mikee and Alan tickled her tee-tee,' Hegburg replies, matter-of-fact. When I tell her Niki's sure abuse by adults is involved, Hegburg disagrees. 'Richard, Elizabeth's response to the doll can be explained by Mikee and Alan.'

Hegburg continues, with a hint of frustration in her voice. 'Richard, she will grow out of her fears by experiencing safe play with other children. There shouldn't be any lingering problems. She'll have to go to school one day, Dad.'

Elizabeth's behaviour with the anatomically correct doll opens a floodgate. Niki feels vindicated, and tonight tells me, 'Elizabeth's sexual abuse started long before Children's Home. Richard, it began with Kacey, progressed to abuse by Dale, which set her up to be taken advantage of by Mikee and Alan. She was conditioned for sexual abuse before Children's Home. She's been taught to masturbate adult males and females, and to be masturbated by them. She's aware of the sex act, erect male penises and ejaculation.'

Niki looks poised to strike if I dare disagree with her chronology of Elizabeth's sexual abuse.

She goes on. 'I came close to abandoning Elizabeth a second time. The first time was allowing her to be sexually abused. The second time was almost ending my investigation before she disclosed. Were it not for my mother and my sister saying they believed me, I would not have pursued this. I would not have had the strength.'

Sunday October 4, 1992

Niki's anxiety ramps back up, as does her questioning of Elizabeth. 'Richard, guess what she told me today. We were talking about the monsters and she said, very, very clearly, "Little Dale touched my tee-tee, opened my tee-tee and punched my tee-tee. And told me I had a bad tee-tee."'

Niki is now questioning Elizabeth about Abigail and Dale's son, 'Little Dale'.

Niki has also ramped up Elizabeth's sex education. Tonight Elizabeth asks, 'Mommy, can we talk more about vaginas and penises and sexual intercourse?'

So Niki reads to her from a children's book, *Where Babies Come From*.

Elizabeth asks, 'Mommy, do I have a vagina? Did I have a penis?' and studies cartoon pictures of sexual intercourse. After this bout of education, she proudly announces, 'Dad, Dad, I'll get pubic hair when I'm older.'

Niki then asks Elizabeth, 'Do you want to talk more about what the naughty people did to you? You'll feel so much better if you talk about it.'

Elizabeth answers with a blank stare.

Niki asks again, 'Are you sure you don't want to talk about it?'

Another blank stare.

After witnessing all this, I can't sleep. This is abuse. It's crazy, sick. What can I do? Finally, I get up at about three in the morning to write. Niki gets up at four, and we talk.

'Richard,' Niki says, 'I will not allow her sexual abuse to go unresolved to cause her problems later in life.' Niki repeats her belief that Elizabeth's behaviour can only be explained by adult sexual abuse, and that her mother and her sister agree with her. 'Richard, you've abandoned Elizabeth. And you've sabotaged my efforts with Schwartz and Hegburg to uncover the truth of her sexual abuse.'

I argue that my having an opinion other than sexual abuse doesn't mean I've abandoned her or Elizabeth. 'And, Niki, I haven't sabotaged you. Schwartz and Hegburg made up their own minds. I've hardly spoken to them.'

Monday October 5, 1992

After work today, we visit Tom Dohne as a couple. Niki mentions the Mikee-and-Alan video. Dohne surprises me by exclaiming, 'So, what's new? We already knew Mikee and Alan hurt Elizabeth.'

Dohne redirects the conversation to the way Niki and I handle our differences of opinion. He summarises our impediments: 'Richard, you are avoidant and withdraw. Niki, you fear abandonment and have dramatic flare-ups.'

Tonight Niki calls her mother. 'Momma! Elizabeth's increasingly bratty behaviour is obviously a result of her sexual abuse disclosures unsettling her.'

I think that's bullshit. Elizabeth exhibits normal bratty three-year-old behaviour, and we don't provide much in the way of boundaries or control.

But I don't say that. I avoid confrontation and withdraw to my diary.

nine

Questioning

Wednesday October 7, 1992

Niki needs answers. She needs to know who sexually abused Elizabeth and the precise nature of the abuse. Niki believes the person with the answers is Elizabeth. So she loads question upon question, brick upon brick, into her three-year-old mind. What ideas and fears are being walled in? What memories are being built? Tonight the interrogation continues.

'Who taught you to pose in a pornographic way?' Niki asks.

Elizabeth answers with a blank stare.

'How did Miss Mabel hurt you? Why is she one of the monsters?'

Blank stare.

Niki, showing Elizabeth photographs of all the babysitters, asks, 'Who hurt you?'

'All of them kept me safe!' Elizabeth exclaims. 'It was Dale! He turned into a girl!'

Niki asks, puzzled, how Dale was a girl?

'He tried to wear a dress,' Elizabeth answers. 'But it was too little. It was my dress. Then he put on his dress. I used my magic wand to change him.'

Monday October 12, 1992

This morning Niki and I visit Hegburg to view the video of Elizabeth's behaviour with the anatomically correct doll. I'm supposed to see Elizabeth go into a sexual frenzy. In the video, she calmly explores the female doll's anatomy and playfully says, 'I'm going to tickle your tee-tee.'

After viewing the video, I ask Hegburg, 'Could we contaminate the disclosure process by asking Elizabeth if certain people have done certain things to her?' I'm angling for Hegburg to tell us we shouldn't question Elizabeth.

'You should certainly not introduce names or activities,' Hegburg replies, adding, 'There's no evidence from my sessions that Dale and Abigail have hurt Elizabeth. Niki, I can't report them to the Department of Human Services.'

As Hegburg says this, I wonder why on earth Elizabeth hasn't told Hegburg something like, 'Dale showed me his penis,' given all of Niki's questioning. My next thought is that Niki's questioning puts people's lives at risk. This thought worries me, so I say, 'Anyway, we wouldn't have a legal leg to stand on, because we've questioned Elizabeth about Dale.'

'We have not!' Niki erupts.

I'm stunned. 'Niki, I've heard you ask Elizabeth if Dale abused her.'

'I did not! I'll check my notes. Elizabeth talked about Dale before I questioned her.'

Wednesday October 14 – Wednesday October 21, 1992

A week of relentless questioning. 'Elizabeth, who are the naughty people?' Niki asks. 'If we knew their names we could have the police put them in jail. I just wish you would tell us their names. I wish you would tell us what they did to you.'

Elizabeth's blank stares don't stop the questioning, so she makes up stock answers, which she delivers robotically. The ones I hear are 'Miss Mabel, Miss Mabel, Miss Mabel'. 'Five Miss Mabels'. 'They hit me in the eye and they hit me in the tummy and they hit me in the tee-tee.' 'Dale hit me in the eye and in the tummy and in the tee-tee with a baseball bat.' Finally, she will tell Niki, 'I don't want to talk about it,' or, 'I'm Pinocchio and I can't talk.'

Niki thinks 'I don't want to talk about it' means 'It's too scary to talk about.' So she asks Elizabeth, 'Why don't you want to talk about it? Is it too scary to talk about?'

Elizabeth answers, 'Yes, it's too scary to talk about.' Soon after that, her stock answer is revised to, 'I don't want to talk about it, it's too scary.'

I'm watching a live drama that Elizabeth makes up as she goes.

When Elizabeth gets bored repeating her stock answers, she invents a pantomime. In answer to, 'What did the naughty people do to you?' her clenched right fist moves in deliberate arcs, in sync with her script. 'They hit me in the eye,' and her right fist arcs to her eyes. 'And they hit me in the tummy,' and her right fist arcs out from her eyes into her tummy. 'And they hit me in the tee-tee,' and her right fist arcs to her tee-tee. Within a few days this pantomime is rehearsed and perfected, but the questions keep coming. After acting out this same abuse script, this same pantomime, over and over, her eyes anxiously plead, Please don't ask me any more questions.

Elizabeth thinks she owns the pantomime, owns the script. But she's a puppet, a desperate three-year-old puppet, jiggling in a tragic performance, attached to strings controlled by Niki. Watching this grim drama, my mind screams, Niki, this is abuse!

But I say nothing.

Thursday October 22, 1992

This evening I sit beside the bathtub watching Elizabeth and Jenny soak clean, a nightly routine. They play with floating toys and we talk and laugh, as usual. Then Elizabeth says, 'Daddy, I just love to play with your penis.' She speaks in a slow, deliberate, scripted way and looks at me intently, watching for my reaction.

I'm annoyed. 'Elizabeth, what you just said is not funny, not a joke.' My voice is raised and Elizabeth sinks slowly down her side of the bathtub, to avoid eye contact. 'Elizabeth, sit back up and look at me,' I say brusquely. 'Have you ever played with anyone's penis?'

'Yes!' she shouts, smiling, 'The monster's penis!' When I ask her who is the monster, she shouts, 'Miss Mabel!'

'Then why did you say you played with my penis?'

'No, no, I never said I played with your penis. I said I played with the monster's penis.'

I pick up Jenny, go into the kitchen, and tell Niki what Elizabeth has just said. 'Niki, was there any questioning today with Elizabeth about playing with penises?' I ask.

'No,' she replies. 'Elizabeth's statement is her way of flirting with you. Richard, she also flirts with me. She says she loves to play with my vagina. It's all flirty behaviour, conditioned by her sexual abuse. Now, finally, it's being acted out on you. I'm convinced she's played with a man's penis.'

Then, together, we ask Elizabeth, 'Why did you say you like to play with Daddy's penis?'

'No, no,' Elizabeth answers, 'I said I played with Miss Mabel's vagina.'

Niki then calls her mother, her sister and her friend Sandra. 'Richard is finally starting to experience Elizabeth's promiscuous sexual flirtation,' she tells them.

Bullshit. These are not the flirtatious statements of a sexualised, sexually abused three-year-old. An intelligent, brainwashed three-year-old girl is talking about playing with penises and vaginas in an attention-seeking way, because that's what she's continuously asked to talk about.

But I don't say any of that either.

Wednesday November 4, 1992

Today we visit Hegburg for an update. Elizabeth has told Hegburg the story about my mother pushing her into a swimming pool and being saved by my father. Niki says she believes the story.

'I don't believe it,' I say. 'It's absurd. And we know Elizabeth makes false statements.'

Hegburg dives into the discussion with some strokes of clarity. 'Children take questions and statements made to them and rebuild them into their own reality. The questions and statements become true for them. Only when they reach a certain age can children separate fiction from reality. Either in the questions or statements made to them, or how they process what they see and hear.'

Did Niki hear a single word? Does she separate fiction from reality? I wait in silence.

'Do you see any evidence of sexual abuse in your therapy?' Niki asks Hegburg.

Hegburg says the only thing she can report is the intrusive behaviour of Mikee and Alan. 'The most important therapy for her will come from a good bond between you two – her parents – and a nurturing home environment. Don't treat her as a victim. Make her feel normal, treat her normally, set appropriate boundaries on her behaviour and encourage normal independence.'

After seeing Hegburg, I feel a buzz of hope. Can we turn this Titanic around? This evening Niki is also positive. 'I suppose we may never know about Elizabeth's sexual abuse. As long as she shows improvement, I'm happy to close the book.'

Then, out of the blue, Elizabeth tells us, 'Mommy, Daddy, Miss Mabel didn't really hurt me. Miss Mabel was really my friend.'

Is this the icing on the cake?

Wednesday November 11, 1992

The respite lasts a week. Today, when we visit Dohne, Niki suddenly unloads.

'Richard, you just fought against all my efforts to uncover Elizabeth's sexual abuse. You say nothing happened. You make it nothing!' she cries. With fierce determination, she insists, 'The terror and disintegration I saw in Elizabeth cannot be the result of Mikee and Alan. Or ear surgery. Or my pregnancy. Or Jenny coming into the family. It has to be more than that. It's because of adult sexual abuse!'

Because I don't agree with her, Niki says she feels abandoned by me.

Dohne thinks he needs to explain to me Niki's fear of abandonment. 'Richard, Niki's father abandoned his family. So Niki has a strong reaction to a father, you, discounting a mother, Niki.' Dohne is reading to me from *Abandonment for Dummies*.

Now I want Dohne to read to Niki from *Obsession for Dummies*, because, from the facts and evidence we have, that's what Niki's beliefs amount to.

But his next comment is, 'I'll leave Elizabeth's diagnosis in the hands of Hegburg, but in my opinion, we'll never know for sure what caused Elizabeth's anxious behaviour.'

Niki's reply stuns Dohne, and me. 'Well, I think Elizabeth might have multiple personality disorder because of her sexual abuse.'

Dohne can't frame a reply before Niki adds, 'Surely there's some way for the police to investigate Abigail and Dale?'

Dohne answers that question quickly enough. 'Niki, that's not going to happen.'

Saturday November 14, 1992

This morning the girls remain asleep until quite late, and Niki and I enjoy a rare and wonderful Saturday morning lie-in. In our relaxed state she asks, in a friendly though serious tone that I interpret as a genuine, heartfelt enquiry, 'Richard, are there gaps in your past I don't know about? Are you really who you say you are? Do you have multiple personality disorder?'

These are strange questions to ask after four years of marriage, but I know she feels confused, unsure and threatened about many things at the moment. It feels silly to try to prove I am who I say I am. Part of me feels amused by her queries – like another weird thing has just happened in my new life of weirdness. So I simply respond with humour. 'Niki,' I joke, 'I'm not an escaped axe murderer. I'm not Dr Jekyll and Mr Hyde.'

Sunday November 15, 1992

Tonight Elizabeth brings me her Ken and Barbie dolls and a pink piglet. 'Dad, Dad,' she tells me, 'the boy is Prince Charming and the girl is Cinderella. The piglet is their baby.' She then puts Prince Charming on top of Cinderella and says, 'Dad, Dad, he has his penis in her vaginal to make a baby.' Elizabeth smiles. She's proud to know all about making babies. Or pink piglets, at least.

Monday November 16, 1992

Tonight Niki shares with me the result of today's questioning. 'Richard, Elizabeth said, when Kacey babysat, she was nice before I left the house. But after I left, Kacey turned into a bad person. I wonder if Kacey has multiple personality disorder?'

I wonder – has Niki gone bonkers?

Multiple Personality Disorder

Wednesday November 18, 1992

America has gone bonkers. Bestselling books, movies, TV talk shows, newspapers and magazines all broadcast that beneath a veneer of civilised society lurk cesspools of incest, sexual abuse and satanic ritual abuse. This abuse induces a coping mechanism whereby victims split into multiple personalities, or 'alters'. After all, just look at all the abuse victims being diagnosed with multiple personality disorder.

This popular focus on multiple personality disorder has made some people rich. Maybe greed is driving the hysteria. Or is it simply as Paul McHugh, director of psychiatry at Johns Hopkins University, later states in the foreword of the book *Hoax & Reality: The Bizarre World of Multiple Personality Disorder*: 'We will all look back ... and be dumbfounded by the gullibility of the public in the late twentieth century and by the power of psychiatric assertions to dissolve common sense.'

Greed and gullibility were certainly the driving forces behind the success of the 1973 publication of *Sybil*. This bestseller by Flora Schreiber was based on psychiatrist Cornelia Wilbur's diagnosis of multiple personality disorder in her long-time patient Shirley Mason. The naive public of the day were unaware that Schreiber, Wilbur and Mason had perpetrated a fraud to create Sybil Incorporated, agreeing to a three-way split of profits from sales of the book, dolls, movies, T-shirts, board games and other paraphernalia. They even discussed a Sybil musical.

Superb marketing of the Sybil hoax set off a firestorm of similar psychiatric diagnoses. Hundreds of thousands of cases of multiple personality disorder flooded out of therapists' offices. Most of these diagnoses were eventually considered a product of the patient's susceptibility to the therapist's suggestion, and a form of hysteria in which patients imitate a condition they've read about in books or seen in movies.

In the meantime, my family mirrors the craziness in America. If Elizabeth's been ritually sexually abused by a Bartlesville cult, surely she deserves to have multiple personality disorder. Or at least to have been abused by someone who has multiple personality disorder, probably Kacey.

Tonight Niki tells me her friend Sandra has multiple personality disorder. Sandra recommends we consult Dr Kramer, a psychiatrist in Tulsa who specialises in this disorder. 'Richard, I've made an appointment with Dr Kramer for next Monday. I've reviewed my journal. It all fits! My notes have lots of statements by Elizabeth about people changing, things changing, babysitters changing.' Niki believes we need to consult an expert on multiple personality disorder, 'to find out if Elizabeth's therapy is adequate'.

'And Richard,' Niki goes on, 'if Kacey has multiple personality disorder, we need to understand what she's done to Elizabeth. Today I asked her about Kacey. It took a few attempts to get her to remember Kacey, but once she did, I asked her if Kacey ever changed. Elizabeth said she changed into a boy and she got angry.'

Thursday November 19, 1992

Today we see Dohne, and Niki kicks off. 'Kacey having multiple personality disorder explains Elizabeth's disturbing behaviour in ways the known stressors don't. We need to see Dr Kramer.'

Dohne isn't convinced. 'Niki, Elizabeth's behaviour is the result of the sum total of all the known, and unknown, stressors in her life. We'll never know how the mix worked, how it was all processed in her mind.' Dohne says multiple personality disorder is highly controversial, extremely rare and very difficult to diagnose. 'Niki, don't immerse yourself in multiple personality disorder. It's a rugged and complicated terrain.'

Home again, and as soon as we walk through the door, Niki says to Elizabeth, 'Let's play babysitters.' She picks up a Ken doll and a Barbie doll and tells Elizabeth they're Prince Charming and Cinderella who can, 'go to the ball because they have a babysitter'. Niki then walks Prince Charming and Cinderella out of their dollhouse and asks Elizabeth, 'Are we at the babysitter's house?'

Elizabeth answers with a blank stare. This play is rushed. She isn't sure what the storyline is. I'm also perplexed.

Niki perseveres. 'Are we at Kacey's house?'

Blank stare.

'What is Kacey doing?'

Blank stare.

'Is Kacey's father there?'

Blank stare.

'What is Kacey's father doing?'

Blank stare.

'No!' Elizabeth suddenly shouts. 'The babysitter's not Kacey! It's Miss Mabel! And Cinderella and Prince Charming are dancing at the ball.'

This gives Niki an idea, so she calls her mother, excited. 'Momma, Elizabeth probably watched Kacey and her father dance naked together. And her father was masturbating against Kacey's stomach. This fits Elizabeth's talk about tummies being cut with a penis.'

What? I'm dazed. What a sick and bizarre image to conjure up. 'Niki, I can't imagine that happening, least of all in front of Elizabeth.'

'Well,' Niki flashes back, 'she definitely understands the sex act from watching it happen, because she talks about the man on top of the woman.'

This is absurd. 'Niki,' I remind her, 'you taught Elizabeth about the man on top of the woman. You showed her cartoon drawings of sexual intercourse.'

'Elizabeth knew about that before I showed her the drawings!'

'Niki,' I plead, exhausted, 'I'm very worried by your focus to find out what happened. It feels like you're pressuring Elizabeth for answers.' I'm not angry, just pleading.

'I am not pressuring Elizabeth!' Niki shouts, 'She has to go through full disclosure in order to heal.' Niki calms and adds, 'Richard, now we have the answers. Don't you see that? It all fits. Multiple personality disorder abuse by Kacey fits. This searching for answers is what I'm good at – uncovering past hurt to figure out what happened.'

Pleading again, I say, 'Niki, that sort of investigation and questioning might work with adults, but it's probably not the same with three-year-olds.'

'Well, I think it's the same!' Niki shouts.

Friday November 20, 1992

Today Niki cancels the appointment with Dr Kramer. I don't ask why. This evening, she takes a pad and pen, sits beside Elizabeth in the living room, and says, 'Let's write a story about the naughty babysitters.'

As Niki starts her usual barrage of questions, Elizabeth looks more and more anxious. Eventually, she stands up, walks to her bedroom, and buries herself under pillows. Niki and I follow. Elizabeth pokes her head from under her pillows and asks, 'Mommy, are you happy with me?'

'I just want to find out what happened to you,' Niki replies.

'Niki, your questions make her anxious,' I plead.

'Richard, she was already anxious,' Niki replies. 'I thought writing a story about the naughty babysitters would relieve her anxiety.'

Tuesday November 24, 1992

Tonight Niki tells me, 'Elizabeth's anxious. I need to take her to bed for a talk.' After the bedroom talk, Niki comes back to the living room, where I'm seated on a couch, stands in the middle of the room, and announces, 'Richard, that does it! We're going to find out exactly what happened. You know what Elizabeth just said? She just said, "The monsters told me when I grow up I'm going to marry the monsters." When I asked who the monsters are, she clammed up in fear.'

'Niki,' I say, 'all the videos Elizabeth's been watching end with a marriage.'

'Well,' Niki counters, 'she also has a theme of boys changing into girls.'

'Niki, in her *Beauty and the Beast* and *Aladdin* videos, everything changes into something else. That could explain her talk of things changing.'

'No, Richard, her statements fit perfectly with multiple personality disorder abuse.'

I keep trying. 'Niki, I'm really worried Elizabeth feels pressured by your search for answers. It may be the biggest stress in her life right now.'

'I am not pressuring Elizabeth!' Niki shouts at me, enraged.

Adrenaline floods my body and surges over the wall of my dammed-up frustration. I lean forward, slam my right fist into the floor, look up at Niki, and growl, 'Niki, I am entitled to my opinion. I think you're harming Elizabeth by constantly questioning her.'

Niki storms out of the living room, goes to the girls' room and slams the door. I go to the study to write down what just happened. I'm shaking. I can't think. I can't write. I get on my exercise bike and pedal furiously to release adrenaline. Will Niki now leave with the girls?

To my surprise, Niki opens the study door and initiates a calm discussion. I repeat my concern that Elizabeth feels pressured by her questioning.

'Richard, I'm just telling her I wish I knew what happened. It's critical to find out what happened.' Niki says she wonders if Elizabeth's been programmed by hypnosis, or scare tactics, not to say what happened. 'Like the abusers saying they put a bomb in her stomach with invisible stiches – to stop her disclosing.' Niki goes on. 'Richard, we need to consult specialists on ritual abuse. And we need the police to look into all the people in Bartlesville with the letter 'K' in their names. And we need to look for pornography rings. I would feel totally crazy having all these thoughts if it wasn't for the support of my mother and my sister.'

'Niki,' I reply, 'different specialists will have different opinions. All we'll have are conflicting opinions. Will we be any nearer the truth? These specialists will dig into Elizabeth's head with their picks and shovels for evidence of ritual abuse, not sure where to dig or if there's anything there to find.' I tell Niki I don't want Elizabeth to go through that.

'Richard,' Niki counters, 'if Elizabeth's been ritually abused, she won't be able to verbalise it. And Hegburg can't diagnose ritual abuse or multiple personality disorder abuse. We need a specialist.'

We talk calmly, in circles, for hours, and end where we started. Niki talks freely and honestly within the reality of her obsession. No reason or logic penetrates the shield protecting her obsession.

Wednesday November 25, 1992

Tonight Elizabeth talks to me playfully during her bath. 'Dad, uuummmm, I went dancing with a babysitter. She danced with her daddy. They French-kissed and fell in love.'

This plot sounds familiar. 'Who was the babysitter?' I ask.

'Uuuuuummm …' But she loses interest and plays with her bath toys.

After the bath, Niki decides to try to breastfeed Elizabeth – who stopped breastfeeding almost two years ago. 'If she wants to breastfeed, it must be a legitimate need related to her abuse and to her damaged bonds with me. My sister thinks breastfeeding Elizabeth is even more important than breastfeeding Jenny, given the abuse she suffered.'

'I haven't finished nursing yet,' echoes Elizabeth, between gulping attempts to breastfeed. Then she looks up at Niki and asks, 'Are you happy with me now, Mommy?'

'No,' Niki replies. 'No, I'm worried about you. I want to know what happened to you. Did you nurse from the monsters?'

Elizabeth answers with a blank stare.

Thursday November 26, 1992

Today is Thanksgiving holiday and Niki's friend Sandra joins us from Tulsa with a pile of literature on multiple personality disorder. While Elizabeth sits close by watching videos, Niki and Sandra openly discuss Elizabeth's ritual sexual abuse, pornography abuse, multiple personality disorder abuse, and who the Bartlesville abuse perpetrators might be. I wonder if Elizabeth overhears their conversation.

I get my answer. Elizabeth walks to where I sit and matter-of-factly says, 'Dad, let's have a meeting and talk about Elizabeth's monsters.' This is followed by a stream of consciousness monologue. 'Dad, the monsters shoot me. But they're nice monsters. They play with me. I shoot them. It's a game. They shoot me in the tee-tee. I like it. They come here when you go to a meeting. They boink me in the eye and in the tummy and in the tee-tee. They tell me Mommy doesn't love me and Daddy doesn't love me. Their names are Newester and Dewester.'

Monday November 30, 1992

Today my crazy parallel universe gets crazier. Niki calls me at work, ecstatic. 'Richard, I'm so happy I could spit. Elizabeth just disclosed what happened to her. I've written it all down':

She woke up and started calling me Uncle Billy. She said, 'He turns into a woman. And Yvonne. He was big and black and blue and huge and we made love. I was left all alone at their house. You left me at the people house, the party house. We had lots of fun there. We played games. We all got big big big and then we got little bitty again and came back. Miss Mabel the babysitter took me there, and her dad. In a car like papa's that was red. I was scared there. I was all alone, no one came. They said others would be there and I was all alone. I wanted you there. I'm scared to tell you. They said you didn't love me and Daddy didn't love me. They had movies there at the hospital, movies with me. And like FernGully to watch.'

Billy is Niki's father's brother – Niki's uncle – and Yvonne is Billy's wife.

'Niki,' I say, 'this makes no sense to me.'

'Richard, it fits! Billy and Yvonne have a two-storey house, and so does Kacey. And Kacey's father has a red truck. It all fits. Nothing else could explain it. Elizabeth is finally opening up, and it's the result of me re-establishing our broken bonds by breastfeeding.'

Niki calls back later, this time from her mother's house. 'Richard, you won't believe what we're finding out. Meet me here for dinner.'

I arrive at her mother's house, anxious. Niki updates me. 'We discovered the house opposite Kacey's was their previous family home, and it's painted blue. And there's a car with a Texas licence plate parked outside.'

I don't understand the significance of these discoveries.

'Richard,' Niki patiently explains, 'Elizabeth always refers to a blue house, so this house could be the one used for her ritual abuse. And a pornography ring could operate out of Texas.'

Wednesday December 2, 1992

Tonight Elizabeth's behaviour is out of control. I watch her spiral downward, from refusing to wear clothes, to refusing to eat with us at the table, to whining for attention, to running wild around the living room, to tripping on a toy, to landing on the hard wood floor in a screaming heap of writhing three-year-old.

Niki picks Elizabeth up, breastfeeds, and says, 'I'm only nursing you because I know you've been hurt. I understand the pain you went through with the naughty babysitters.' Niki then explains what Elizabeth's experiencing. 'I'll tell you the proper name for it; it's called a flashback. You are remembering when a naughty babysitter hurt you.'

Niki then takes Elizabeth to bed, to delve deeper into flashbacks. So I play with Jenny in the family room. Jenny now loves my 'I'm-gonna-get-ya' game. She waddles away, laughing her head off, while I pretend to chase her.

Elizabeth hears our play from the bedroom, abandons flashback therapy, jumps out of bed, runs to the living room, and shouts, 'Chase me too, Dad! Chase me too, Dad!'

Niki returns to the living room, despondent. 'Richard, we need to treat Elizabeth like her development stopped at thirteen months. From now on, we have to think of ourselves as having twin thirteen-month-old girls, one suffering arrested development.'

Niki also tells me that, from now on, in her parenting of Elizabeth, she's proceeding as if abuse by someone with multiple personality disorder is a given. 'Hegburg doesn't know anything about multiple personality disorder abuse. And Elizabeth obviously has post-traumatic stress disorder. Hegburg should at least diagnose post-traumatic stress disorder.'

eleven

Goodbye, Tom Dohne

Thursday December 3, 1992

For years, Tom Dohne has provided welcome counsel to Niki for chronic fatigue syndrome, for her parents' fraught relationship, for our communication issues, and now for Elizabeth. Niki considers Tom Dohne an ally and fellow wise counsellor. Today that ends.

We visit Dohne as a couple and Niki opens proceedings, declaring, 'I'm angry!' She then says, 'Elizabeth's obviously suffered a major trauma and I'm tired of carrying the emotional burden. All her behaviour fits the model of ritual abuse and multiple personality disorder abuse.' Niki tells Dohne she's re-booked to see Dr Kramer.

'Why have you gone back to multiple personality disorder?' asks Dohne. 'It's controversial and hard to prove or disprove. And how would therapy for Elizabeth change?'

Dohne then steps, fatally, into the minefield protecting Niki's obsession. 'Niki, I hear you trying to play two roles, mother and therapist. Niki, nobody can do that, not even a trained therapist. I wouldn't attempt to do that. Doing that is dangerous for Elizabeth, and too great a burden on you.'

I wait for the fireworks. But not for long.

'I am not acting as a therapist to Elizabeth!' Niki shouts. But she wants to shift the conversation back to the source of her anger. 'Richard is not emotionally supportive. He spends all his time flopped on the couch.'

What? I have lots of flaws, but laziness is not one of them. 'Niki,' I say, 'that's not true. And I'm very emotionally involved.'

'Tell me your feelings, then,' Niki replies, as if I'm her patient.

That's a surprising request, but okay, since she asked: 'Niki, you've reached your own abuse diagnoses, and I think your constant questioning of Elizabeth, to prove your diagnoses, could harm her.'

Anger bubbles up from wherever I lock it away. 'Niki, it scares the shit out of me!' I growl. 'Elizabeth could be totally fucked-up by you screwing with her mind!'

My anger turns to panic. I can hardly breathe. My vision shrinks to a tunnel. I don't hear much. Then I hear distant voices. I take a slow, deep breath, get a grip, calm down, and say, 'Niki, Elizabeth gets anxious because of your questioning. She even asks, "Mommy, are you happy with me?" and you reply, "No, I want to find out what happened to you."'

'That's a lie!' Niki shouts, 'I never said that!' Then she unleashes. 'You have unresolved issues. You are in denial. You don't talk with me. You don't talk with the girls. You don't try to find out what happened to Elizabeth.'

'Niki,' I reply, 'I have questioned Elizabeth when she said she was hurt. It's only happened a few times. She usually talks about Mikee and Alan, or makes playful, nonsensical statements like "five Miss Mabels". Or she doesn't want to talk about it.'

'But, Richard, you see, she is trying to tell you something,' Niki remonstrates. 'The five Miss Mabels are part of the multiple personality disorder abuse, part of Kacey's multiple personalities.'

Dohne re-enters the minefield. 'Niki, a multiple personality disorder diagnosis is all-inclusive and hard to disprove.'

'That's a male problem!' Niki retorts.

'Do you think Tom Dohne thinks that way?' he asks, sounding confused and hurt.

Niki doesn't answer, so Dohne sums up. 'You're both concerned about Elizabeth. You need to try to come together and listen to what the other person is saying. Richard, you need to listen more to Elizabeth's anxiety. Niki, you need to listen more to Richard's concerns.'

***

I return to work and Niki goes to her mother's house. Then we meet at a restaurant. We order food but can't eat. 'Richard, I cannot go to Australia with you until we can work together,' Niki says. 'And Dohne was completely out of line. I'm not trying to be a therapist to Elizabeth.'

'Niki,' I ask, 'will you try to understand my concern that you might be pressuring Elizabeth and making her anxious by questioning her?'

'Everything fits perfectly into multiple personality disorder abuse,' Niki replies, and starts to explain her theory.

I interrupt and say she's not answering my question.

'Yes, I am!' Niki growls. She tells me multiple personality disorder abuse of Elizabeth happened, and she'll expect an apology from me when I see the truth, when I see she's right. 'And, Richard, I can't keep carrying the emotional burden of Elizabeth's abuse.'

***

At home, Niki says she's really happy. 'I finally understand what's bothering me. Richard, it's your lack of emotional parenting. I know you work long hours and do a lot of housework, but I need you to be engaged in the emotional parenting. That's the core issue for me.'

'Niki, I'm ex-*haus*-ted,' I say, 'but I'll do my best. On your side, will you avoid questioning Elizabeth? It makes her anxious.' I'm pleading again.

'Richard,' Niki responds with arrogant certainty, 'I'm totally comfortable with the way I parent Elizabeth. At times, I know, I've probably gone overboard. I've wanted to shake it out of her. But I'm certain she knows things she's too scared to talk about.'

'Niki,' I say, calmly, slowly, trying to lower the voltage, 'your questions imply something bad happened, and she's supposed to have answers. What if she has no answers? What if she can't answer your questions? Then she thinks you're not happy with her.'

'It's Elizabeth who brings it all up!' Niki shouts. 'It's not me. It's not my questioning.'

Discussion seems pointless. I want this conversation to end. I drift over to play with Elizabeth, who holds a plastic frog. I joke and say, 'Elizabeth, kiss the frog and turn him into Prince Charming.' Those words trigger a blinding flash of the obvious – the absurdity of Niki's theory that Elizabeth has been abused by someone with multiple personalities. Niki is distressed because Elizabeth talks about people changing, things changing.

People changing, things changing, is a part of three-year-old Elizabeth's reality – a reality fed by a daily diet of movies involving bizarre stories and impossible characters who assume weird and frightening forms: beasts, frogs, genies, pixies, fairies, mermaids, witches, dragons, goblins, wizards, phantoms, scarecrows, giants and more. Not only do they change, they miraculously fly, disappear, reappear, live under water, and obey magic wands and pixie dust. Monsters lurk as ferocious demons and devils, shadows and slime. Animals have human personas: bears, lions, rabbits, elephants, dinosaurs. There's even a spider called Charlotte.

I change my play from kissing the frog to pretending it'll jump if we tickle its bottom. Sitting beside Elizabeth on a couch, I ask her to tickle the frog's bottom. Then I throw the frog into the air, as if it jumped of its own accord.

Elizabeth screams with delight. 'Do it again, Dad! Do it again, Dad!'

Each time the frog jumps away, she runs to collect it, runs back and jumps into my lap. Then Elizabeth wants to jump like the frog, so gets down on all fours in front of me, arches her bottom into my face, and says, 'Tickle my bottom, Dad! Tickle my bottom, Dad!'

I look up and tell Niki, 'If Elizabeth bent over, put her backside into my face, and asked me to tickle her bottom, I might wonder about sexual abuse. Isn't it amazing how easily children's behaviour can be misinterpreted?'

Niki doesn't answer.

Saturday December 5, 1992

Late this morning we attend a children's Christmas party at the Bartlesville Country Club, courtesy of Niki's parents. I take Elizabeth to sit on Santa's lap.

'Daddy, I asked Santa for a Beauty the Beast doll,' she boasts.

Elizabeth always omits the conjunction 'and' when she talks about *Beauty and the Beast*. Then she wants to touch the goldfish in a small fishpond and run around with her cousins. It looks like normal behaviour to me. But as we're about to be seated for lunch, Niki and her mother suddenly announce, 'Elizabeth's anxious. She's not feeling safe. We have to leave!'

Niki and her mother then frantically bustle Elizabeth out of the restaurant and into our car. Charlie and I are left standing at the table, looking at each other like stunned witnesses to a road accident.

'Richard, they're a different species,' he says. Charlie has a one-liner for every occasion.

Our family dynamic now revolves around Elizabeth, and she knows it. And I think she feels anxious about it. How can a three-year-old manage so much power? She can't. She behaves like somebody elevated to rule who has no idea how to rule. She's always scanning, always hoping to see that we're pleased by her decrees. All she sees today are frantic responses from Mommy and Nanna. Why aren't they happy with me?

***

At home, Niki tells me, 'I need to settle Elizabeth by nursing.' The next thing I hear is Niki saying, 'I don't like the sexual way you're nursing. I will not nurse you if you suck and touch my breast in a sexual way. Who taught you bad touch? Was it Kacey? Was it Kimberley?'

Blank stare from Elizabeth.

Niki looks up at me, desperate. 'Richard, it makes me feel crazy thinking Elizabeth was sexual in this way with someone else.'

Yes, Niki, I say to myself, this is crazy. I'm surviving craziness one day at a time. I'll survive today. And I will get up tomorrow morning, and I will survive tomorrow. This is all I can do.

And, no, I don't say that to Niki.

Sunday December 6, 1992

Late this morning Niki plays a puppet game with Elizabeth. This game started a year ago, when I used a hand puppet to pretend to be imaginary characters. Elizabeth thought it was great fun. Now Niki uses the hand puppet to question Elizabeth about the monsters. 'Richard, did you hear that!' Niki says, excited.

No, I didn't listen. I've zoned out. I'm exhausted. Depressed. Silent. I wait for Niki to tell me.

'She talked about a pool. Maybe it's the pool your mother pushed her into?'

I've had enough. 'Niki, I know you love the girls. I know you're doing what you think is right. But all your questions and talk about the monsters and naughty people keep Elizabeth stuck. Why can't you let her be a normal three-year-old kid? Niki, I want this to stop,' I plead.

As I say those words, a trapdoor opens and I fall through into bottomless darkness and despair. I feel helpless to stop this craziness. I begin to cry, which surprises Niki, and we talk calmly. I keep saying I'm worried about her constant questioning of Elizabeth.

Niki's obsession is, however, unwavering. 'Richard,' she replies, 'how could Elizabeth know so much about sex and talk so much about sex, without having been sexually abused?'

Then Niki tells me she and her mother have arranged to meet, today, with Mr and Mrs Bruce, whose son, Peter, is a Bartlesville sexual abuse victim. 'We might learn about who abused Elizabeth,' she says.

So Niki and her mother visit the Bruces, whose son was apparently sexually abused by his Bartlesville paediatrician. Niki and her mother harbour grave suspicions about a connection between babysitter Kacey and Peter's sexual abuse, because the attorney who acted on behalf of the paediatrician is also acting for Kacey's father in a lawsuit against Niki's father. And the paediatrician now lives opposite the Parkers, who are bankrolling Kacey's father in his legal battles against both Niki's brother, who's accused of raping Kacey, and his lawsuit against Niki's father.

I think I got that right. This small-town intrigue is mind-boggling.

I have a calm and relaxed few hours playing with the girls while Niki and her mother meet the Bruces.

When Niki returns, Elizabeth screams for her attention and wants to nurse. 'Richard, that's what I have to put up with all day long,' Niki says. 'Her behaviour is obviously not normal. All because of sexual abuse.'

Niki then bathes Elizabeth, asking her questions about 'Newester', 'Dewester', 'French-kissing', 'naughty people and monsters', and on and on.

After her bath, Elizabeth gets a school bag and tells me, 'Dad, I'm going to school.'

'What are you going to learn about?' I ask innocently.

'Jesus, Batman and tee-tees,' she replies. 'I'll go to school in a bus driven by Charlie.'

'Is Charlie my father?' Niki asks.

Blank stare.

Niki has an idea and checks the phone directory. 'Oh my God!' she shouts, 'Kimberley's father is also named Charlie.' Niki calls her mother to share her discovery, then takes Elizabeth to bed. 'I need to find out if there's anything more she wants to talk about.'

After this bedroom talk, Niki looks worried. 'Richard, Elizabeth just told me Dewester was brought to our house by Charlie the bus driver.'

Elizabeth interrupts Niki. 'And I was safe,' she says. 'Dewester was good. Nothing bad happened to me. I was not hurt by Dewester.'

Elizabeth speaks with emphasis, confidence and assurance. What an amazing thing to witness. Elizabeth realises her mother will be anxious unless she, the child, reassures Niki, the mother, that everything was okay with Dewester.

Then Peter Bruce, the Bartlesville abuse victim, calls Niki from California.

Niki describes Elizabeth's supposed symptoms, and asks Peter, 'Now, don't you think that's strange behaviour for a three-year-old? I just want to put it all out of my mind. I really don't want to even think about it. I'm only doing it because I believe Elizabeth needs to work through her sexual abuse. Peter, don't you think Elizabeth needs to work through her sexual abuse?'

Gauging by Niki's enthusiastic nodding, it looks like it's an affirmative from Peter. He agrees Elizabeth needs to work through her sexual abuse.

Niki continues. 'My husband's concerned about making Elizabeth work through her sexual abuse. He's a PhD in geology, but he's not familiar with the therapy process. I'm a retired counsellor. Peter, I don't think my husband understands what's best for Elizabeth. Do you?'

More enthusiastic nodding from Niki. It's another affirmative from Peter. I don't understand what's best for my daughter Elizabeth.

Niki hangs up the phone, euphoric. 'Richard, my approach has just been vindicated by an abuse survivor. You're in denial.'

I'm depressed.

Hello, Penny Blake

Monday December 7, 1992

I'm depressed and I'm on the madness train. Niki waved goodbye to Tom Dohne at the last station and waves hello to Penny Blake at the next station. After Niki visited the Bruces yesterday, they contacted Penny Blake, who works for a child advocacy service in Bartlesville. This morning Niki calls me at work, elated. 'Richard, Penny Blake just called. She agreed with my ideas about ritual abuse. And she knows people in Bartlesville who are involved in ritual abuse.'

Blake also told Niki to purchase the *Dungeons & Dragons* board game, because teenage Satanists use it. And not to contact the police.

'Why on earth not?' I ask. 'If this sort of thing is going on, it should be stopped.'

'I don't know why not,' Niki says. 'Penny just said she would only talk with me unofficially. Won't it be great to get some answers?'

'Yes, that would be wonderful,' I reply, with a hint of sarcasm that eludes Niki.

What I really feel are panic and rage. Who the hell is Penny Blake? How the hell can Penny Blake have a single damn clue about our situation? Or know if Elizabeth suffered ritual abuse? How can a responsible health professional reach such a devastating conclusion in a phone conversation? Who are these nut jobs?

Niki calls again, even more hyped. 'Richard, you have to take the girls to Uncle Billy's Christmas party tonight. I need to buy the *Dungeons & Dragons* game and work on my ritual abuse notes.'

I arrive home to euphoria about Penny Blake. 'At last!' Niki exclaims, 'I'm finally talking to someone who speaks my language. Why didn't I think about teenage babysitters playing cult board games? It's so obvious!'

Niki then notices Elizabeth scribbling on a sheet of paper and asks, concerned, what she's drawing.

'A drawing of people for Daddy,' Elizabeth answers, happy.

Niki asks, in a sombre voice, who the people are.

'Just my friends, Mommy,' Elizabeth answers in an exaggerated, happy tone, trying to say, 'Don't worry, Mommy.'

Niki then leaves to buy the *Dungeons & Dragons* board game, and returns, frantic to rip open the box. Meanwhile, I load the girls into the car to leave for Uncle Billy's party. As I exit through the garage door, Niki looks at me, stunned, and says, 'I can already see stuff Elizabeth always talks about.' Then, when I'm through the garage door, I hear her shout, 'The five is here! The five is here!'

I return inside. Niki shows me a picture with five people in it, counting them off with her forefinger: 'One, two, three, four, five. Elizabeth is always saying "five".'

The trapdoor opens again and I plunge into despair. Niki has just made an abuse interpretation of Elizabeth's recent habit to say 'five'. 'Niki, I just taught Elizabeth to count to five. So everything is now "five". If it's "five", then it's good.'

After about an hour at Uncle Billy's, Elizabeth's bored and commands, 'I want to go home!' I say we'll leave soon, but she shouts back, 'No! We have to go home now!'

Uncle Billy, watching this exchange, tries to entertain Elizabeth, saying something playful. Elizabeth won't be dissuaded and shouts, 'Uncle Billy boinked me!'

Uncle Billy looks at me, puzzled, and asks, 'What did she say I just did to her?'

I'm embarrassed. How do I begin to explain Elizabeth's bizarre accusation? Part of me wants to unload five months' worth of bitter frustration, right here, right now, right into his lap. Instead I just mumble, 'Elizabeth's confused, it's nothing important.' I manage to distract her with a swivel chair game. But then, when it is time to leave, she doesn't want to go home. I have to carry her to the car, kicking, screaming and punching.

At home, the board game is open on the dining room table. Elizabeth makes a motion to grab the box. 'Niki,' I say, 'we should let Elizabeth see this game for the first time with Hegburg. It would be impartial and she could make a video.'

I hold my breath. I envisage days of Niki questioning Elizabeth about the board game. Niki considers my suggestion. And agrees. She hides the board game in her car.

Then talks to me about Penny Blake, how tuned-in Penny is to satanic ritual abuse. 'Richard, she thought Elizabeth's behaviour could not result from just molestation. She was impatient with me, in an "I'm a busy woman, don't waste my time" kind of way. Or, "Let's not beat around the bush, of course we're dealing with satanic ritual abuse."'

'Niki, I worry we're heading toward a self-fulfilling prophesy,' I reply.

But there's no room for doubt in Niki's mind. 'Richard, my sister has friends who are incest victims with unresolved issues as adult women. They're still in therapy trying to remember what happened to them as children. I want to be able to tell Elizabeth exactly what happened to her when she was a child. I'll keep going until I have all the answers.'

The madness train rolls on.

thirteen

I Want An Expert

Tuesday December 8, 1992

Niki and I are in an undeclared tug of war. She pulls on her end of the obsession rope, dragging Elizabeth, who's in the middle, inch by inch, day by day, toward the winning line of abused victimhood and lifelong therapy. I dig in my heels, hold on to my end of the rope and try to keep Elizabeth in the field of normal. Niki's winning. When therapists, unasked, hold onto my end of the rope, Niki cuts them loose and pulls the rope further and further toward victimhood. If she could just find a therapist to help pull on her end of the rope, help drag Elizabeth into victimhood and lifelong therapy, she could claim victory and vindication.

After the Penny Blake and Uncle Billy events, I don't sleep. How do I keep Elizabeth in the field of normal? I go into my office at 3 am to think and write. Niki calls my office midmorning. 'Richard we still don't have a diagnosis from Hegburg. We need an official diagnosis.' With her next breath she says, 'Hegburg's play therapy isn't the correct therapy for ritual abuse. Richard, I want an expert in ritual abuse to diagnose Elizabeth.'

Wednesday December 9, 1992

Today I visit Hegburg alone. 'Faye, Niki believes Elizabeth's suffered sexual abuse, pornography abuse, multiple personality disorder abuse and probably satanic ritual abuse, and is questioning her along these lines. She said you're okay with the questioning.'

'There may have been some miscommunication,' Hegburg replies. 'Dwelling on Elizabeth's trauma will only perpetuate her anxiety. You don't need all the answers for her to move on. I need to discuss parenting issues and appropriate questioning with Niki. Elizabeth desperately needs boundaries and structure in her life.'

While I'm with Hegburg, Niki visits a psychiatrist, Dr Blair, in Tulsa, to discuss her theory that Kacey has multiple personality disorder. We meet at her mother's house when she returns. Upset and teary, Niki tells her mother in a morbid tone that Dr Blair supported her diagnoses of ritual abuse for Elizabeth and multiple personality disorder for Kacey. 'Oh my God! Elizabeth will need lifelong therapy!' Niki and her mother then say, in stereo.

During this discussion, Elizabeth sits nearby, watching *Gulliver's Travels*, her latest favourite video. She picks up on the sombre tone, looks anxious, comes over to me, and asks in a worried whisper, 'Dad, what's going on?' I give her a lame answer – 'We're just talking, pumpkin' – then take her to another room, to play.

At home, Niki's agitated, and repeats her mantra that Elizabeth will need lifelong therapy. I counter with Hegburg's comment about moving on, not dwelling on the trauma.

'Richard, I'm doing everything humanly possible to help Elizabeth!' Niki protests. 'I can't do anything more. It's not like I'm causing her problems.'

Thursday December 10, 1992

Today Niki begins her crusade to find a ritual abuse expert to diagnose Elizabeth. Tonight she tells me, 'I want a full assessment, with parent input and follow-up therapy. And I called Penny Blake again. Richard, she agrees with me. Elizabeth's obviously been ritually abused.' When I ask Niki how Blake diagnoses ritual abuse, she answers, 'Blake said you just know! And she said there are two witches in Bartlesville, and they wouldn't hesitate to murder.'

'There have been witch-murders in Bartlesville?' I ask. 'How does Blake know that?'

'I don't know!' Niki shouts. 'But we need a house alarm!'

Later, Elizabeth and I play make-believe in the bathtub. 'Dad, Dad, there are sharks in the water!' She screams with delight as I make a toy shark chase her. Then she smiles and says, 'Dad, when I grow up, I'm going to be a man.'

I smile back and agree, 'Yeah, sweetheart, you know what, I think you are.' Elizabeth laughs, then picks other silly things to be when she grows up, laughing harder each time I agree with her. Niki overhears our play and, with a worried look, tells me, 'Richard, this is all part of her multiple personality disorder abuse.'

Friday December 11, 1992

Here we go again. The next day, Niki calls my office, subdued and serious. 'Richard, Elizabeth said you scare her again.' Niki tells me Elizabeth wanted to go to the YMCA swimming pool. 'I told her, "Daddy can take you tomorrow." She said, "No! He turns into a mean person. A fairy godmother called Joanna turns him into a mean person." Richard, I can't handle much more of this.' Niki says she called Hegburg, who told her Elizabeth's play therapy indicates I'm a nurturing father.

After this conversation, I also call Hegburg, who says, 'You two are reaching some kind of decision point.' I wonder what decision point Hegburg has in mind. Pistols at dawn? I ask her if Niki will ever accept a diagnosis other than ritual sexual abuse. 'Niki will interpret Elizabeth's statements and behaviour the way Niki wants,' she replies, without elaborating.

After speaking with Hegburg, I join Niki at her parents' house. She wants a private talk before we return home. 'Richard, we're both at the end of our patience. We need an expert diagnosis of ritual abuse so we can move ahead.' Niki goes on. 'Elizabeth said she was scared of you because Joanna turned you into a mean person. Who's Joanna?'

Why do I need to explain this? 'Niki, Joanna is the bad lizard in the video *Rescuers Down Under*.' This calms Niki's fears, and we head home – where I'm greeted by burnt books and smashed porcelain ducks.

'Elizabeth said there were scary monsters in her room,' Niki explains. 'She got her Snow White and Sleeping Beauty books and pointed at the witches. Then she pointed at the porcelain ducks. So we burnt the books and smashed the ducks.' Niki tells me these items must have a connection to her ritual abuse. Elizabeth chimes in, excited, 'Dad! Dad! I burned all my scary monsters.'

Sunday December 13, 1992

This morning, Niki and Elizabeth go to church, and I drive, with Jenny, to Birch Lake. I park beside the lake, look out over a still, grey, misty winter scene, and quietly weep. Baby Jenny sleeps in her car seat beside me, oblivious to the drama swirling around her. I look at Jenny and wonder if she'll also be dragged into madness. Please, not Jenny as well.

Back home, I tell Niki I want a normal family life again.

'Well, we'll never have one,' she answers, brusquely. 'Elizabeth's ritual abuse will take years of therapy to heal.'

Monday December 14, 1992

Today we travel to Tulsa to meet Dr Kramer. Niki types a revised five-page list of Elizabeth's ritual abuse symptoms, as well as an explanatory letter:

> We have speculated … about the female teenage babysitter being a multiple personality … She (Elizabeth) is now beginning to clearly indicate that the female babysitter "changed," changed from nice to naughty, from being a girl to being a boy (scary and mean), to being Newister, Deweyster and Blueister (the main monsters who hurt her …) She (Elizabeth) indicates she could change this person with her magic wand and with pressing a button. Much of the confusion we have all felt in trying to understand what happened to Elizabeth would be greatly clarified if this babysitter did indeed prove to be a multiple personality.

I wonder who the 'we' in the letter refers to, but don't ask.

Some experiences are unforgettable. I'll never forget meeting Dr Kramer. Probably in his mid-to-late fifties, Kramer is tall, lean, and professorial. He invites us into a well-appointed office that shouts success: beautiful wooden desk, bookshelves, windows with panoramic views over the Tulsa skyline. We sit opposite his desk in well-padded leather chairs.

Then, in a detached manner, he looks down onto his desk at a blank sheet of paper. We wait for him to look up and talk to us. We wait. And we wait. I begin to wonder, is this guy nuts? Has he had a stroke? I look at Niki quizzically. She seems a little puzzled, but not too bothered. So we wait some more. After a few minutes, I can't restrain a muffled laugh. Is this a joke? Does he want to see how we react in an unusual circumstance?

Finally, I decide to break the silence, and ask, 'Are we in a game where the first person to speak loses?' Kramer then talks to us like everything's normal.

Niki outlines her abuse theories and Elizabeth's symptoms. I discuss other, more benign sources of trauma. Kramer says that while it appears a trauma has occurred, he doesn't see a strong resemblance in Elizabeth's symptoms to those in his other ritually abused patients. He tells us the ear surgery scare and molestation by older boys could have been significant traumas, but thinks some of her behaviour could be explained by dissociative states.

Discussion moves on to Kacey suffering multiple personality disorder, her apparent switch in character around Niki's brother, and Niki's observation of changes in Elizabeth's behaviour when she babysat. Kramer is receptive to Kacey having a background of abuse and suffering multiple personality disorder.

As our meeting wraps up, Kramer invites us to join the Tulsa chapter of the Multiple Personality Disorder Association. 'I'm on the committee,' he boasts.

fourteen

Satanic Ritual Abuse

Could a reasonable, rational, educated parent believe their child, at one and two years old, has witnessed and participated in torture, pornography, sexual abuse, eating faeces, drinking blood and urine, human sacrifice, dismemberment, eating cooked body parts and elaborate cult ceremonial rituals? Could this reasonable, rational, educated parent believe satanic cults operate undetected throughout American society, breeding crate-loads of babies for ritual sacrifice? Could this reasonable, rational and educated parent also believe their child witnessed and participated in these horrors while in the care of babysitters and day care centres for just one to three hours, once or twice a week, to be greeted by their parents intact, unmarked and coherent?

Niki believes. She also believes an expert therapist will be able to diagnose this ritual abuse one or two years later, in three-and-a-half-year-old Elizabeth.

How do people lose grip on reality?

Four centuries ago, the scientific method revolutionised how we can comprehend the world around us – how we can comprehend reality. By this method, reason and logic are combined with ever more sophisticated technologies to conduct experiments. These experiments accumulate data, accumulate evidence. This evidence is used test the validity of our ideas and hypotheses about the world around us, and slowly surrenders the knowledge we need to understand reality. Many realities remain difficult to grasp and incompletely understood – but we begin to understand why. As we penetrate the unknown, we create the space and grace for knowledge to replace superstition, for love to replace fear, for function to replace dysfunction.

The slow, dogged and often difficult pursuit of knowledge is not for everyone. For some, the mind is faulty, the wiring is imperfect, and the use of reason and logic is impossible. For others, a wilder ride through reality is their preferred route – along winding paths of fantasy or down dark alleys of magic and mysticism. For many, ignorance prevails because the pursuit of knowledge requires a dedication to learning, and the opportunity to learn may be unavailable, or, if available, too much like damn hard work. And finally, there are the gullible, those led astray in their perception of reality by frauds and hoaxes.

The satanic ritual abuse hoax began with the bestseller *Michelle Remembers*, published in 1980 and co-written by Canadian psychiatrist Lawrence Padzer and his patient (and eventual wife) Michelle Smith. Through years of therapy, Padzer recovered Michelle's repressed memories of phantasmagorical satanic torture in a coven led by her Satanist parents, when she was five years old. Just as the bestseller *Sybil* convinced hundreds of thousands of gullible patients they possessed multiple personalities, *Michelle Remembers* triggered an explosion of recovered memories of satanic ritual abuse.

Police and FBI investigations of tens of thousands of accusations of satanic ritual abuse failed to uncover a single case that could be proven with any physical evidence. *Michelle Remembers*, as with *Sybil*, was eventually shown to be a fraud, concocted by the authors. But not before a firestorm of fear and panic about the rise of Satanism had spread across America – and smashed through our front door.

Tuesday December 15, 1992

Today Niki's exhausted. She's called around the country, searching for an expert to diagnose and treat Elizabeth's ritual abuse. I return home early to give her a break from childcare. As I arrive, Niki leaves for the bookstore to purchase *Breaking the Circle of Satanic Ritual Abuse*. This evening she tells me, 'Richard, this book explains exactly what Elizabeth's been saying about feet and hands and fingers being cut off.'

What? 'Niki, I've never heard Elizabeth say things like that.'

Wednesday December 16, 1992

This morning, Niki calls me at work, pumped. 'Richard, what Elizabeth does fits exactly with satanic ritual abuse. The way she paints herself with lipstick, her talk about adult sexual activity and the "Red Man" and the "Blue Man" and statements like, "They painted themselves pink," "They were dripping with chocolate," "Mikee and Alan marked me up." Richard, it describes people and herself being painted for ritual abuse ceremonies.'

Later we meet Hegburg for an update. This is our 'Goodbye Hegburg' day – the last time Niki will sit in her office. The madness train is about to leave Hegburg at the station.

Hegburg kicks off with the good news. 'Elizabeth's play this morning was normal and happy. I'm really pleased.' Then there's the sting in the tail: 'Niki, she needs more structure and boundaries in her life; set mealtimes and bed times. She's at a testing age and needs more control over her behaviour. Otherwise she'll lose the sense you can provide safety.'

Hegburg's blunt assessment surprises me. Her next statement is a stunner.

'Niki, have you considered whether you suffer from intergenerational transference of shame? Are you projecting the sexual abandonment by your father onto Elizabeth?'

I'm gobsmacked. What will Niki say? She considers her response for about fifteen seconds, then tells Hegburg, 'I understand what you're talking about.' End of discussion.

So Hegburg shifts topics to Niki's search for a ritual abuse expert. 'Niki, ritual abuse is a new and controversial field. Finding an expert will be difficult. You need to be careful. You need objective, factual analysis, not zealots with fixed agendas. And an expert diagnosis would be difficult to reach for a three-year-old. Ten different experts could give you ten different opinions. And therapy and healing for a three-year-old should still involve non-directed play therapy and a calm home environment.'

Hegburg then addresses Niki's questioning of Elizabeth. 'You must avoid revivifying trauma,' she says. 'Niki, making her remember trauma by questioning her delays healing. She will grow beyond her trauma, whatever it was, into a normal, happy child, if you let her heal. Keeping her stuck by rehashing these events, whatever they were, won't help. You don't need all the answers, which anyway, is impossible for such a young child.'

Like Schwartz, Hegburg has nailed it. And challenged Niki's behaviour.

I wonder if Niki heard a single word Hegburg just said? My answer arrives immediately.

'Faye, I've been able to work with Elizabeth down through her various levels of trauma,' Niki replies, with an air of professional conviction, 'starting with Mikee and Alan, going down to Dale and Abigail, and then down to Kacey. Each time I've worked with her through one of these levels I've thought it was the last level. But then, *thud* – Elizabeth drops down to a new level of disclosure. And now she's disclosing satanic ritual abuse, and going into dissociative states, talking about people cutting off heads and feet and hands. She's witnessed people having their heads cut off! Babies being killed! Animals being tortured! I don't want to work with her with this stuff.'

Niki goes on. 'There are similarities between information in the book *Breaking the Circle of Satanic Ritual Abuse* and Elizabeth's statements. I think the Parker house is used for ritual abuse. Elizabeth recognised the house, calling it the "high school". She even pointed out a side entrance to the house. Faye, we should pass this information on to the police.'

Niki begins to sob. 'The thought of Elizabeth suffering satanic ritual abuse torments me. Where was I? Her mother. I didn't protect her. I let this happen!' Niki wails.

'Niki, a police investigation is unlikely,' Hegburg replies. 'They would need more than the word of a three-and-a-half-year-old about events when she was a one or two-year-old.'

Hegburg faces the same dilemma I face – how to conduct a rational discussion with Niki about the absurdity of her beliefs. I notice Hegburg takes the same route as me – avoidance. Neither of us are able to tell Niki her ideas are nuts.

***

When I arrive home from work, Niki's furious. 'Richard, I'm not happy with Hegburg. She's let us down. She just said to provide structure and boundaries. We need support for Elizabeth's satanic ritual abuse. Richard, I can't go on. I need help!'

'We can hire help,' I reply.

'That's not what I mean!' Niki shouts. 'Elizabeth's disclosing satanic ritual abuse. I need help dealing with that! My nerves are shot. I need time alone.'

Niki disappears through the garage door – poof! Elizabeth sees Niki leave without her, and throws a tantrum. First she lies on her back, arching, kicking and flailing. Then she rolls over and over, slapping herself in the face with both hands as she rolls. Then she stands up and kicks and hits at the garage door. Then she kicks and hits at me. It's distressing.

To calm her, I make up a story. As she sucks in air with gulping, sobbing breaths, by some miracle, her attention locks on to my story. 'Old Man Winter' is outside. He breathes out cold air, which is why the air outside is cold, and why we need to keep the garage door closed. When Old Man Winter cries, it causes snow. Elizabeth calms and joins in the spirit of storytelling, asking questions about Old Man Winter. Then she wants to go search for Old Man Winter. So we drive around town, look at Christmas decorations, but we can't find him. Home again and Elizabeth asks, 'Daddy, are you Old Man Winter?'

I laugh, 'No, I'm not, I'm Daddy.'

Thursday December 17, 1992

This morning, Niki calls me at work, excited to tell me the Bruces know of a man, Rick, who now lives in Albuquerque, New Mexico, and who suffered satanic ritual abuse in Bartlesville when he was a child. 'And I knew Rick!' Niki exclaims. 'I just called him but he won't share any information with me over the phone. His ritual abuse is only now coming to the surface through recovered memory therapy.'

Niki wants to go to Albuquerque to speak with Rick. 'Richard, there may be a link between what he suffered and what happened to Elizabeth.'

I feel panic. This Albuquerque news could lead us further down the garden path of satanic craziness. 'Niki, let's get the expert diagnosis first, then, if necessary, travel to Albuquerque.'

'But we need this information first,' Niki argues, 'and we could have Rick's therapist send a letter to our expert.'

I need a dose of Dohne to calm my nerves, but he's more agitated than I am. 'I think I've lost Niki,' he tells me. 'And Hegburg says you visited *the* Dr Kramer in Tulsa. Richard, *the* Dr Kramer that you visited is a nut job, a bona-fide kook.'

This evening I drive the girls around town to look at Christmas decorations while Niki calls the abuse victim in Albuquerque. 'Richard,' Niki tells me later, 'he won't share any details with me over the phone. I need to fly to Albuquerque.' She then shifts topics to home security. 'A police sergeant Hinchcliff is referred to in *Breaking the Circle of Satanic Ritual Abuse*. I want you to call him about our security.'

Friday December 18, 1992

Today, when I call Sergeant Hinchcliff and explain Niki's request for security information, he asks, 'How old is Elizabeth?' When I tell him three-and-a-half years, he says, 'I've never heard of a child that young involved in satanic ritual abuse. The youngest is about four.' When I tell him Elizabeth would have only been one or two years old when abuse could have occurred, Hinchcliff laughs at me, 'That didn't happen!'

I ask if he'll speak with my wife. He will.

Niki calls and I relay Hinchcliff's sceptical comments. She's unperturbed. She wants to tell me about a ritual abuse expert in the psychiatric unit at Oklahoma University. 'I called a Dr Bonnell and she asked if the FBI were involved. I told her I know ritual abuse occurred – I just don't have all the details yet. Richard, eventually the FBI will need to be involved. And I found another expert, Dr York, at the University of California in Los Angeles.'

At home, Niki tells me, 'I called Hinchcliff. He was rude. He said he'd never heard of a two-year-old involved in satanic ritual abuse. Well, he's wrong.'

To counterbalance Hinchcliff's negativity, Niki tells me about her meeting today with Penny Blake. 'After seeing Elizabeth for just five minutes, she had no doubt she'd been ritually abused. She saw important things, like dilated pupils. Richard, I could really communicate with her.' This opens a floodgate of resentment. 'Richard, everyone else sees Elizabeth's ritual abuse. Why are you in denial? I feel so unsupported by you.'

Niki later offers a multiple personality disorder explanation for my state of denial. 'Richard, Elizabeth behaves differently with me and with you. She has two alters. Her alter with me shares the terror of her ritual abuse. Her alter with you hides her abuse. How would you feel if you knew she had watched people being murdered, watched their legs being cut off, been forced to drink blood, forced to eat body parts, forced to have a man's erect penis in her mouth!'

This is hysterical. 'Niki, I won't believe those things happened unless we can prove it. If we believe those things happened but they didn't, it would harm Elizabeth.'

'Well, I believe they did happen!' Niki shouts.

Saturday December 19, 1992

Today I take the girls to a shopping mall to visit Santa, then we drive to Woolaroc Ranch to look at buffalo, Indian teepees and walk through the museum. Travelling from the shopping mall to Woolaroc, I drive past the Parker house, the epicentre of satanic ritual abuse in Bartlesville. I ask Elizabeth, 'Do you know that house?'

'Is that where the monsters live?' she replies.

'I don't know,' I ask, 'do they?'

'Nah,' Elizabeth answers in a disinterested tone.

Sunday December 20, 1992

Niki and her mother spend today speculating about individuals in Bartlesville who are Satanists. They map out their current and previous street addresses and identify an intriguing cluster. They also observe clicking sounds while making telephone calls and wonder if our phone lines are tapped.

Tuesday December 22, 1992

Niki's search for a ritual abuse expert is not going well. She calls me late afternoon, tired and downcast. 'The message from everyone I speak to is we won't be able to prove anything. Nobody's going to be able to prove anything. So what are we trying to achieve? What's our objective? What answers can we get? Do we need answers to move ahead with Elizabeth's healing? The therapists recommended we just focus on good parenting.'

Niki goes on. 'I want to understand how to parent Elizabeth if ritual abuse occurred. If this is our goal, why not just go to Barbara Tillman for an assessment of Elizabeth and parenting advice? It would be so much easier than travelling outside of Bartlesville. Richard, could you please call Hegburg for advice about Tillman?'

So I call Hegburg and share my concern that Tillman might over-diagnose ritual abuse, since Paul Roland recommended her. Hegburg admits she's already consulted with Tillman, without disclosing Elizabeth's identity. 'Richard, she's a children's advocate. Tillman's agenda would be Elizabeth's interests. She would not over-diagnose.'

I relay this conversation to Niki and we agree to see Tillman. Niki makes an appointment for a parent meeting on Wednesday January 6, 1993.

**

Over the last six months Niki has shared her belief Elizabeth was sexually abused with paediatrician Dr Linda Doyle. I have not been privy to their conversations. Today, Dr Doyle provides a three-page report detailing Elizabeth's medical history. Portions of her report address Elizabeth's possible sexual abuse:

> At the age of 2-1/2, Elizabeth had problems with complaining of her vaginal area hurting. She was examined and found to have only slight irritation but no evidence of any trauma or traumatic abnormalities to her vaginal area ...
>
> By the time she was a little bit over 3 [July 1992] ... there was some evidence of (sic) brought to the parents' attention from the way Elizabeth was acting. There were some other sources that there was a possibility of a problem with sexual abuse.
>
> On 8/30/92 [August 30, 1992] ... her genitourinary examination showed ... no evidence of trauma and there was an intact hymen. When I asked in questioning Elizabeth if anyone had hurt her bottom or did anything to her tongue, she told me no ... however we did do throat cultures, vaginal cultures at that time and we did get a large amount of E. coli which was colon normal bacteria which had apparently from irritation invaded the vaginal area ... I know that other pathogens can be there so she was checked for gonorrhoea and Chlamydia and both of those tests came back negative.
>
> ... finally on 10/15/92 [October 15, 1992] I questioned Elizabeth, she told me, 'monsters go in my pee pee with a stick and my bottom and

pointed to where she 'poo poos.' … I asked her if they put the stick on
the inside or the outside and she stated they use this stick on the outside.
… I rechecked her back again on 12/11/92 [December 11, 1992] and
… her examination was normal …

In my opinion, Elizabeth has been sexually fondled or abused. There
certainly has been no evidence of genital extreme trauma, the hymen is
intact … She has had multiple episodes of vaginal irritation and vulvitis
although no evidence of vaginal trauma has ever been witnessed on her
examinations. I have no idea if her repeat vaginal irritation has anything
to do with this or not because many times normal girls at this age from
lack of wiping, playing in sandboxes etc. can also develop the same type
of vulva irritation.

I wonder about Dr Doyle's assessment. Niki is desperate for professional
validation of her beliefs and Dr Doyle has no doubt felt the full force of
her personality. The medical evidence Linda cites seems either inconclu-
sive, or points in the opposite direction to her opinion about sexual abuse.

Thursday December 24, 1992

It's Christmas Eve. Niki and I prepare the girls' presents and arrange the
living room to make it appear Santa's visited. It's a beautiful arrangement,
which Niki does so well. We should be happy. We should feel blessed. We
have abundance.

And we have distress. Niki cries and sobs, 'Richard, Elizabeth did her
"save me" thing again today. It's her call for help during her ritual abuse,
when she was forced to have penises in her mouth. I need painkillers to
get the images out of my mind.'

In Elizabeth's 'save me' pantomime, she lies on the floor, reaches out
her hand and playfully calls out 'save me.' After her first Oscar-winning
performance, I asked which movie she was copying. I knew the answer.
'It's Beauty the Beast, Dad!' Elizabeth replied, annoyed at my ignorance.
Beauty reaches out her hand to save the Beast from falling off the castle
roof. Why can't Niki understand this?

Saturday December 26, 1992

Today I entertain the girls while Niki shops for Boxing Day bargains. We take a road trip. I love our road trips. They're calming and uncomplicated. Elizabeth and I talk and laugh about normal stuff. First we drive to Tulsa Airport to watch the planes, then to Tulsa Zoo.

Niki arrives home mid-afternoon, tired from shopping, and needs a nap. Elizabeth wants her attention. Niki takes her to bed. Elizabeth won't sleep. Finally, they return to the family room. 'Elizabeth's behaviour was sexually inappropriate.' Niki says, angry. 'She said, "Let's make love." Richard, this happens every time you take the girls for any length of time.'

Niki returns to bed, and Elizabeth and I watch *FernGully*. 'Dad, I get scared by the monster Hexus,' she says. I suggest we turn off the video, but Elizabeth replies, 'No! Hexus is my drippy chocolate monster.' In the movie, Hexus is a brown, oozing slime.

Again, I imagine the cornucopia of distorted reality in Elizabeth's young mind: terrifying images of good fighting evil, heroic children in life-threatening situations – fighting anthropomorphic monsters. Her latest favourite video is *Duck Tales, The Movie – Treasure of the Lost Lamp*, about a genie and a beast who continually change form. It's violent and bizarre and she watches it endlessly.

Monday December 28, 1992

Tom Dohne has loaned me a couples-in-crisis book, *Making It Through the Night*. Reading this book, I feel hopeful Niki and I can get back to our loving relationship. Tonight I mention the book to Niki as a possible read. I get a bucket of ice water dumped on my head.

'Richard,' Niki says scornfully, 'as a trained counsellor, I already know and understand the content of that book, without reading it. Does that shock you? I have an excellent understanding of myself. I am a fair and decent person, who would not purposefully misrepresent the truth, who is only seeking the truth. I have been through years and years of therapy and gone through the long and difficult process of self-discovery.'

Niki takes a deep breath and goes on. 'Richard, your problem is you have not tried to understand the anguish I feel at the thought Elizabeth was ritually abused. I know I have my issues as a result of my family and my upbringing, but I've worked very hard to resolve these issues and recognise the role they play. Through this difficult experience with

Elizabeth, we'll learn that I'm a good mother and you're a good father. Although, I have wondered about you abusing her. And you don't open up to me. You don't express your feelings. Maybe you should be tested for underlying pathologies. I'd recommend the Minnesota Multiphasic Personality Inventory test.'

fifteen

The Behaviour War

Thursday December 31, 1992

Elizabeth has a strong and courageous temperament, the sort that's admirable until it's focused, full blast, full strength, directly at you. She's no pushover.

In our household, Niki sets the rules of behaviour. She has a loving, kind, 'motherhood and apple pie' approach to parenting. Every hurt or illness brings to bear the full force of medical and pharmaceutical science. Any anguish attracts therapeutic assessment and counselling. The girls know their mother cares deeply for their wellbeing.

Niki's focus at present is to nurture Elizabeth in a way that allows her to disclose her ritual abuse. There's no structure, no discipline and no boundaries around her behaviour. Elizabeth pretty much does what she wants, when she wants. She wears what she wants – usually nothing – eats what she wants and has those around her do what she wants. When I occasionally try to discipline her, Niki reminds me that Elizabeth's testing behaviour is due to her ritual abuse, and so we have to back off from discipline. Combine this loose approach with Elizabeth's naturally strong temperament and her three-year-old testing phase, and the result is a nightmare of bad behaviour. Elizabeth is out of control.

It's early morning, New Year's Eve. I'm on vacation. Niki sleeps in and I take both girls to the living room.

'I'm cold!' Elizabeth shouts, naked.

I suggest she puts on some clothing.

'No!' she says, 'I want a blanket.'

So I wrap her in a blanket on the sofa, and she watches her *Bambi* video. 'I'm cold!' she shouts again.

'Elizabeth, please put on some clothing,' I tell her. 'It's winter.'

Elizabeth is defiant. 'No!'

I try to reason with her using a storyline from *Bambi*. 'Elizabeth, Bambi's daddy saves Bambi's life by telling him he must get up as the fire approaches. I'm your daddy, and like Bambi's father, sometimes I have to tell you to do things for your own health.'

'No! I won't put clothes on!' she shouts, and runs away, laughing. Not wearing clothes is now a test, a game, and she wants me to chase her. So I pretend to play chase with her to her room, but then make her put on panties and a T-shirt. She resents my discipline and shouts, 'No! I don't have a daddy who saves me!'

'Yep, pumpkin,' I reply, 'you have two parents, a mummy and a daddy.'

'No! I only have one parent, not two parents. I don't have a daddy! And I don't like you!'

Niki, now awake, overhears this part of our exchange. 'Richard, what did Elizabeth just say about not having two parents, not having a daddy?'

'Elizabeth's being contrarian,' I answer casually. 'She's angry I made her wear clothes.'

Niki erupts. 'Richard! You always discount Elizabeth's disclosures.'

I'm stunned by Niki's rage, but stand my ground, and say it's my opinion Elizabeth is being contrarian, is testing me, and is angry because I made her put clothes on.

'Richard, it's hopeless to even try to have her wear clothes in the house. I've given up.'

'Niki, I agree, it's not a huge issue, but if Elizabeth learns to get her way by throwing tantrums, it sends the wrong message.'

This afternoon I take Elizabeth to the movie theatre, to see *Aladdin*. As we leave through the foyer she says, 'That was fun, Dad,' and wraps her arms around my legs with a hug. A joyful moment for me. Then she wants to drive to an ice cream parlour, but we need to head home – we're off to a party. 'No!' Elizabeth shouts, 'we can't go home! The monsters are at home! I want ice cream!'

We've been invited to a New Year's Eve party at Dr Linda Doyle's. As we prepare to leave, Elizabeth won't allow Niki to dress her. She becomes so disobedient Niki swats her on the bottom. This calms her, and she asks, 'Mommy, were you fussy when you were a little girl?'

'No,' Niki replies, 'I could never have behaved the way you do. The only reason I'm putting up with it is because I think you were hurt.'

At the party, Elizabeth enjoys playing with Linda's daughter, Shelby, who is about the same age. I check on them a few times. One time they're searching for monsters in a sleeping bag, using a flashlight. Niki then invites Shelby to spend the night with us. Her father, Matt, a full-time househusband, packs an overnight kit and comes to our car, giving Shelby a hug goodbye. He looks unsure about this arrangement. We drive home happy – singing lullabies to baby Jenny in a car full of party balloons.

At home, Elizabeth and Shelby play dress-up and pretend games. In one game, Shelby says, 'There's a lion in your bathroom,' and goes to the bathroom door. 'I'm closing the lion cage, so now we're safe.' The girls laugh. I take photos of their play.

All's well until Shelby puts on Elizabeth's new dress-up high heel plastic shoes. Elizabeth wears Shelby's child bra, so it looks like they're sharing. But Elizabeth wants her slippers back. 'No, Shelby's wearing them,' Niki says.

Elizabeth becomes enraged, stands erect, arms rigid at her sides, fists clenched, and screams into Shelby's face for her shoes.

Shelby ignores Elizabeth. I'm flabbergasted by her composure. Elizabeth then spirals out of control, so Niki carries her, kicking and screaming, back to her room to calm her.

'I don't like Shelby!' she continues to scream, 'I want her to go home!'

Niki then calls me to the bedroom. When I enter, Elizabeth redirects her rage at me, kicking, spitting, hitting and screaming she doesn't like me.

'What should we do?' Niki asks.

'It's probably a combination of sugar, tiredness and upset over her shoes,' I reply.

Niki puts Elizabeth on her breast and she falls asleep instantly. I go back to the family room to be greeted by Shelby's continued surreal composure. I'm embarrassed. I feel like I need to apologise.

Niki joins us and Shelby says, in a mannered tone, 'I'm ready for bed now.'

Is this kid for real?

Matt told us Shelby falls asleep after she's read to. Shelby wants me to read to her. I read for about ten minutes, her eyes close, and off to sleep she goes.

And the post-mortem begins. 'Richard, Elizabeth's fit makes perfect sense in terms of a ritual abuse,' Niki tells me. 'Her fit was a flashback. A flashback from ritual abuse and pornography abuse. There was a specific sequence of triggers.'

Niki maps out the sequence of triggers, drawing an upward stair-step chart on a piece of paper: over-stimulation at the party; leaving the party with another baby; paying attention to Shelby in the car; party balloons; the girls taking their clothes off to play dress-up; photos being taken; Elizabeth putting a bra on. 'Richard, this sequence fits exactly with what she experienced in ritual abuse ceremonies. She had a flashback.'

Friday January 1, 1993

Today, Elizabeth and I watch the movie *It's a Wonderful Life*. She asks me about George Bailey growing up. I explain, 'When we grow up we learn to do things for ourselves, and then to do things for other people. Just like George Bailey.'

Elizabeth becomes upset. 'I don't want to grow up,' she cries.

'Elizabeth has said that countless times,' Niki tells me. 'It's one of the main reasons I think she was ritually abused.' Then she asks Elizabeth, 'Why don't you want to grow up? Did the bad monsters scare you about growing up?'

'Yes, the bad monsters scared me,' Elizabeth replies, adding, 'Mommy, there are bad monsters and good monsters. The bad monsters hurt me for a little while, and then the good monsters were nice to me.' And then, out of the blue, she adds, 'I want to go to Australia.'

We're transferring to our Australian office, midyear. I assume Niki's already mentioned this to Elizabeth.

'It's paradise in Australia,' Niki replies. 'There are no monsters. They'll all be left here.'

'But what about my good monsters?' Elizabeth asks.

Sunday January 3, 1993

'Richard,' Niki tells me today, 'the key to Elizabeth's healing is to focus on love and safety and security. We can't be too strict. We must listen respectfully to her legitimate requests, like not wearing clothes. Denying her legitimate requests will crush her sense of self.'

I tell Niki that Elizabeth desperately needs boundaries in her life, so she can learn self-discipline.

Niki disagrees. 'Richard, the focus should be on love, safety and nurturing. A strong sense of self will grow from that.'

Tuesday January 5, 1993

Today Niki calls my office, distressed. 'Richard, I talked with my sister this morning. Carmen told me Ester is the maiden name of Kimberley's mother. Maybe the "ester" in Newester, Dewester and Brewester is Elizabeth's way of saying "Ester"?'

Niki tells me she then drove Elizabeth along the street where the Ester's live, 'to see if she recognised a monster house. Richard, she said, "That's a monster house! And that's a monster house! And that's a monster house!" all the way along the street.'

Niki goes on, 'So I drove back more slowly and she said, "That's a monster house! And that's a monster house!" to a white house and a green house.' After more questioning, Elizabeth apparently chose the green house as the monster house. 'Richard, the green house was the Ester house!'

This evening, Niki calls Rick in Albuquerque, to ask if he thinks there's a connection between his and Elizabeth's abuse. Niki tells me, 'Rick's reply was, "Does one hand know about the other?" He thinks he and Elizabeth were abused by the same Satanists. Richard, we have to find out if the people I suspect abused Elizabeth are the same ones who abused Rick. It would prove she was abused. Richard, we have to go to Albuquerque.'

I'm tired. I've had little sleep. I've had hour after hour, day after day, week after week, of ritual abuse. 'Niki, wouldn't it be better to work with Tillman first?'

'But Richard, the Albuquerque information would help Tillman know what type of ritual abuse Elizabeth suffered, and who did it.'

'Niki, if Tillman thinks ritual abuse isn't likely, then we don't need to go to Albuquerque.'

Niki's now angry. 'Richard, I've been working my butt off to get answers about Elizabeth's abuse, when I would much rather be playing with the girls, like you can. If you don't want to go, I'll go by myself.'

Niki sees how tired I am, and suggests I go to bed. I try to sleep, but Niki and Elizabeth talk loudly about the monsters. Then Elizabeth tells Niki our ceramic rabbit is a monster. So Niki opens the back door and smashes the rabbit on our rear patio paving. 'You don't have to worry about that monster anymore,' she says.

This beautiful baked clay ornament was a handmade gift from Carmen's husband, a talented sculptor. It met its untimely end as a shattered monster. I'll miss it.

Niki then tells Elizabeth, if there are other monsters in the house, 'get them, and we'll smash them too.' So Elizabeth runs, laughing, to find more monsters, more ornaments to smash. A 'monster smash-a-thon' of ornaments occurs on our back patio.

Elizabeth then shifts topic to being in jail and eating poopy. She knows this gets a good reaction from Niki. 'Mommy, they put me in jail and made me eat poopy and drink tee-tee because they ran out of food. But eating poopy tastes nice,' Elizabeth says. 'The monsters ate poopy too!'

Somehow, among all this poop, I fall asleep.

sixteen

Barbara Tillman And
The Ritual Abuse Swamp

Wednesday January 6, 1993

Things didn't work out as Niki had hoped with Faye Hegburg, so
Elizabeth will soon see a new therapist, Barbara Tillman. Faye prepares
a report (Appendix 2) for Tillman, based on her five months of twice-
weekly play therapy with Elizabeth. Her summation states:

> My concern for Elizabeth at this point is that we allow her to recover
> according to her needs and at her pace. If we burden her with our adult
> need to understand and 'know', we may keep the trauma alive for her.

Niki wants to keep Elizabeth's trauma well and truly alive. This afternoon
we meet Tillman for the first time. Niki hopes she'll be the therapist
who'll finally get it right about Elizabeth's ritual abuse. 'Tillman should
see this obvious diagnosis,' she tells me.

Tillman's modern office is located in an annex of the Bartlesville hospital in which Elizabeth was born. Somewhere in her fifties, short and
round, she has a wise and friendly smile and a no-nonsense demeanour.
Her eyes twinkle with the joy of life. She presents as caring, competent
and professional. I'm not looking at a nut job.

Niki tells Tillman that Hegburg can only conclude Elizabeth experienced inappropriate play at day care. 'But I believe there's been ritual
abuse. Our family's been in crisis since last July, and we'll probably relocate

to Australia, midyear. We need resolution. Can you help?'

Tillman summarises her training and thirty-plus years of counselling experience, and then stresses, 'It's difficult working with three-and-a-half-year-olds. I can't promise answers. Working with such young children, the answers are not black or white.'

Tillman wants to see Niki and me for a few weeks before seeing Elizabeth, whose sessions with Hegburg will continue until she starts with Tillman. We schedule two parent meetings per week. Tillman also wants to read our diary notes. She may also seek input from Hegburg, Schwartz, Foster, Dohne, Roland and Doyle. We leave her office feeling positive.

This evening Niki's upbeat and speculates about 'a possible curse on my family', outlining their problems and setbacks over the years. 'I wonder if there's a curse at work, set in motion by people who seek power and money at the expense of my family? Is this curse now at work on Elizabeth?'

Thursday January 7, 1993

This morning Niki calls my office to discuss travel to Albuquerque. 'Richard, I don't think we're together on this. It's important we're together on this.' Then she calls again to tell me we're booked to travel to Albuquerque next week, next Wednesday, January 13.

Today, Elizabeth told Niki she thinks the monsters will come back. This evening, Niki has an explanation for Elizabeth's thought. 'Richard, I think it's related to her happier mood. A book I'm reading on satanic ritual abuse explains a cult technique where everything is said in opposites.' Niki says she told Elizabeth the cult tricked her by telling her that if she's happy, they'll come back.

I wonder, did Elizabeth grasp this bizarre explanation? Does Elizabeth think the monsters are somehow her fault, because she's happy? Is Niki taking Elizabeth deeper and deeper into an impenetrable swamp of grotesque behaviour and twisted logic, with no clear signposts showing her the way back out? Will Elizabeth be able to dredge this swamp out of her mind?

Friday January 8, 1992

When I arrive home today, the mood is playful. Elizabeth runs back and forth between our Christmas tree and Niki, who holds open a large black garbage bag, into which Elizabeth throws and smashes our Christmas ornaments. 'This is cheap therapy,' Niki tells me.

After all the ornaments, or monsters, are smashed, Elizabeth sits on Niki's lap. 'I didn't know the monsters were hurting you,' Niki tells her. 'I would never have let the monsters hurt you. I didn't know Kacey and Kimberley came here and hurt you.'

Well, I think to myself, Elizabeth, if you didn't know that Kacey and Kimberley were monsters who came here and hurt you, surely you do now.

Saturday January 9, 1992

This morning, Niki says she accidently pricked her finger and Elizabeth saw the blood. Elizabeth then told Niki, 'The monsters gave me blood to drink. I liked it. I'm a bad girl.'

Niki goes on, 'Richard, I absolutely did not ask her any questions about drinking blood. I don't want to visualise the gore she's disclosing. It makes me want to kill someone, retch, scream, sob hysterically.'

Later, after Niki tells Elizabeth how pretty she looks, she responds, 'No! I'm not pretty!' and then unloads a brain dump from the swamp. 'I eat tee-tee and poo-poo and blood. They come to see me at my blue school. Miss Mabel and Miss Karly were nice. They took their hands and went way, way down my body and pushed my tee-tee and poo-poo and blood out and I ate it. They made me eat tee-tee and poo-poo and blood and junk food and popsicles and it was nice. It's still in my tummy.'

Niki asks more questions, but now Elizabeth's disinterested. 'I want to stop talking about it,' she tells Niki. 'I'm Pinocchio, who can't talk.'

What broken pipes are leaking swamp sewage into Elizabeth's head? Today, I plumb through Niki's books, pamphlets and newsletters on satanic ritual abuse. They are loaded with exactly the same bizarre statements Elizabeth makes about being cut, drinking blood, eating faeces, being tied to trees, and on and on. I wonder, does Niki read these accounts, ask questions, and then later Elizabeth spouts Niki's questions as unsolicited statements? I don't know.

While I scan Niki's library of Satanism, she reads a copy of my diary notes, the notes we've given Tillman, along with Niki's journal. My diary is a huge dialogue dump of what I hear and see, not the annotated commentary you're reading now.

'We definitely have different perceptions about what happened to Elizabeth,' Niki says, as she reads, getting more and more upset. 'Richard, you paint me as a mother brainwashing her child. All you do is make yourself sound wonderful. Your notes read like someone preparing to go to court, to present a legal case. You look at me with a magnifying glass. You look for flaws, while I'm locked in an immense battle for the soul of our child.'

Niki's right. I have recorded in detail our journey since last July. I felt threatened, and wanted a very good record of events. It's also been my way of coping with the craziness. I sense this is an unfolding story, with many more chapters to go before what might be a very bad ending. I want to be able to tell this story accurately.

Niki goes on. 'Richard, I'm exhausted from what I think is a heroic effort on my part. But you see me as crazy, and driving Elizabeth crazy. You're always the one with the healthy, fun interaction with the girls. I'm always the one making paranoid comments. You never make an empathetic comment about Elizabeth's pain or my pain. Nor is love ever mentioned. Why did you even marry me?'

When Niki calms down, we talk about our very differing beliefs. Then we hug and say we love each other and are committed to working together, with Tillman, to find the answers.

As soon as we reach this truce, our family dynamic plunges back into the abuse paradigm. Elizabeth has a new toy sword, and wants to take her sword, find some monsters and cut their necks. This perks Niki up, so we drive Elizabeth, sword in hand, around town, to find some monsters. Elizabeth directs – we follow her every instruction: straight, left, left, right, straight, until she's completely lost. We can't find any monsters. This isn't fun anymore.

So Niki says, 'Let's drive past Kimberley's house.' As we slowly approach Kimberley's house, she tells Elizabeth, 'Now, take a good look. Tell us if you see the monsters' house.'

'Yes, this house is the monsters' house,' Elizabeth replies, bored. Then tells us, 'I'm sleepy.'

'But you're supposed to direct us,' Niki says.

'I can speak while I'm asleep,' Elizabeth replies. Then falls asleep.

'Elizabeth's in a self-induced trance,' Niki says, anxious. She thinks passing Kimberley's house has made Elizabeth go into a trance. Home again, and Niki carries Elizabeth to her bed. But suddenly, she's awake. 'It must have been a self-induced trance!' Niki exclaims.

Sunday January 10, 1993

Today is wonderfully stress-free and the evening starts well. Niki packs away the Christmas tree and I play Annie Lennox's *Diva* album. The music is fast-paced and Elizabeth begins to dance. Niki and Jenny join in, and I clap. Baby Jenny simply turns in circles between dancing Niki and Elizabeth. It's gorgeous. Elizabeth then gets groovy and wiggles her hips. 'Where did you learn to dance?' I ask, innocently, thinking of all the dance shows on TV.

'At high school. Miss Mabel taught me,' Elizabeth answers, while dancing.

'Should we take photos of you?' Niki asks. 'Is that what they did at the high school?'

'No, they didn't take photos,' Elizabeth replies, still dancing.

Niki asks Elizabeth if she can teach her to dance. So Elizabeth tells Niki to pull her tummy in, pull her boobies up, push her boobies down, pull her T-shirt up over her boobies, wiggle her hips, and bend down and touch her toes.

'Elizabeth wants me to striptease!' Niki exclaims, shocked, then asks Elizabeth what she wears when they dance at high school.

'A towel,' Elizabeth replies.

'I have absolutely no doubt Elizabeth's been made to perform erotic dances and striptease,' Niki tells me. 'I feel sick and enraged. Richard, what are you feeling?'

'Niki, we shouldn't sexualise the behaviour of a three-and-a-half-year-old,' I reply. 'Maybe it was copied from a TV exercise program, or MTV?'

'Okay,' Niki challenges, 'then what about Elizabeth saying she drank blood and drank tee-tee and ate poo-poo? Where did that come from? Certainly not from me! I have no doubt Barbara will diagnose ritual abuse once she reads my journal.'

'Niki, yes, they are bizarre statements,' I agree. 'But I told her not to play with her tee-tee and poo-poo when I was potty-training her. And that if she ate poo-poo she would get sick and have to go to hospital. Maybe it's just a contrarian comment?'

'Richard, it's probably good only one of us believes this happened. At least one of us can function.'

Monday January 11, 1993

This evening Elizabeth watches 'Beauty the Beast'. I sit with her in the family room, reading a newspaper. 'Daddy, who's your monster?' she asks.

I say I don't know, and ask who's her monster.

'Newey Dewester,' she replies.

When I ask where he lives, she points at the TV screen and says, 'There. There in the woods.' Wolves are running in the woods. I ask where the monster is.

'He's in the castle,' she answers as a scary castle appears on the screen.

'Tell me when you see the monster,' I say.

Elizabeth covers her eyes, two fingers slightly apart to just see what's happening. The Beast enters a room of the castle. 'There's my monster!' Elizabeth shouts. 'There's Newey Dewester!'

Tuesday January 12, 1993

Today, we have our second meeting with Tillman. Niki starts with Elizabeth's erotic dancing, and her amazement that, 'Richard just doesn't see it.'

'I don't want to sexualise Elizabeth's behaviour,' I reply. 'Asking Niki to "lift her boobies" while dancing might sound erotic to us, but it could be innocent from a child's perspective. Who knows why she said that? I don't know.'

'I hesitate to tell you this story,' Tillman says, but tells it anyway. 'There was a study conducted in which psychiatrists, unknown to the staff, were admitted to a mental institution with fictitious diagnoses. These "patients" behaved normally, not feigning any mental illness. However, the institution's psychiatrists interpreted their normal behaviour as confirming their fictitious diagnoses.'

Tillman has just told us our beliefs bias our views. Alarm bells go off. I feel conflict coming. I taste conflict coming. Tillman has challenged Niki's belief about erotic dancing and cautioned her against preconceived notions. Oh dear. After the prolonged and agonising build-up to enlist Tillman to diagnose Elizabeth's ritual abuse, I see an early head-on collision between Tillman and Niki.

Our session goes from bad to worse. Tillman then cautions Niki against sleeping in the same bed as Elizabeth. 'It sends her the message she's in control,' Tillman says.

'She's needy due to illness,' Niki replies, tearful. 'I'm trying to be the best mother I can.'

I jump in to support Niki. 'We try to protect each other's sleep,' I say, 'and Niki sleeping with Elizabeth only started with her ear infections.'

Tillman sympathises and says her motherly instincts controlled her actions with her own sick children. 'But,' she says, 'as a general rule, I caution you against routinely sleeping with your three-year-old daughter instead of your husband.'

Then the coup de grâce. 'Niki, I've read your journal. Contamination of Elizabeth by your questioning will make it difficult to reach any conclusion as to what happened.'

'I only asked questions as a concerned mother,' Niki replies. 'I had no resources to turn to for help when Elizabeth was disintegrating. And now she's disclosing eating poo-poo and drinking blood. This is even worse than the sexualised behaviour and masturbation my mother and sister were so concerned about.'

'Early masturbation in young girls is reason for concern,' Tillman says. 'Girls usually need to be taught self-stimulation, as opposed to boys.'

'And Elizabeth has a constant fear of monsters,' Niki adds.

Tillman downplays children's fears of monsters. She cites the case of a young girl who was terrified by toilets. 'Someone told her monsters lived in toilet bowls. She thought the water swirling down the bowl was the monster. A child's terror about monsters can be huge in response to something quite innocent.'

Tillman then asks, 'Are you two still seeing Tom Dohne as a couple?'

'No, we're not,' Niki answers firmly, without elaborating.

This evening, Niki's not happy. 'Richard, I'm out on a limb. I feel very exposed and very vulnerable by taking a strong stance on ritual abuse. Tillman needs to focus on Elizabeth's ritual abuse, not my parenting.'

seventeen

Albuquerque

Wednesday January 13, 1993

The day after our second session with Tillman, Niki and I fly to Albuquerque to meet Rick, a Bartlesville victim of ritual abuse. Niki hopes to learn the identity of the Bartlesville ritual abusers, and to learn more about the nature of Elizabeth's abuse. She hopes Rick has the answers.

Rick meets us at the airport then drives to a church where his therapist waits. In his mid-thirties, trim, blond, handsome, highly educated, intelligent and articulate, Rick has a detached, ethereal manner. His speech is monotone and emotionless, like he's on medication.

At the church we descend concrete stairs to a dusty, dimly lit basement littered with storage boxes and church paraphernalia, piled high between foundation pillars. One area of clutter has been cleared to allow enough room for an old sofa, two recycled chairs, a desk and a side table with kettle, teabags, unwashed mugs, instant coffee and half-eaten sandwiches.

Waiting for us in his therapeutic palace is Jake, a Master of Divinity. Maybe in his late twenties, Jake looks like an eccentric missionary: long hair, long beard and dishevelled clothing.

Niki and I take the sofa, Rick and Jake the chairs. Jake opens proceedings with a warning about the spread of Satanism across America, especially into Oklahoma. 'North-east Oklahoma is a recognised satanic ritual abuse hotspot,' he says.

'How do you know this, Jake?' I ask.

'For an area to be considered satanically active, it must have identified satanic ritual abuse cults operating over a period of at least ten years.'

'What evidence do you have that this is the case for north-east Oklahoma?' I ask.

'I have a network of contacts in the field,' Jake replies.

Jake sarcastically dismisses any question I ask that challenges the reality of Satanism taking over America. And sitting before us is Rick, whom Jake has awakened through recovered memory therapy to his childhood of satanic ritual abuse. If I'm not convinced about the looming satanic takeover, I should listen to Rick's story.

Rick speaks in a precise, rote, unemotional and unhesitating way, as if performing a recital. He focuses into the distance, disengaged from his audience.

His wife left him seven years ago for another man. After the divorce, he began a journey of self-discovery, sensing there was much he didn't understand about himself. He suffered terror in water. He was a loner, independent and obsessively self-reliant. He used swearwords he couldn't recall learning. He replayed certain movie images over and over in his mind. He had been hurtful to other children. He had difficulty falling asleep and suffered cold sweats. He had an obsessive interest in the Holocaust.

Rick grew up in Bartlesville and his childhood paediatrician was Dr Luke Daniel. Early last year, someone pursuing a child abuse accusation against Daniel asked Rick if he could provide any useful information to assist in the court case. Rick had no memory of abuse by Daniel.

He then began to recall memories of an auntie laying a knife blade on his forehead and dragging it down and across his face. Six months ago he asked Jake, his church counsellor, a question about his memories. Jake felt there might be more to Rick's memories, and so therapy commenced. Rick has since recovered memories of ritual abuse at the hands of Daniel, his auntie, and other adults he cannot yet identify.

He was left by his mother at a babysitter's house in Tulsa, Oklahoma, at two years of age. Inside the house were his aunt and Daniel. He was drugged, tied to a chair, and forced to watch as people performed sexual acts: homosexual, heterosexual and women using dildos. Then a woman performed oral sex on him. Non-participants stood in the shadows, as observers or instructors.

A knife was inserted into his mouth and down his throat, and he was told that if he spoke about what had happened, they would kill him. When his mother collected him from the babysitter he was in shock. He assumed his mother would know what had happened, just by looking at him. His mother never found out. The abuse went on and on.

He has since recovered memories of human sacrifice. At least three babies per year were killed and their bodies put through meat grinders. Adults were also sacrificed. He participated in group sex, torture, drug use, pornography and group masturbation. He was stripped naked and locked in a room with naked men and forced to masturbate them. He was placed in a bathtub full of ice, becoming hypothermic. Daniel then lifted him out of the tub and held him to his naked body. Rick remembers clutching to him, front to front, for warmth. He was then turned around and sodomised. Other children were involved, but he can't yet identify them. The children gave the adults nicknames: 'Ugly Face', 'Shit Face' and 'Poop Face'.

The torture grew to cattle prods and electric shocks to his genitals. He was tied to trees. A rope was inserted into his colon and they said his intestines were going to be pulled out. He had animal entrails spilled onto his body as they pulled out the rope, to make him think they were his intestines. He was told they were going to cook and eat him. He was made to watch a turkey cooking in an oven. Then he was placed briefly into the oven. The turkey was then torn apart and eaten, to make him feel like he was being torn apart and eaten.

He was told they were breaking the bones in his body, while hearing the snapping sound of breaking sticks. A wet cloth was placed over his mouth and water poured over the cloth. This caused loss of consciousness. On regaining consciousness, the process was repeated until he said he wouldn't tell his mummy about his abuse.

He watched animals tortured and disembowelled. He was injected with saline solutions. He was a bridegroom in a wedding ceremony. The cult assigned him a 'mommy' and a 'daddy' and he brought them gifts. They preferred blonde, blue-eyed Caucasians. He participated in the torture of other children and animals, and now feels remorse at the suffering he caused. He was conditioned to 'behave badly' to warrant beatings, after which they said, 'He was good for being bad,' and received their affection. Crying spoilt the abusers' pleasure, so they limited the abuse to get maximum enjoyment without excessive crying.

He was conditioned by hypnosis to respond to signals to leave his house at night, to join the abusers. The signals were single taps on his window or single rings on the telephone. He also gave a house key to his abusers so they could enter his house. The abuse continued until he was seven years old.

At the end of Rick's recital, Jake says, 'The abusers were trying to get closer to Satan. By hurting others, they gain power unto themselves.'

Rick has tried to share his memories with his parents, but they don't want to be disturbed by this information. 'They weren't there for me during the abuse,' Rick says, 'and they're not here for me now.'

I dwell on Rick's story during our flight back to Oklahoma. He told his story as he believes it – an impossible tale of abuse. A buried story, lived by a two-to-seven-year-old boy, and now dug up by a shovel-wielding, crusading Satanist hunter.

Niki, on the other hand, wonders, 'Richard, how can Elizabeth recover from her ritual abuse? First we need to let her tell her story, then let her cry and feel her feelings. We need to empathise with her terror. And we need to believe her.'

Then Niki says, 'I'm so relieved I can tell Carmen not to worry anymore about our father. My sister worried Rick might say our father was a cult member.'

Travelling at hundreds of kilometres per hour, thousands of metres above the ground, I feel solid inside this aluminium icon of science and engineering, this capsule of faith in rational thought. I wish I could take this feeling with me when I leave the plane. I've just lived through another crazy day in my new life of craziness.

eighteen

Back To Tillman And The Swamp

Thursday January 14, 1993

The day after Albuquerque, Niki and I attend our third session with Tillman. We're on a ritual abuse mission, with not a moment to lose. Before the session, Niki says, 'Richard, you have to tell Tillman we want answers about ritual abuse, not parenting.'

So I kick off, telling Tillman, 'We hope we can focus on finding out what happened to Elizabeth.'

We discuss when, and for how long, Elizabeth would have been available to abusers, and conclude it was only until early 1992, and wasn't a long span of time; day care centres and babysitters for a few hours, once or twice a week. We discuss aspects of Elizabeth's behaviour that could be considered normal and developmental, versus behaviour that might indicate abuse. Tillman thinks Elizabeth saying she eats poopy is developmental. She's more concerned about Elizabeth's constant monster talk. Tillman mentions play objects she'll use to aid disclosure – knives, swords and scissors.

'Elizabeth used to cut herself a lot with scissors.' Niki says. This is news to me, but I don't say that. 'Barbara,' Niki goes on, 'Elizabeth's terror triggers are clear indicators of ritual abuse. She's scared at Halloween and she's scared of Santa Claus.'

Wait a minute. I took Elizabeth out trick or treating last Halloween. She wore a pink fairy outfit and sure seemed happy to me, and still talks about 'the time I dressed up and collected candy with Daddy.' And she loved asking Santa for a 'Beauty the Beast' doll a few weeks ago at the country club. But I don't say any of that either. I'm not allowed to sabotage Niki with the therapist.

Niki then suggests a forensic examination of Elizabeth, to look for physical evidence of abuse. Tillman counsels against this, to avoid distress for Elizabeth. Her attitude throughout the session is cautious and professional.

When I arrive home from work, Niki's distraught and angry. I ask what's wrong. 'I'm not getting any support from Tillman,' Niki answers. 'I called the Bruces. I pleaded with them to tell me if they know anything else about our situation, to help prove to Tillman that Elizabeth's been ritually abused. They just said they'd think about it. Richard, I feel like I'm going crazy.'

Niki sobs while I hold and comfort her. 'Elizabeth's obviously been ritually abused,' she cries. 'I need help uncovering what happened. I'm exhausted taking a lone stance and being made to feel I'm crazy by therapists like Schwartz and Hegburg. I have needs too, you know. And they're not being met!'

'Niki,' I reply, 'put Tillman to the test. Explain your feelings and ask for support.' Niki calms down, agrees to try this, and asks that I not attend the next parent session. She'll take her mother instead, to help convince Tillman that Elizabeth's behaviour isn't normal.

Later, Elizabeth says, 'Daddy, you know what the monsters did that makes me sad? They put me in jail and put a fire in it and hurt my back.' When I ask her how big the jail was, she answers, 'This big!' arms wide apart, almost as wide as her smile.

Niki's listening. 'Richard, I'm so pleased Elizabeth is finally disclosing her sadness to you. I'm exhausted by her just burdening me with her terror.'

Sunday January 17, 1993

Midafternoon, and Niki wants to drive around town 'to see if Elizabeth recognises any monster locations'. As we drive past Kimberley's house, Elizabeth asks, 'Is this Kimberley's house?' and then tells us, 'Kimberly was nice. She protected me from the monsters. She bipped and bopped my monsters.'

I take directions from Niki. We end up in the countryside, on the perimeter of town. It's late afternoon and the light has faded. A winter chill weighs on an eerie, grey, leafless scrub oak forest. Niki tells me to turn left into what looks like an abandoned brick factory. Dilapidated tin sheds and hollowed-out concrete buildings sit beneath lifeless brick chimneys and surround a puddled and potholed gravel clearing. I feel like I'm in a scene from the *Rocky Horror Picture Show*. A car occupied by two innocent baby girls, a simpleton driver and a deranged navigator, heads blindly into industrial devastation. Unfortunately, I'm not doing the *Time Warp*.

What does Niki honestly think Elizabeth might say? 'Yes, I remember now! This is the place. The monsters incinerated babies inside those chimneys.'

We head home through Bartlesville's older suburbs. Niki points out a corner house that, on a previous search, Elizabeth identified as a monster house. This time she says nothing.

Wednesday January 20, 1993

Today, Niki calls me at work, distressed. 'Richard, I'll be glad when Barbara provides answers. Elizabeth doesn't want to return home from my parents' house. She says the monsters live in our house. She wants to stay at Nanna's and play with Wilson.'

Niki's sister, Carmen, has travelled down from Omaha with her two-year-old son, Wilson, to stay with Niki's parents. The family is rallying to support Niki's brother in his upcoming sexual assault trial. Why does Niki need Tillman to explain Elizabeth's desire to stay at Nanna's house and play with cousin Wilson?

This evening, Rick calls Niki from Albuquerque. After a long conversation, they agree Niki will mail him a letter with the names of her Bartlesville suspects, and he'll try to recall, in therapy, whether these people were connected with his ritual abuse.

Her long talk with Rick is followed by another long phone conversation with the mother of a ritually abused child. The mother's contact details came from the ritual abuse newsletter *Believe the Children*. They talk and share feelings about their stress as the mothers of ritually abused children. 'My husband doesn't understand ritual abuse,' Niki tells her. Later she tells me, 'It's universal that the father is sceptical and doesn't understand the emotional burden of ritual abuse. The mothers always carry the burden of emotional grief, just like I have.'

I'm tired. I've been awake since 3 am. This evening I've entertained both girls during Niki's two long phone conversations. Elizabeth has a cold, Jenny has ear infections and I'm recovering from bronchitis. Mainly, I'm just tired. I want to scream, Niki, it's not a matter of understanding, it's a matter of interpretation! We just interpret the same information very differently. I am very emotionally engaged, because I'm very worried about the impact of all this on Elizabeth. But, as usual, I say nothing.

Thursday January 21, 1993

Today Niki meets with Tillman, alone, and takes with her a typed two-page list of forty-three stressors that impact her, as the mother of a ritually abused child. Niki wants Tillman to understand, appreciate and empathise with her stress.

After the meeting Niki calls me at work, distraught. She still feels no support from Tillman. 'Richard, she doesn't get what I'm saying about the stress I'm under. I cried when she told me I was pressing too hard with Elizabeth and complicating things. I don't like the assumptions she's starting out with about me. I'm supported by people who think like I do. Ritual abuse is clear as a bell to them.'

Niki's devastated. Tillman isn't the therapist she craves – a therapist who will diagnose ritual abuse, proclaim Elizabeth an abused victim needing lifelong therapy and Niki an amazing mother. 'Niki, if you're unhappy with Barbara, let's go elsewhere,' I reply.

'Barbara purchased some more toys that will allow Elizabeth to disclose,' Niki says. 'And Carmen said Tillman is probably a child advocate and not a parent advocate. So I'll waive judgement until after she works with Elizabeth.'

When I arrive home, Niki sits on the living room floor, sobbing. 'Tillman doesn't understand the stress I'm under, knowing Elizabeth's been ritually abused,' she cries. 'She's got a negative attitude toward me. I haven't been supported by any of the therapists. It's just so unfair. I get more support from Rick than Barbara.'

Niki then shares Rick's latest recovered memories, relayed to her last night. 'What Rick experienced fits exactly with Elizabeth's erotic dancing.

He remembers orgies where he would dance around a room, masturbating naked men. I told Rick that Elizabeth uses a lever-pulling arm motion when she dances. He said this equates exactly to the act of stimulating penises. Richard, I believe Elizabeth had to masturbate naked men who were lined up in a room, while she did erotic dancing.'

Niki continues with Rick's memories. 'A high priestess had sex with a dying man on an altar. They pulled out his heart and intestines and showed them to him to increase the power of the sacrifice. The man's penis became rigid and the high priestess had sex with him and received his power when he ejaculated and died. And blacks came from a Louisiana coven, and educated the Bartlesville coven about sacrificing black children.'

Niki goes on. 'Rick and I speculated about why Satanists have targeted my family. He thinks we have shame in our background. He said satanic forces jump onto shame. Or maybe our spiritual approach makes us vulnerable. He said to just accept Christ as our saviour and let Christ keep us safe.'

As I listen to all this nonsense, a hidden, hopeful part of me wants to assume Niki realises Rick's stories are bonkers – beyond belief by any rational person – that these are manufactured memories recovered by a charlatan therapist from an unstable individual. But it seems Niki believes Rick's stories, and uses them to picture Elizabeth's abuse.

'Niki,' I say, 'anybody who participated in such incredibly sick activities, or thinks they did, is delusional. Niki, Rick is not normal.'

Niki enthusiastically agrees. 'Yes! Yes! You'd have to be crazy. And that's why I'm so worried Elizabeth will be crazy.'

Niki has missed my point, and goes on. 'Elizabeth's come under the influence of a cult that wants to sabotage our bonds with her. I discussed Rick's information with Tillman, but she doesn't think a cult exists in Bartlesville. But Rick's memories prove a cult is here. And now this cult is persecuting my family.'

'It's a complicated issue to unravel,' I reply, in an offhand way. I want to end our conversation. It's pointless discussing this delusional nonsense.

'No! No, it isn't complicated!' Niki shouts. 'It's obvious to me. What Elizabeth says makes perfect sense. I absolutely believe Elizabeth's been ritually abused. If I find out she hasn't, I must totally misunderstand child behaviour, and have very poor judgement as a mother.'

I try to defuse this powder keg. 'Niki, please don't be so hard on your-self. Don't personalise the issue. Don't back yourself into a corner to the extent of feeling like you're a bad mother if ritual abuse hasn't occurred.'

But Niki's adamant. 'Richard, if ritual abuse hasn't occurred, I'll need to work on myself. I'll have to find out how I got things so wrong.'

Niki has bet her motherhood on winning this hand of ritual abuse, gambling that her ritually abused child, the full house of horrors she thinks she's been dealt, will beat what Schwartz and Hegburg and I were dealt, a normal child, ace high. If she wins, she thinks she'll be vindicated as a good mother. Niki has gone all in. But really, it's not her motherhood she's betting, it's Elizabeth's life she's pushed forward on the poker table. It's Elizabeth's life that's at stake.

Friday January 22, 1993

This evening, Niki needs to talk to me, for hour after hour, about her predicament with Tillman. She's utterly distressed that another thera-pist doesn't support her belief in ritual abuse, and, worse, thinks she's pressuring Elizabeth. 'I deserve some compassion and support from Till-man,' Niki says, 'for what I've gone through with Elizabeth.'

'Niki,' I reply, 'maybe you asking Tillman for support about your list of ritual abuse stressors made her feel like you were asking her to agree with your belief in ritual abuse?'

I'm not sure why Niki's already butting heads with Tillman, but I have a hunch it's her journal, provided to Tillman. It paints a clear picture, an enormous mural, of her questioning, contamination and brainwashing of Elizabeth.

Saturday January 23, 1993

Niki's distress escalates. Tonight, when I arrive home, she unloads. 'Barbara said her strategy would be to assume Elizabeth's normal, then look for indications of abnormal behaviour. Richard, I think she's just looking at my parenting. Trying to see what impact I've had on Elizabeth. She's biased against me. I don't want Elizabeth to see Tillman if she's biased against me.'

'And, Richard, I thought you were a nice person. But since this crisis began I have my doubts. Now, after seeing Tillman, I have doubts about everybody. Am I hysterical? Are you a child molester? Is Elizabeth mentally ill? Did I make her mentally ill?

'I called Rachel and Sandra today. They were amazed at Tillman's attitude toward me. They said I shouldn't go back to her. Richard, I'm a good mother and I won't be devalued by her!'

Niki pauses, considers her next statement, then shouts, 'Richard, I demand to be believed by Tillman!'

'Niki,' I reply, 'we must be heard but we can't demand to be believed.'

Niki persists. 'Well, therapists should at least believe what the parents hear from their own children. They should at least believe the children. Richard, if I don't like Barbara, Elizabeth will pick up on my vibe and she won't disclose. And then Tillman won't diagnose ritual abuse. And I won't accept her diagnosis.'

'Niki, you've just set Tillman up for failure. It's pointless continuing with her.'

Sunday January 24, 1993

This evening, Niki tells me, 'At church this morning I had an idea to explain Elizabeth's talk about drinking blood. She participates in communion, which talks about drinking the blood of Christ. I wonder if she picked up on that statement?'

I'm impressed Niki thought of that. Is there hope?

Later, Elizabeth smiles and says, 'Dad, I have five mean monsters. They took a piece of glass and cut me all over. Then they cut me with scissors and knives. Then they tied me up to a tree. I love to be itchy. The tree made me itchy. Then they boinked me in the eyes, and in the tummy, and in the tee-tee, and in the bottom, and in the knees, and in the feet, and in the head, and then they wanted to cook me and eat me for dinner, in a fire, in their oven.'

And hope fades away.

Tuesday January 26, 1993

Niki's brother's sexual assault trial is this week. It's a trial by judge only.

Today Niki tells me, 'The judge just advised Chuck to alter his plea to no contest. It boils down to whether there was sexual consent and who's telling the truth. The verdict will be handed down on March 16.'

Niki attended the trial to support Chuck, while Elizabeth and Jenny were cared for by Daisy, Niki's mother's housekeeper, who also occasionally helps us with housecleaning. Niki continues on the phone. 'Daisy told me something about Kacey today. Once, when Daisy cleaned our house and Kacey was babysitting, she saw Kacey take Elizabeth into her bedroom when she was crying. Richard, when she told me that, I exploded inside. I visualised Kacey abusing Elizabeth.'

While Niki sobs on the phone, I think to myself, who knows what Kacey was doing? Maybe she was just trying to comfort Elizabeth – get her down for a nap by lying with her. Which is exactly what Niki told Kacey to do. Because that's exactly what Niki does.

We see Tillman in the afternoon and Niki describes her upset at hearing Daisy's comments regarding Kacey. She again cries and sobs.

'I need to clarify my status with you both,' Tillman says after Niki regains her composure. 'In the previous two sessions with Niki, I've sensed you, Niki, have been on the defensive regarding our relationship. I gave you positive feedback. I said you'd done well to have Elizabeth disclose and heal so much. However, where appropriate, I will make comments about parenting and normal versus abnormal child development, as well as suggestions on how best to interact with her – for example, by not asking her questions. And I can't support Niki in her belief in ritualistic abuse until I've worked with Elizabeth. That would be professionally irresponsible.'

'I understand,' Niki replies, compliantly. 'I certainly want an unbiased assessment. But it felt like you were just focusing on parenting. I hope you will work with Elizabeth to get a sense of the trauma she's experienced.'

'Elizabeth has suffered a trauma,' Tillman says, 'and unless you fire me, by not coming back, you've got me. I will work hard to uncover what happened. I'd like to see Elizabeth twice per week, starting tomorrow, and also continue seeing you both, once per week. I don't need any more journal notes. If Elizabeth's still impacted by her trauma, it will be expressed during her sessions with me.'

'Please read my December journal notes,' Niki pleads. 'That's when Elizabeth disclosed her ritual abuse.'

Tillman agrees to read Niki's December notes, and closes the session saying she wants to relieve Niki of the burden of working with Elizabeth. 'Niki, I want you to pull back now and let me work with her.'

'I didn't want to work with her,' Niki replies, 'but all this stuff came up and she was dwelling on it twenty-four hours a day. I didn't make it come up.'

'I hope you will pull back now,' Tillman says.

nineteen

Elizabeth Sees Tillman

Wednesday January 27, 1993

Elizabeth ended therapy with Hegburg last week. Today she begins therapy with Tillman. Niki takes Elizabeth to Tillman while I babysit Jenny. It's freezing outside, with snow on the ground. Elizabeth wears a tight, thin summer dress and plastic high heel slippers. Does Niki *want* her to look like the perfect porno star?

Niki remains with Elizabeth during the session. 'It went very well,' she tells me. 'Elizabeth found Barbara's toy knife and gun. Tillman wants to be alone with her tomorrow. We'll tell her I'm waiting outside while she does some drawings to show me later. But I don't get it – why the big deal about wanting me out of the room?'

Thursday January 28, 1993

Today Niki calls me at work, ecstatic. 'Elizabeth had a great session with Barbara. She did the same things with Barbara that she does with me. She played out themes Barbara said definitely indicate anxiety. She made a hospital and said there was a naughty lady and shot the naughty lady and broke up the hospital. And she drew a lady with a baby in her tummy and stabbed the picture.'

Niki's now happy with Barbara. 'I knew Elizabeth didn't disclose to Hegburg. She was great for stabilising her, but she didn't have the experience to get her to disclose. Today, Barbara looked at me in a way that made me feel like she connects with me. Richard, I'm so relieved. And to think I almost didn't go back to her.'

This evening, Elizabeth and I play in her bedroom. She's Jessie, the daughter in the *Prancer* video. In the movie, Jessie's mother has died, but we never learn why. And a reindeer, Prancer, has a bullet wound from a hunter. I'm Prancer, with a leg wound. Elizabeth tends kindly to my leg wound using pillows and blankets. Then she talks about the dead mother. 'Jessie's mother didn't die,' Elizabeth tells me, 'she had another baby. Jenny is the other baby. Mommy had another baby too. When Mommy had the baby in her tummy she was very sick. But Mommy didn't die. And she had Jenny.'

Sunday January 31, 1993

Tonight Niki surprises me with a confession. 'Okay, Richard, I did ask Elizabeth questions about Kacey and Abigail and Dale and Children's Home and all the others. But, honestly, I haven't asked her questions about ritual abuse. It's all come from her. I've just finished reading *Michelle Remembers*. The stuff Elizabeth talks about is exactly the same as the satanic ritual abuse in this book.'

Thursday February 4, 1993

Today I take Elizabeth to Tillman. Before we leave home, Elizabeth proudly brushes her teeth, her hair and puts on her dress. As we drive she says, in a serious tone, 'You know, Dad, I used to have monsters, but I don't anymore. Just my baby doll; she still has monsters.'

At Tillman's office she exclaims, 'Barbara has putty!' then rushes past Tillman, who stands at her office door, telling me, 'Wait outside, Dad.'

Friday February 5, 1993

This evening, peeling an apple, I cut a finger and exclaim 'Ouch!' Elizabeth is concerned and sympathetic, and wants to know what happened. She wants to see the cut. It's not a big cut, but it's bleeding. I ask if she's seen a bleeding cut before? 'No,' Elizabeth answers without thinking. But, then, after a moment's thought, she smiles and exclaims, 'Yes! Yes, the monsters cut me!'

Monday February 8, 1993

Tonight Niki tells me that today Elizabeth asked, 'Mommy, why do you want me to talk to you about the monsters?' Niki says she told Elizabeth,

'It's good to talk stuff like that out of your system, and to make sure other boys and girls aren't hurt like you were.'

'Niki,' I say, 'maybe she meant, why are you so interested to talk about the monsters when she doesn't need to talk about them?'

'That may be true,' Niki agrees.

Wednesday February 10, 1993

Tonight Niki tells me she feels like our crisis is over. 'Richard, Elizabeth's behaviour is within the realm of normal. Her terror is gone. Unless Barbara tells us something tomorrow that puts us back into crisis, I want to resume a normal family life.'

Thursday February 11, 1993

Today we'll meet Tillman to hear her thoughts on Elizabeth. Last night, Niki felt like the crisis was over. Not this morning. 'I'm very anxious,' she tells me, 'I'm worried Tillman will blow me off.'

When I arrive at Tillman's office, early afternoon, Niki's not there. Tillman and I shoot the breeze and wait. What we don't know is that Niki's called to say she can't make it.

Eventually, Tillman reviews Elizabeth's therapy with me. She says Elizabeth separates well from Niki, and then lists her play therapy methods: using putty, reading stories, drawing pictures and playing with anatomically correct dolls. Tillman also allows free play – whatever Elizabeth wants to do. Free play comes with two rules: Elizabeth must help pick up the toys afterwards and she must not hurt Barbara or herself while she plays.

'First of all,' Tillman says, 'Elizabeth has lots of energy. She's strong, active, bright, inquisitive and has a good memory. Second, she has anxiety, which is reflected in her drawings, rough play and poor self-control.' Tillman talks about Elizabeth drawing a baby in a mummy's tummy and hitting the drawing.

Tillman goes on. 'Third, she can be rough. She said she was "the monster" and was going to hurt me. I told her she's not allowed to do that. She tried to hit me, so I held her hands. Then she bit my hand. I didn't react other than to say, "You're hurting me." She was surprised

when I said that, and stopped biting me.' Tillman says she's amazed by
Elizabeth's strong will and that, 'She sure wants it her way.'

Tillman then offers some general observations. 'Elizabeth's very interested in family and sickness topics. She asked me where my mother is. I
told her my mother was no longer alive. She struggles with the concept of
"alive" versus "dead". She wants to know why sometimes the mommy is
not there. There's significant anxiety around mommies being sick or dying.

'Elizabeth also comes up with a lot of monster talk, but there's nothing sinister in it. And when she played with the anatomically correct dolls,
there was nothing of concern. I asked her some questions about the
naked doll and questions about Miss Mabel, but she said nothing unusual. I can't link any of her behaviour or statements to sexual abuse.'

So far, Tillman's comments have been fairly clinical – things she might
have said to Niki and me. This now changes. 'Richard, I see the tremen-
dous stress Niki's under. She's convinced Elizabeth's been ritually abused,
and isn't receptive to comments about other possible stressors – especially any comments about parenting. I have to walk a fine line.'

Tillman goes on. 'It wouldn't be good for Elizabeth to go from
therapist to therapist, but I feel like I could lose Niki if I discuss other
stressors. And I'm worried she'll think I'm saying she's a bad mother if
I don't diagnose ritual abuse.' Tillman says she feels like Niki will only
accept one diagnosis, ritual abuse, 'and that's a real dilemma for me.'

Now I'm uncomfortable. I sense Niki's somehow here, in the room,
with us. And I don't want to begin a dialogue with Tillman about Niki.
Tillman has just told me she recognises Niki's ritual abuse obsession,
without calling it that, and brought me into her confidence. But I haven't
got a clue how to solve Tillman's dilemma. Which is also my dilemma.

It gets worse. 'Richard, I need to speak to you in confidence. There's
no control on Elizabeth's behaviour. When she leaves my office, where
I set rules and limits, she's wild again. Niki doesn't control her. Children
need structure and limits otherwise they feel crazy. It's stressful for
them. Elizabeth feels in control of your family and this might be her
biggest stressor.'

Tillman continues. 'A lesser stressor is baby Jenny. Elizabeth's
expressed anxiety about Niki's illness during pregnancy. About Jenny

coming into the family, and about sharing Niki's attention. She plays out numerous themes along these lines.'

'What about the terror?' I ask. 'I've seen a couple of Elizabeth's night terrors.'

'I can't say what caused this terror,' Tillman replies. 'But I know children between eighteen months to three years old have temper tantrums that can spin out of control into terror. They can't control their emotions. This can be terrifying.'

I return to my office wondering how this will play out. I have a rough idea. I call Niki and relay Tillman's comments, leaving out Tillman's dilemma, and her thoughts about discipline. Niki's pleased Barbara has at least identified anxiety. 'That's a start,' she says.

* * *

When I arrive home, Niki's combative. 'Richard, Elizabeth isn't disclosing to Tillman, probably because she's not comfortable with her. She doesn't want to leave me to go into her office.' When I tell Niki how excited Elizabeth was to go into Barbara's office last Tuesday, Niki's angry response is, 'Well, then, you take her from now on!'

I try, diplomatically, to discuss discipline. Niki becomes exasperated. 'Richard, when Elizabeth was going through her terror, I wasn't concerned about discipline. I just wanted my child back. I had to let her know who her mother was. All my bonds with her had been broken. But now that the terror phase has passed, yes, we need to focus on discipline. But her acting out makes perfect sense following her disclosures of ritual abuse.'

Later in the evening, Niki asks my opinion regarding a draft letter-to-the-editor she's written to a magazine, responding to an article on childcare for working parents. Her draft states, 'We have a daughter who has disclosed to us abuse of the most perverted kind that she suffered at the hands of caretakers.'

'Niki,' I say cautiously, 'from a generic viewpoint, your letter helps parents to be cautious to the dangers of child abuse in childcare. But I disagree with the way it infers, as truth, that abuse of the most perverted kind did happen to Elizabeth.'

My comment enrages Niki. 'Well, I know it's the truth! As a mother and retired counsellor, I have confidence in my judgement. I'd be amazed to be so wrong. Richard, Elizabeth is telling us what happened to her. All we have to do is believe her. How come Penny Blake and Rick's counsellor and my mother and my sister believe Elizabeth? Why can't you believe Elizabeth?'

I want to get away from Niki's rage. Instead, I sit down on a sofa and silently hold onto my anxiety. 'Do you have an internal dialogue going on that you need to share?' Niki asks, in a superior tone of voice. She's calmed down.

'Niki, we have different opinions about this,' I reply. 'I don't interpret things the way you do. Elizabeth says things like "someone cut me" and "someone burnt me", which are obviously untrue. And if all we need to do is believe what Elizabeth tells us, why aren't the therapists reaching the same conclusions as you? And why is satanic ritual abuse so controversial?'

'Richard, the cult abusers use trickery,' Niki answers in a friendly, persuasive and patient tone, to display tolerance toward my ignorance. 'They convince children they've been cut and burnt. And it's such a new field, most therapists don't even understand it. And they just don't want to believe it. And we know Mikee and Alan abused Elizabeth. I think Mikee and Alan are the names of other abusers. Cult abusers.'

twenty

Out in The Cold

Tuesday February 16, 1993

Prejudice has a bitter taste. Forced to swallow it, the body wants to rebel. You learn not to take it too personally, but it always tastes bitter. I tasted prejudice in my younger years as the son of a Dutchman in Anglo-Celtic Australia. And I taste it now, as a man and as a father. Some men are violent, cruel and abusive, but Niki's continued suspicion I might have abused Elizabeth leaves a bitter taste whenever I'm given a mouthful.

Bartlesville is snow-covered, so this afternoon I head home early for snow play with the girls. Niki has baked some bread, 'your favourite'. I don snow jacket and gloves and am just about to head outside when Niki says, 'Richard, I'm glad you're playing at home with the girls. When you take them away on weekends, it plays right into my fear that you might be the abuser.'

There's a bitter taste in my mouth. 'Niki, do you honestly think I'm abusing Elizabeth?'

'It's a possibility,' Niki replies. 'But if I really believed it, I wouldn't be around. I just don't want you taking Elizabeth away for long trips. Your Saturday trips are as much separation from Elizabeth as I can handle.'

I'm hurt and I'm angry. 'Niki,' I reply, 'if I'm going to abuse Elizabeth, then Saturday is as good a day as any other day.'

Elizabeth's impatient to play in the snow, so I join her outside, dazed. Will this nightmare ever end? I play with Elizabeth, but she gets cold and returns inside. I shovel snow off our driveway, then just stand in the snow, in despair. Until Niki opens the garage door and asks, 'Are you coming inside?'

'I'm really hurt by what you said,' I tell Niki. 'I can't be a husband or a father under these circumstances.' I begin crying. Niki interprets my statement as a threat to leave. 'Niki, it's not a threat to leave. But I can't go on being a husband if you think it's possible I'm abusing the girls, and I have to live under restrictions or curfews. That's absurd.'

We go inside and talk. And cover the same ground, over and over. 'I don't believe you're abusing Elizabeth,' Niki says. 'If I did, I would've left you. But, Richard, I believe Elizabeth's been ritually abused. I believe it with every fibre in my body. And because you don't trust my judgement, because you don't agree with me, it's made you an abuse suspect in my mind, to some degree. And why do you need to go all the way to Tulsa? I get anxious when you're so far away with the girls.'

Elizabeth overhears Niki talk about Tulsa and asks, excited, 'Dad, Dad, can we go to Tulsa?'

I couldn't have scripted the timing of her question any better. 'Sweetheart, we have to wait till Saturday. Why do you want to go to Tulsa?' I ask.

'To go to the zoo!' Elizabeth answers.

Niki looks deflated. 'Elizabeth obviously has a good time on your drive trips. But they're no fun for me. I hated my one trip to Tulsa Zoo with you.'

Niki goes on. 'Richard, I know I'm susceptible to paranoia. I've considered just about everybody in terms of, could they be the abusers? I've even searched inside myself to see if there's any possibility I'm a multiple personality, and if I've abused Elizabeth, but I don't remember abusing her.'

'Try to imagine our positions reversed,' I ask Niki. 'Imagine you hold my beliefs and I hold yours. And I tell you I don't want you taking the girls for daytrips because I think it's possible you might be abusing them.'

'I can't imagine it that way,' Niki replies. 'If our positions were reversed, I would believe you. I would know you have good reason to believe so strongly in what you believe, because you have training and good judgement in such matters.'

I tell Niki we operate differently, that I need my own analysis to reach an opinion, especially a belief in ritual abuse of Elizabeth. 'Niki, my concern is you could pass your abuse belief on to Elizabeth. If the abuse occurred, well, then, okay. But what if it didn't? You'll have implanted a false belief. What unnecessary harm and damage will that do to Elizabeth?'

Niki agrees. 'Yes, it's a dilemma. But I will trust my instincts until someone proves otherwise.'

'Niki, no-one can prove a negative. No-one can prove it didn't happen.'

'A forensic medical examination would help,' Niki says. 'I spoke today with Dr Doyle. She suggested a forensic examination under anaesthetic. Or maybe we'll just have to wait until Elizabeth grows up and tells us herself what happened.'

Elizabeth's now in the bath and feels ignored. 'Mom! Mom, come and visit me!' she shouts.

'I will in a minute!' Niki shouts back.

Then Elizabeth shouts in a rote, unemotional monotone, 'Mom! Mom, come here! I want to tell you about my monsters and my bad dream. They put me in cold water and tied me to a tree and cut me all over and burnt me and stuff.'

Niki goes to the bathroom.

Wednesday February 17, 1993

Elizabeth continues twice-weekly therapy with Tillman. Niki and I reach a kind of stasis: acceptance of opposing opinions regarding what can ever be known about what might have happened to Elizabeth. A truce prevails, with underlying, unresolved tension.

For Niki, there is also an ebb and flow of emotions. One pendulum swings between optimism about the future and pessimism about the past, which hides the black unknown of what happened. Another pendulum swings between desperation to illuminate the black past and acceptance of its opacity.

Today, after Elizabeth's session with Tillman, Niki is happy. 'Richard, Elizabeth talked about Kacey and acted out knives, jails and being cut. I hope there'll be more disclosure.' Then, in the evening, she says, 'Elizabeth's as normal as I can remember. Maybe we'll never know what happened? Maybe we'll have to mark it down as a mystery and move on?'

The ebb and flow.

Thursday February 18, 1993

Tonight Elizabeth asks, 'Mommy, why am I going to see Barbara?' Niki tells Elizabeth it's to help her with her monsters. So Elizabeth goes into monster talk about cut and broken necks. Niki asks if she's seen people have their necks cut. 'Yes!' Elizabeth replies.

Saturday February 20, 1993

Today Niki tells me, 'Elizabeth's her old normal self again. There's no monster talk. Maybe there's no need for more therapy? Barbara just thinks we're not disciplining Elizabeth. Well, I hope she understands we're being much firmer now.'

Monday February 22, 1993

By tonight, Elizabeth's recovery is over and it's back to busy monster talk. Then Niki tells me, 'There's a passage in the book I've just read, *Too Scared to Cry*, where the author, strolling on the beach, observes a little girl killing her doll. She buries her baby doll in the sand, which shows the little girl was abused.'

'Why?' I ask. 'I grew up on a beach. You bury things in the sand.'

'Richard, it was this psychiatrist's opinion the girl was killing her doll. Maybe you have unresolved trauma in your own family and that's why you buried things in beach sand.'

twenty one

Madness And Depression

Tuesday February 23, 1993

This morning, in my office, I scan Niki's latest abuse guidebook, *Too Scared to Cry: Psychic Trauma in Childhood*. The author, Lenore Terr, believes most disturbed childhood behaviour is caused by trauma, especially sexual abuse. Every page reads, to me, like hysteria. Are there any voices for reason out there? I feel lost in a fog of madness.

Then the fog clears. I put down Terr's book and pick up yesterday's *Wall Street Journal*. Richard Gardner, clinical professor of child psychiatry at Columbia University, New York, and an expert on child sexual abuse, has published an opinion piece entitled 'Modern Witch Hunt – Child Abuse Charges'. As I read Gardner's article, the crazy, jumbled events of my life over the past seven months crystallise around a controversy raging in America's child abuse establishment regarding the over-diagnosis and false diagnosis of child sexual abuse. What I learn is that this controversy is raging in American psychotherapy and social work, raging in American law enforcement and the courts, and raging in my own home.

Professor Gardner's article details cases of blatantly false and fabricated accusations of child sexual abuse by overzealous judges, social workers, prosecutors, psychotherapists and hysterical parents. According to Gardner, these false accusations have resulted in lengthy jail sentences for innocent caregivers, relatives, parents and teachers. He cites as an example the conviction and sentencing of elderly grandparents Raymond and Shirley Souza to life in prison for perverted sexual acts on three of their grandchildren:

The accusations began when one of the Souzas' daughters had a *dream* in which she envisioned her parents and her brother sexually abusing her when she was a child. In the dream her mother had a penis. She concluded that the dream indicated that she had actually been sexually abused as a child by her parents and that the Souza grandchildren had probably been abused as well. She suggested that her siblings question the grandchildren. Thus began the wave of hysteria that ultimately resulted in the Souzas being found guilty ...

On the basis of my examinations of the Souzas, I was convinced that there wasn't a scintilla of evidence that they committed these crimes ... I carefully reviewed many of the documents in this case, especially videotapes of the interviews with the grandchildren conducted by the prosecutor's overzealous examiners. I found the interviews to be coercive, with the use of many leading questions and the selective ignoring of comments by the children that would have led any unbiased examiner to question whether these allegations had any merit whatsoever.

Gardner's article concludes with a section entitled 'The New Hysteria':

The U.S. appears to be witnessing its third great wave of hysteria. The first, the Salem Witch Trials, in 1692, lasted only a few months. Nineteen people were hanged before it became apparent that the accusations were suspect. In the 1950s, at the time of the McCarthy hearings, hysteria over the communist threat resulted in the destruction of many careers. Our current hysteria, which began in the early 1980s, is by far the worst with regard to the number of lives that have been destroyed and families that have disintegrated.

After reading this article I feel depressed. How will my family crisis end? What will happen to Elizabeth? Will this hysteria prevent her living a normal life? She already believes something bad has happened to her. Growing up is hard enough without this added burden.

I show Gardner's article to Niki this evening. 'That's just a biased putdown of legitimate concerns about sexual abuse,' Niki says. 'That's why we need a forensic examination. If Elizabeth's been ritually abused, as I believe she has, there'll be some sign of it.'

Friday February 26, 1993

This evening Niki reads *The Bondage Breaker*, a book about confronting the power of Satan. I read *Newsweek*. One article covers the murder of two-year-old James Bulger in England, and shows a security camera photo of the toddler being led to his death from a shopping mall. The image is horrific; it nauseates me. Niki also reads the article and tells me, 'Elizabeth's suffering was worse than that boy.'

The boy was beaten to death and left to be run over by a train. Is Niki insane?

Monday March 1, 1993

This evening I watch Niki make a playdough husband on our living room floor so Elizabeth can re-enact a cult marriage ceremony. Niki worries that Elizabeth was married to a cult member during her ritual abuse. This marriage theme is a replay of a cult script from Rick, or one of Niki's satanic guidebooks – I'm not sure which. Elizabeth is excited by this play.

'Tell me what you wear when you get married?' Niki asks.

Elizabeth answers with a blank stare. So Niki asks, 'Do you get married with a veil?'

Another blank stare.

Then Elizabeth shouts, 'No! I just want to make a baby in my tummy,' and lifts her T-shirt to mate with the lump of playdough. 'The man's penis goes in the woman's vaginal to make babies,' she tells us.

'Nobody should touch your tee-tee!' Niki exclaims, upset by Elizabeth's action to mate with the playdough man.

When I point out that Elizabeth did not say someone had touched her tee-tee, Niki responds, angry, 'Richard, she's behaving very provocatively toward the playdough man.' When I ask Niki if that's because she taught Elizabeth how sexual intercourse makes babies, she shouts, 'I don't know! That's part of the confusion.'

Elizabeth then turns her playdough husband into a ball, and says, 'This is the mean monster. It's really mean. It shoots a baby, like, clunk!' And wallops the side of her head with the ball, a glazed look in her eyes.

'That's a naughty monster,' Niki then says, 'let's kill it!'

So Elizabeth throws the playdough ball onto the floor and shouts 'Bam! Bam! Bam!' as she jumps up and down on the playdough ball – on the monster. Then she jumps up and down on books and toys that are scattered around on the living room floor, shouting, 'Kill the monsters! Kill the monsters! Bam! Bam! Bam!'

As I watch, I think to myself, this is completely nuts. I wonder, will our crazy family life just go on like this? Will it get worse before it gets better? How bad can it get?

Wednesday March 3, 1993

Dr Doyle has requested the Tulsa Justice Center conduct a forensic examination of Elizabeth, and this morning Niki takes Elizabeth to the centre to help her feel relaxed with the set-up. Elizabeth remembers her previous visit and asks, 'Is this where the scary table is?'

In the afternoon, Niki and I see Tillman. 'Elizabeth's become familiar with me and is testing limits,' she says. 'She wants to take her clothes off and show me her tee-tee. I asked her if someone else had seen her tee-tee and she said no.' Tillman goes on. 'If a child without Elizabeth's contaminated background behaved this way, I would be concerned about sexual abuse. But with so much questioning about her tee-tee, and if people have touched her tee-tee, or hurt her tee-tee, I can't interpret sexual abuse.'

Thursday March 4, 1993

Today is 'babies in the attic' day. True believers of satanic ritual abuse tell the tale that babies are bred and kept – usually in crates in attics – ready for ritual sacrifice.

This afternoon, Niki calls my office to pass on the news that Elizabeth reported there were babies trapped in her mother's attic. A quick inspection revealed no babies. However, Elizabeth was convinced there were babies trapped in an attic somewhere in Bartlesville, and wanted to find them. 'So, Richard, we drove around town. We drove past Kacey's house, but she didn't react. But, at the Phillips Hotel, she said, "That's the attic house!" Richard, I think Elizabeth's referring to an attic in the hotel where babies are being abused.'

Friday March 5, 1993

This morning Niki calls my office, solemn, sombre, serious, with dramatic news. 'Richard, Elizabeth's just disclosed her sexual abuse to Dr Doyle.'

Niki tells me that Elizabeth told Dr Doyle that she should check her tee-tee, and then disclosed to Linda that, 'Monsters boinked her in the eyes and in the tummy and in the tee-tee. The monsters were Newester, Dewester, Blewester and Brewester, and they stuck sharp things up her tee-tee. And they put their fist up her tee-tee. Then someone punched her in the tee-tee and cut her tee-tee and then sewed up her tee-tee.'

Niki's sombre mood then shifts to elation. 'Richard, Elizabeth has disclosed to Linda! I can't believe it. This takes it out of the realm of suspicion. It's now a fact. It's no longer, "maybe yes" or "maybe no". Elizabeth's disclosure to a doctor, to Linda, makes it a fact! I'm beside myself happy. I'm so happy I could spit. I've been saying prayers and thanking God. Richard, I've been vindicated!'

Niki goes on. 'It's out of our hands now. Richard, we need an attorney. I told Linda, "Nobody has paid any attention to me. But now, thank God, you have." I feel such enormous relief. Someone finally agrees something bad happened to my baby.'

Niki tells me she told Linda all about ritual abuse, and told her to look at all the possibilities, including everyone and everything. 'Linda was amazed,' Niki says. 'She wondered how many other children had been abused, and she'd missed it.'

Niki wonders why, today, Elizabeth has finally disclosed? 'Maybe her disclosure yesterday about the babies in the hotel attic brought it out of her?' Niki says she drove home from Dr Doyle's past the Phillips Hotel and Elizabeth talked more about the attic. 'She told me there were people in there getting married, like Robin Hood, Maid Marian and Mermaid Ariel.'

I listen patiently to all this madness, then finally ask, 'Niki, what has Elizabeth said to Linda that she hasn't said before? Why is telling Linda different to telling Barbara?'

'I don't know why it's different!' Niki shouts, angry, 'but it is!'

Saturday March 6, 1993

Tonight I've planned a treat for Niki and me. Restaurant dinner, then a jazz concert at the Bartlesville Community Center. The trumpeter is Wynton Marsalis. When Julie, an adult babysitter, arrives, Elizabeth screams, 'I don't like Julie anymore!' Julie visibly flinches. I know how she feels.

Elizabeth's screaming escalates, so Niki takes her to her room. Then returns. 'It's not going to work out,' she says. So I pay Julie for a night's babysitting and she leaves.

Then, without forethought, I say, 'Why don't I take Elizabeth to the concert?' Elizabeth controls the house, is the mistress of the house. Maybe that's why I say it?

Elizabeth's instantly happy. 'I'm going to have a date with Daddy. I'm going to the trumpet movie with Daddy.' I had told her that Mummy and I were going to see a trumpeter.

Niki, initially happy with the idea, has a change of heart, asking Elizabeth, 'Aren't you tired? Don't you want to stay home?' But she really wants to go. As we leave, Niki tells me, 'Drive past the Phillips Hotel. See what her reaction is.'

We drive past the hotel a couple of times. The first time Elizabeth doesn't respond. The second time I ask if she knows that place? 'Yes, it's the hotel,' she says. Has she been inside? 'No,' she says. I ask if she's sure? 'I'm sure,' she answers.

Elizabeth behaves well at the concert. We're seated in a top row and look down at the stage, at hundreds of milling patrons as they find their seats. Elizabeth sits upright, adult-like, asking intelligent questions about proceedings. Finally, the bright lights dim and coloured lights illuminate the stage. Elizabeth takes it all in her stride. The trumpet music is loud, so she puts fingers into her ears. Eventually she falls asleep in my lap. We leave at the first break, around 9 pm.

At home, Niki's tired. 'Jenny's been no fun. Was Elizabeth scared at the concert?'

'She wasn't scared at all,' I reply, 'but she thought we were going to a movie.'

Sunday March 7, 1993

A beautiful early spring day. I play in the garden with the girls. Elizabeth collects rocks from around her sandpit, puts them into her toy trolley and tells me, 'I'm collecting rocks to cook dinner for Mommy, Daddy, Jenny, Nanna, Poppa, Gerard, Dell, Carmen, Wilson and Chris.' She then takes a few rocks inside and tells Niki she's going to cook them.

'Where have you eaten rocks before?' Niki asks, anxious. Elizabeth's not sure how to answer that question, and tells Niki she just wants to cook the rocks. 'You haven't eaten rocks.' Niki says. 'Your teeth would be broken.'

Later Niki confronts me, hostile. 'Richard, I'm very concerned Elizabeth did not enjoy the concert last night. So let's not do that again.'

Monday March 8, 1993

I wake early, utterly distressed. What's happening is madness. Later, I call Tillman from my office. I don't know what else to do with my anguish. 'I know the stress you're all under,' she says. 'I had a hard session with Niki this morning. I said I need to see her as much as I see Elizabeth. Richard, I don't want to lose Niki. If I do, it's all lost.'

It's all lost? I'm watching my beautiful daughter being brainwashed by her mother, by the woman I love, by the woman I married, to believe she's an abused victim. I don't understand what's happening. I feel helpless to save Elizabeth from madness. And the therapist who's supposed to unravel the madness has just told me that unless she gets Niki to let go of her obsession, unless she can persuade Niki to allow Elizabeth to be normal, then she, the therapist, thinks it's all lost. She also feels helpless. Are we both helpless witnesses to a tragedy?

At home, I'm surprised to find Niki in high spirits. 'Richard, this morning Barbara asked me to treat Elizabeth as if ritual abuse didn't happen. To treat her as if she's normal. I told her I'd try. But, afterwards, I realised I can't do that. Elizabeth needs an avenue for disclosure. All my ritual abuse contacts say the most important thing is to listen to the children, and to believe the children.'

Niki goes on. 'Barbara doesn't understand ritual abuse. I need to go over my journal with her, page by page. I'm a good mother. I can figure it out. Elizabeth's behaviour only makes sense in terms of ritual abuse.'

Tuesday March 9, 1993

Niki calls me at work, happy and upbeat. 'Richard, I've just spoken with Beth Vargo from Believe the Children in Chicago. Vargo said Barbara's approach about structure and discipline was correct. She said ritually abused children need structure and limits, even more than normal children.' Niki's excitement grows. 'And Vargo told me there's a ritual abuse conference in Chicago in April. I want all of us to go, including Barbara.'

Niki then shifts topic from the April conference to electric shock torture. 'Richard, yesterday Elizabeth said her legs didn't work because the monsters hurt her legs. Something about shocks put into her legs. Electric shock torture fits exactly with her game of cycling her legs under the sheets. She says she's running. Richard, I wonder if it's because of ritual abuse with electric shocks?'

After hearing my wife tell me a Satanist cult may have tortured our daughter with electric shock equipment, I hang up the phone and resume work as a geologist. This is now my daily life, my daily shuffle, back and forth between madness and sanity.

This evening, Niki cooks a wonderful dinner and we all sit down together. Niki suggests we each take turns to say grace. When it's Elizabeth turn, she says, 'God, please heal me.' Hearing this, I feel like I've been punched in the guts. Three-year-old Elizabeth thinks she's been abused by naughty people and prays for God to heal her.

Then Niki says, 'Elizabeth's excited to go back to the scary table. I told her they use the scary table to help find the naughty people who hurt children. And I asked Elizabeth if Jenny had monsters, and she said yes. Richard, Jenny should be forensically examined as well.'

This conversation occurs in front of Elizabeth and Jenny. I begin shaking, vibrating. This is madness and brainwashing. Niki has convinced Elizabeth she's a victim of the naughty people and needs to get up onto the scary table so they can look inside her tee-tee and find the naughty people. And now Niki wants to drag Jenny into this madness as well.

I swallow mouthfuls of anger. I choke it down. I stop it flying up my throat and out into Niki's face. I can't keep swallowing. 'Niki, what exactly did you tell Elizabeth about the Justice Center?' I growl brusquely, drops of anger leaking out.

'I can't remember exactly,' she replies, curt and dismissive.

'Niki, saying things like that just make her believe she's been abused. And that's wrong.'

'It's Elizabeth who says this, not me,' Niki hisses back. 'I'm just repeating what she's said all along. And I will allow her to act out her terror, regardless of what Barbara Tillman says. And I'm tired of being abused by you!' Niki shouts.

'I'm just expressing my opinion,' I say. 'This is difficult for me.' I lift up shaking hands.

'Why are you shaking?'

'Because anger upsets me.'

'Well I'm upset too!' Niki shouts. 'I have emotions too. I'm a good mother. I will not tolerate being cast as a bad mother.'

Wednesday March 10, 1993

I wake at 3am, acutely distressed. Around midday I leave on a business trip for South Carolina. I'm severely anxious, in despair, numb, robotic. My world shrinks to the space I occupy – a taxi, a hotel room. I feel powerless beyond the reach of my arms. I feel trapped inside a bubble of madness, unable to use logic to live my life. In my hotel room I pray on my knees, for a second time, that somehow this crisis can end.

Thursday March 11, 1993

Tonight, when I call home from South Carolina, Niki's combative. 'Richard, I'm convinced Elizabeth suffered ritual abuse. I think you're in denial about your own sexual abuse. You need to appreciate my judgement. You need to develop trust in my insights. Richard, you don't understand me. You don't know where I'm coming from when I work with Elizabeth. One day you'll know I was right.'

Then, with less venom, 'Elizabeth's been talking a lot about last Saturday's concert and the loud trumpets. She said it was okay. And she's missing you. This has relieved my concerns about you abusing her last Saturday.'

Friday March 12, 1993

Home from South Carolina, and I'm greeted by rage. 'Richard,' Niki shouts, 'I talked with Linda Doyle today. Tillman told Linda that Elizabeth's been contaminated by me! She painted me as hysterical. Why do I have these problems with Tillman?' Niki points a finger at me and shouts, 'Well, I think because of you! Whenever your views are expressed, the therapist sides with you! But when I can get my message across, without your interference, they see my point of view.'

Niki calms and explains what's expected of me. 'You now have to use your strong communication skills, as head of this household and as my loving husband, and support me against Tillman. You must insist I'm not treated as hysterical. If I'm going to progress from wondering if you're abusing Elizabeth, you can't think of me as hysterical.'

Later, Elizabeth wakes and comes into our room. With an anxious expression, veiled by a smile, she says, 'Mom, Dad, I need to tell you something. A long, long, long, long, long, long time ago I had monsters. But I was dreaming, and they're gone now.'

I wonder, is this bright young girl trying to initiate a peace settlement between her arguing, stressed-out parents? Is she trying to remove the source of her parents' conflict, her monsters?

Saturday March 13, 1993

This morning Niki hands me a brochure for the Chicago conference: *From Heartbreak Through Healing – Facing The Reality of Sexual and Ritual Abuse of Children.*

'Richard,' Niki says with messianic conviction, 'there are few things I have ever in my life, and will ever again in my life, feel so strongly about. Richard, I want to attend this ritual abuse conference.'

I cannot bear the thought, let alone the reality, of attending a ritual abuse conference. When I imagine the experience, it blends into and magnifies my daily nightmare, then morphs into a horror spectacle – milling crowds celebrating ritual abuse. Cheerleading nut-job therapists, like rock stars on a stage, jumping up and down, whipping ritual abuse fans into a frenzy: 'Go Team Satan!' 'Go Team Ritual Abuse!'

And then I see Niki, rushing from booth to booth, gathering armloads of books and pamphlets, all packed with more and more abnormal behaviours and more and more spectacular symptoms, to identify and implant into Elizabeth.

I see Niki's anxiety about ritual abuse escalating, like fuel thrown onto a bonfire. And in the middle of this bonfire, tied to her ritual abuse tree, is Elizabeth, burning at the stake for the sake of a fantasy, an obsession.

Looking at the brochure I want to vomit.

twenty two

Calm And Codependency

Sunday March 14, 1993

After weeks of madness and stress, a respite arrives. Elizabeth's out-of-control behaviour diminishes, Niki's anxiety calms and a therapeutic distraction presents itself.

This morning I catch up on office work. Elizabeth calls, upset. She wants me to come home. Niki takes the phone. 'Elizabeth's going through some kind of revelation about you. That you're her daddy and that you do love her.'

A bizarre comment, but I let it roll by; another weird moment in my new weird life.

At home Elizabeth is well behaved and loving. 'Elizabeth's helping with housework,' Niki says. 'She's eating. She's cooperative. She's wearing clothes. There's no monster talk. She's regaining a sense of predictability about the world, a sense of safety and trust. When I look into her eyes I see her old sparkle. Richard, I see a happy soul.'

After her conversation with Beth Vargo, Niki began imposing boundaries, structure and discipline onto Elizabeth's behaviour, and pulled back on the monster talk.

Tuesday March 16, 1993

Today Niki's brother's ordeal ends. The judge announces a deferred sentence. If Chuck fulfils counselling and community service, he'll have a clean record.

Tonight Niki tells me she also wants our ordeal to end. 'Richard, we could end Elizabeth's therapy and just use the time with Barbara to work through my journal and reach a consensus. I'm still convinced about ritual abuse, but I know we'll never have a smoking gun to pin down for sure what happened. But I still want a forensic examination.'

Wednesday March 17, 1993

And Niki still wants to attend the ritual abuse conference in Chicago. So this morning I call Beth Vargo from Believe the Children. Vargo sounds like a genuinely caring person, whose passion is the wellbeing of abused children. 'The most important thing you can do, regardless of a clear diagnosis, is provide a healing environment for Elizabeth,' Vargo tells me. 'Make her feel loved and safe. Allow disclosure, if she initiates it, but only at certain times and places. And you must stop negative, out-of-control behaviour.'

This afternoon Niki and I have a parent session with Tillman, my first in a long time. 'Elizabeth's play is healthy and happy,' Barbara says. 'I'm really pleased.'

So the session switches to a discussion about how Niki and I communicate. 'There were times I did not trust Richard,' Niki says, 'and wondered if he was the abuser. This issue is now resolved. But he still treats me like a hysterical mother. And he doesn't share his thoughts and feelings. He withdraws, which plays right into my issue with abandonment.'

'I admire the way Niki is always open and honest,' I reply. 'I don't always behave that way. Niki's anger frightens me, so I withdraw. I don't say what I'm thinking or feeling, especially if what I'll say will anger Niki.' I search for an example and, not innocently, pick one in which Barbara has some insight. 'I felt unable to tell Niki I disagreed with her when she told me, "Abuse is now a proven fact," after Elizabeth spoke with Dr Doyle.'

Niki erupts, furious. 'I resent you bringing that up to Barbara!'

Tillman enters the conversation. 'Niki, are you aware that you pounce? Maybe take some time to frame your thoughts before responding angrily?' Tillman then turns to me and asks, 'Richard, do you know what codependent means?'

I don't.

Barbara explains the term, and says she thinks I'm codependent. I hear her words, but they make little sense. 'I have a strong sense of self-worth,' I reply, 'but anger feels life-threatening. That might sound paradoxical, but there you go.'

Niki jumps back into the conversation, enthusiastically announcing, 'I'm a recovering codependent.'

By this evening Niki has shifted paradigms. 'Richard, if we make a commitment to work together on codependency, I can move on from ritual abuse.'

What Faustian bargain is this? Niki's offer to trade one diagnosis of ritual abuse for two diagnoses of codependency sounds like a good deal. Maybe I should shake hands on it. But I know I'd be kidding myself if I thought it was a done deal. Because by tomorrow, or the next day, or next week, Niki will want her ritual abuse diagnosis back. I know that. I say nothing.

Then I read up on codependency. What I'm supposed to suffer from doesn't sound good. A relationship in which I'm controlled by another person, probably someone with a pathological condition, typically narcissism. I supposedly place a lower priority on my own needs and am excessively preoccupied with the needs of others, and overly compliant.

Thursday March 18, 1993

Today Niki calls me at work. She sounds grounded, rational, even-keeled, friendly. She sounds like the Niki I married. 'Richard, I picked up a pamphlet on normal childhood fears at Dr Doyle's. I'm wondering if Elizabeth's fears were the result of something benign, like her known traumas, and maybe not ritual abuse. Maybe we can get to the bottom of this with Barbara.'

Did Niki really say that?

This evening Elizabeth's behaviour is great. Niki has set boundaries and now relates to her as if she's normal. There's no monster questions and no monster talk – no talk of being hurt by the naughty people. And Niki's less anxious, which rubs off on Elizabeth. I feel so hopeful.

Friday March 19, 1993

Tonight Niki and I discuss how disconnected we've become. 'One of my concerns about your opposition to ritual abuse was the sense you aren't open to my strong emotions,' Niki says. 'But working on your codependency will address this, and then I can let go of ritual abuse.'

'Niki,' I reply, 'we desperately need to get some stability and harmony and fun back into our family life. We need to reconnect with our goals.'

Niki then calls Sandra. 'Elizabeth's improved behaviour is a miracle. I can't explain it.'

Sunday March 21, 1993

Elizabeth remains happy and normal. 'It could all boil down to Kacey molesting Elizabeth, along with Mikee and Alan,' Niki tells me tonight.

I feel elated. Is this nightmare finally over?

Then Rick calls Niki from Albuquerque to pass on his latest recovered memories. Niki mentions Elizabeth's 'babies in the hotel attic' disclosure, and Rick tells Niki that he's now recovered memories of 'crate loads of babies in attics, ready for ritual sacrifice'.

Niki then tells Rick, 'Elizabeth now has a fascination with the colour yellow.'

'I also have a fascination with the colour yellow,' Rick replies.

Is this nightmare over?

twenty three

Veronica Oliver-Bell

Tuesday March 23, 1993

This nightmare is not over. Today Niki receives a return phone call from Veronica Oliver-Bell, a social worker in Oklahoma City and true believer in ritual abuse.

'Veronica works with ritually abused children,' Niki tells me, 'and believes cult ritual abuse involves a different disclosure and therapy process. She said we do need to listen to and believe the children. She sounded calm and centred, and took my concerns about ritual abuse very seriously. Richard, I felt listened to.'

Wednesday March 24, 1993

Today Niki and I meet with Tillman. 'Elizabeth is much improved,' she says. 'Her play and drawings indicate far less anxiety. I'm very pleased. We'll never know, for sure, what scared Elizabeth, but there were some significant stressors: ear surgery, your illness during Jenny's pregnancy, the arrival of a competing sibling, seeing Niki distressed believing she'd been hurt, and then you two at odds. Children are very sensitive to their parents' emotions. She would have also picked up that Niki wondered if Richard had abused her.'

Tillman goes on. 'If she experienced abuse, she has well and truly talked it out. You listened to her. You should continue to listen, but don't question her to find an adult understanding, because there isn't one. Questioning a three-year-old about what happened when she was one or two years old will not provide a meaningful answer.'

152

Niki has a completely different perspective. 'Barbara, I believe Elizabeth when she tells me about the monsters and what they did to her. Richard thinks my approach just builds on her fantasy and sends the message she's an abused victim. This has been a huge dilemma for us.'

'Niki,' Tillman replies, 'Elizabeth has learned to get your attention by talking about the monsters. She's so smart, she would have tuned in. And her manipulation is conscious and subconscious. The topic of monsters has now been imprinted in her subconscious. Her bizarre monster statements come from a combination of contamination, children's videos and stories, and her own imagination.'

'Do you have any constructive criticisms to offer me?' Niki asks.

'In the beginning I was afraid I'd lose you,' Barbara replies. 'As the mother, you're the most important person in terms of helping Elizabeth heal.'

'Why did you feel that way?'

'I felt like there was a glitch in our communication,' Barbara says. 'But the best therapy for Elizabeth is a calm, loving and caring family relationship.'

Barbara is shadow-boxing. She wants to focus on Elizabeth's improved behaviour. She wants Niki to close the book on ritual abuse. She wants Niki to let go of her obsession.

Niki won't let go. 'Tillman still doesn't get it,' she tells me this evening. 'She doesn't understand ritual abuse. She hasn't gone over my journal and explained to me why ritual abuse didn't occur.'

Niki then calls her mother. 'Momma, Tillman doesn't get ritual abuse. She isn't an expert in ritual abuse. We need an expert in ritual abuse. Veronica is an expert in ritual abuse.'

This nightmare is definitely not over.

Thursday March 25, 1993

Today Jenny has ear and adenoid surgery. Dr Kaplan tells us, 'We intubate children during surgery. If Elizabeth remembers a tube going down her throat when she had ear surgery, then she was insufficiently sedated.' Niki and I are devastated by this information. It must have been traumatic for Elizabeth to have a black mask put over her face to initiate anaesthesia, and then have a tube pushed down her throat while conscious. This could explain her acute distress following ear surgery.

This evening, Veronica Oliver-Bell calls Niki again to discuss ritual abuse. After a long conversation, Niki's euphoric. 'I want to meet Veronica and discuss ritual abuse,' she tells me. 'I'm praying for a miracle. Maybe Kacey will admit involvement in a cult?'

Listening to Niki I wonder why proving Elizabeth suffered horrific abuse would make her euphoric. The answer I come up with is both simple and complex. The simple part is that this isn't about Elizabeth's abuse, it's about Niki's vindication. She needs Elizabeth to be ritually abused to prove she's right, and not a bad mother. Niki would throw Elizabeth into the lion's den of abused victimhood to prove she's a good mother; a mother who did not brainwash her daughter to believe she's an abused victim, because, 'see, she is an abused victim.' This answer is also complex, because I don't know why Niki's doing this. But I do know it's a tragedy for Elizabeth.

Friday March 26, 1993

Niki talks again today with Oliver-Bell, then calls me at work, besotted. 'Richard, Veronica is the person I need, the person I'd hoped Barbara would be. She listened to me. She agreed ritual abuse fits my observations. I'm going to Oklahoma City next Monday to review my notes with her.' Niki tells me Oliver-Bell doesn't want to interfere with Tillman's therapy. 'She'll just tell Barbara what to be on the lookout for to identify ritual abuse.'

'Niki,' I ask, 'are you expecting a ritual abuse diagnosis from Veronica?'

'Richard, I don't want a diagnosis,' Niki replies. 'Veronica said she couldn't diagnose without seeing Elizabeth. I just want her opinion on my notes, and to see if she can help Barbara. Veronica and Barbara. You and me. We can all work together as a team.'

Niki goes on. 'Richard, I need to speak with someone who listens to me. I have no rapport with Barbara. Since last July, I've had no rapport with a therapist. Schwartz, Hegburg and now Barbara, they haven't listened to me.' Niki flares up, 'They don't get ritual abuse!'

After this conversation, I forecast our future. Oliver-Bell will agree that Elizabeth's statements and behaviour, as recorded by Niki, indicate ritual abuse. Niki's anxiety will jack back up, her interrogation of Elizabeth will start again and Elizabeth's anxiety will return. I'm distressed.

Niki, on the other hand, is excited, animated and happy. When I arrive home she's on the phone with her sister talking about Veronica. Then she tells me, 'My mother's coming with me on Monday to see Veronica.' Then talks to me, hour after hour, about the obvious diagnosis of ritual abuse for Elizabeth.

I could just switch off and not care what Niki does. But I'm caught, with Niki, in the ritual abuse web. I'm fighting to stop the spider. If the spider, the obsession, wraps Elizabeth in its abused victim cocoon, her chance for a normal life is over. So I can't switch off. But I'm exhausted and depressed, so tonight I just sit and listen as Niki goes on and on and on about ritual abuse. Finally, she notices my silence, and asks, 'Why are you so unhappy?'

'Niki,' I answer, 'Veronica can't provide a ritual abuse diagnosis without seeing Elizabeth. And also reviewing our diaries and journals and all the therapist's reports. All she can do is listen to you and be supportive. Then Veronica and Barbara will clash, with Barbara telling Veronica there's been contamination. Then you will feel sabotaged and unsupported and upset and stressed. Which will stress Elizabeth. And so we're back to where we started. Niki I'm tired. Tired from a long week at work. Tired from worry over Elizabeth. Tired.'

Now Niki's angry. 'Veronica knows she can't render a diagnosis. And, Richard, I have unmet needs. For the last eight months my needs haven't been met by any of the therapists. I need someone who supports me, who believes what I say about Elizabeth's behaviour, who knows about ritual abuse, who connects with me on the topic, who agrees it's a possibility. Or can explain why it's not a possibility. I can tell Veronica 'gets it'. And this is my last effort before we transfer to Australia. After this, I'll put closure around my belief in ritual abuse.'

I want to believe Niki. I imagine the perfect scene where Niki no longer obsesses about ritual abuse: where we resume a family life of normal activities, free of conflict over differing beliefs about horrific child abuse; where our two gifted daughters, both blessed with extraordinary potential and opportunity, grow up to be all they can be, and live their own happy and independent lives. But I despair that my vision is a mirage.

'Niki,' I say, 'starting again with Veronica feels like going down a new dark tunnel of uncertainty, with no light at the end. I don't know Veronica. I don't know if she's a rational person who'll give reasoned, commonsense advice. Dohne warned us to be very careful who we engage because the field of therapists dealing with ritual abuse and other spectacular diagnoses is full of nut jobs.'

Niki tries to soothe my concerns. 'Richard, Veronica sounds centred and rational. And I'm also not interested in working with fanatics. You have to trust me about that. I could see Penny Blake was an extremist, so I didn't use her. And Veronica says there are key behavioural indicators of ritual abuse which are always there, no matter how much parental contamination occurred.'

Niki goes on. 'I don't want Elizabeth to see a new therapist. And I'll be happy to drop my belief in ritual abuse if Veronica explains to me why it doesn't fit. Richard, don't you want to know if awful things were done to her?'

'Of course I do,' I reply. 'But short of a miracle, how can we ever know?'

'Veronica can help us know,' Niki says, excited. 'Will you be amazed if it turns out I'm right? Will you be proud of me if we find out Elizabeth was ritually abused?'

Monday March 29, 1993

Today Niki and her mother visit Veronica Oliver-Bell in Oklahoma City and audiotape the session for me. Niki provides Veronica with an edited version of her journal, boiling it down to lists of Elizabeth's bizarre statements and behaviours, devoid of context, devoid of her questioning.

Niki returns, excited. 'Veronica provided the support I've needed. Richard, she believes we have a very serious problem with Elizabeth. She said, "Can we all at least agree we're dealing with a very major trauma here?"'

Wednesday March 31, 1993

Today we see Tillman for a parent update and Niki's pumped. 'Codependency isn't the root cause of our problem,' she asserts, 'it's cult ritual abuse!'

'Children don't live in a vacuum, Mom,' Tillman replies, bluntly, then shifts topics to Elizabeth's improved behaviour. 'She's separating fantasy from reality, and she isn't anxious. And she's loving. She's also putting bound-aries around her own behaviour, learning self-control. I am so pleased.'

Niki doesn't want to talk about Elizabeth's improved behaviour. She wants to talk about Elizabeth's cult ritual abuse. She's in combat mode. 'Veronica gave me the support I need. She agreed with me. She agreed we need to know what happened to Elizabeth. Therapy is different for cult ritual abuse.' Niki tells Tillman that Veronica has benchmarks of behaviour for ritually abused children. 'And I think Elizabeth's behaviour corresponds exactly to those benchmarks.'

'And, Barbara,' Niki goes on, 'Veronica asked what your diagnosis is, and I said I wasn't sure.'

'Niki, I can't say sexual abuse occurred. We'll never know, because of the contamination.'

Niki's uncompromising. 'Well, I think we need to find out if ritual abuse occurred. Barbara, we know it's going on in Bartlesville. My friend Rick is an adult survivor of ritual abuse, perpetrated in Bartlesville. We know a cult is here.'

'Niki,' Barbara replies, 'I met recently with the Bartlesville Child Advo-cacy Council and discussed this topic with Officer Mike Miller, whose specialty is investigating sexual abuse. They believe ritual abuse is not present in Bartlesville.'

Niki ignores Barbara's comment, ups the tempo, points at me, and shouts, 'All the therapists think I'm just a hysterical overreacting mother because of you! Look what happened with Schwartz.'

'Niki, I hardly spoke to Schwartz,' I reply. 'He's a big boy, he made up his own mind.'

Tillman tries to calm Niki by heaping praise on her. 'The reason chil-dren don't recover from abuse is because they don't talk it out, they aren't heard. But, Niki, with Elizabeth, there's been so much talking and hear-ing, if ritual abuse occurred, the trauma's been diluted.'

When we leave Tillman's office, Niki's despondent. 'Barbara and I just don't click. I feel no support from her.' By evening, her despondency has ballooned. Hour upon hour, Niki ploughs over the same ritual abuse ground: 'Tillman doesn't get cult ritual abuse. What's the use of seeing her anymore? What use is she to Elizabeth?'

Finally, late at night, the conversation changes. 'Richard, I need to know you don't think Elizabeth's behaviour is my fault.' Niki is defensive, worried, concerned about being seen as the problem. I suspect Veronica has said something to make Niki feel threatened.

'Niki, there have been stressors outside and inside the home,' I reply.

Thursday April 1, 1993

Today Niki listens to the audiotape of her Monday session with Veronica and drafts a summary transcript, which she hands me as I walk through the door from work. Niki's happy, excited, bubbly, and wants me to read her transcript. Now.

I'm exhausted. Work was busy, I slept poorly and I'm burned out on the topic of ritual abuse. The prospect of another night talking for hour after hour about ritual abuse appals me. I want to beg Niki for mercy. Instead, I just say, 'Niki, I'll read it later.'

Now Niki's furious. She fizzes hostility: pursed lips, taut posture, brusque, curt comments. The tension in the air is suffocating me. I have to defuse it. After dinner I muster the strength to sit down and read Niki's notes. I exaggerate a positive and conciliatory attitude to thaw the icy cloud around Niki. 'Veronica sounds wonderful,' I lie. I figure it's a harmless lie. There are probably no harmless lies.

Niki immediately thaws, warms, her eyes sparkle, and she starts to talk about Veronica's depth of understanding of cult ritual abuse. I see hours of ritual abuse looming ahead of me. It looks intolerable. I don't have the physical, mental or emotional reserves to sustain me through another evening of ritual abuse. With a hangdog, pleading expression, I interrupt her monologue about Veronica and say, 'Niki, I'm so tired.'

I'm trying to say, 'Niki, I don't want to talk about ritual abuse tonight.' But that's not what she hears. She feels dismissed, brushed off, unsupported, abandoned. The atmosphere again becomes frosty, electric with tension. I ask, 'Niki, are you cranky?'

'Yes. I'm tired,' Niki answers, dismissively.

'So am I,' I respond.

'I know that,' Niki replies, and walks off.

Elizabeth, seemingly oblivious to the tension, asks me to watch

FernGully with her. She sits on my lap and the movie begins with scary rock paintings. 'Dad, those paintings don't scare me anymore,' she says, full of pride. 'Remember when they used to scare me?' I heap praise on her for not being scared.

Friday April 2, 1993

I sleep little, and this morning, before leaving early for work, I write Niki a note saying Veronica sounds wonderful. I apologise for being tired.

What I feel is stressed. As I feared, Veronica has reignited Niki's obsession, and her conviction that other therapists have not supported her, not listened to her, not believed her, not believed Elizabeth and missed the obvious ritual abuse diagnosis. I worry Elizabeth's improvement will be reversed.

Niki calls me at work to thank me for my note. 'Richard, we need to find out what happened to Elizabeth. We need to work together. We need to support each other. Veronica can help us.'

The thought of Elizabeth starting over with a new therapist terrifies me. But if we do that, I don't want Niki to censor the truth. 'Okay Niki,' I reply, with a hard edge in my voice, 'let's put all the knowledge we have into Veronica's hands. Let's meet her and let her talk to Elizabeth. And let's give her both of our unedited journals.'

'No!' Niki says emphatically. 'My edited summary of my journal is sufficient information for Veronica to put the puzzle together. Richard, we will not give her our journals.'

'Niki, this puzzle is complex. Veronica needs to see all the pieces of the puzzle in their proper context. She needs our unedited journals.'

Niki is adamant. 'No! The journals just go back to the microscope effect. They provide information that biases the interpretation against me, and against ritual abuse. No matter how unbiased the therapist, your strong communication style, especially your journal, would put doubt into any therapist's mind about me. Veronica will not see our journals, only my summary.'

When I arrive home, Niki hands me a letter:

I want to share with you the pain I have felt. In this crisis with Eliza-beth, I feel that you have not believed me. I also feel that you have not

believed Elizabeth. Not only have you not believed us, but you have
written extensively about WHY we should not be believed. This has
been extremely painful for me and I would guess painful for Elizabeth
as well … it now has to stop.

We must believe what each family member is saying. We do not have
to agree with them, nor take it as literal truth. But we must believe
that they are communicating something of value to the best of their
ability …

I am also very disappointed to conclude that through this crisis, you
have shown very little respect for me: for me as a human being, as your
beloved and loving wife, as a loving mother, as a competent healer in a
crisis situation, as a woman with some wisdom and strength …

… We are all of us imperfect human beings. We should use that fact
to bind us together, not tear us apart. Life is so difficult – we need one
another to thrive in spite of it. Please help me find the ways we can
correct our current course and build a loving, healthy, happy future for
us one and all.

After reading the letter, I look up and tell Niki, 'Thank you. I understand
this is how you feel. But I don't agree that I've been intentionally abusive
or unsupportive. I've simply struggled, in my own dysfunctional way, to
keep my own opinions intact.' Then I ask, 'Niki, what happened yesterday to bring your feelings to a head?'

'I spent all day working on my transcript, and you weren't even interested to read it,' Niki replies.

'Niki, I did read it after dinner, and I did say Veronica sounded wonderful.'

'I feel you've been very abusive toward me,' Niki says, 'by not believing
me and not supporting me. And by writing a journal that only explains why
I should not be believed. Richard, you have actively worked against me.'

'Niki, my communication, my diary-writing, is dysfunctional,' I agree.

Niki relaxes and we take the girls out for pizzas. Eating pizza, I wonder
about our dilemma. Our beliefs are polarised. From my perspective, Niki
is obsessed to achieve a diagnosis of ritual abuse for Elizabeth, which I
think is a hysterical overreaction. If I had spoken out honestly at every
interaction between Niki and Elizabeth that I perceived as unhelpful or
contaminating or brainwashing or abusive, then we would have been in

almost constant conflict, an untenable situation for me. So, mostly I said nothing and just wrote.

Hence Niki's assessment of me is correct. I have written a diary that explains why she should not be believed. But I think my assessment of Niki is also correct. Niki is obsessed with a fantasy.

twenty four

The Veronica Tapes – Part One

Sunday April 4, 1993

Today I push a cassette tape into my car stereo and listen to Niki and her mother talk with Veronica Oliver-Bell. They agree Elizabeth could have suffered cult ritual abuse. The foundation of this abuse construct is hysteria. As I listen, I hear obsession layered onto hysteria and falsehood layered onto obsession. Trapped inside this fantasy edifice is Elizabeth. Niki has found her therapist.

Niki tells Veronica that at fourteen months of age, when Kacey babysat, Elizabeth started to stimulate herself sexually, developed a sexual aura, and her behaviour disintegrated. Niki's mother agrees. Faye says she knows how girls go through 'you know, just the discovery of their sexual self. This was totally different. This was as though an adult had taught her.'

'She also did these "twirlies",' Niki adds. 'She just seemed to over-stimulate herself. I was scared to death to be around her … she was wild. She chased wildly and danced – this strange little dance from when that particular babysitter was with us.'

'That's pretty suspicious,' Veronica agrees. 'Where is this particular girl now?' she asks.

'She's in Bartlesville,' Niki replies. 'She and my brother have been in court. She pressed charges of sexual battery against him.'

'Are you primarily suspicious of this one person?' Veronica asks.

'Definitely!' Niki replies. 'I mean it would be one thing if … I was sitting around and saying … "Did Kacey do this? Did Kacey do that? What about Kacey?" But I have tried very carefully to not mention her name. If I ever mention Kacey's name, I will try and mention other babysitters' names. But I rarely mention any babysitter's name because I tried not to confuse things … I have tried very conscientiously to not plant seeds of any particular person in her mind, because I want to know as accurately as possible what has happened to her … We have all been so afraid of contaminating anything. And my husband is so sensitive – even if I am just sympathetic with her, he thinks I'm questioning her.'

Niki then tells Veronica about Elizabeth's disclosures. 'She has talked about a Red Man and Blue Man. She's talked about Newester, Dewester, Blewester. She's talked about a woman with white hair, the naughty lady, the bad lady, good and bad monsters … She went on to disclose really bizarre stuff about an attic house with real live babies in it. In boxes!'

'You definitely have some reasons to be suspicious,' Veronica says. 'Now, what is the status of things with, for example, DHS [Department of Human Services]?'

'They just plain old dropped it,' Niki answers. 'First we consulted Paul Schwartz. After three sessions, he didn't know what to make of anything … more than maybe Mikee and Alan being inappropriate with her. He didn't say anything about ritual abuse. But by then I was really getting hysterical thinking that was what was happening.'

Niki's mother knows why Schwartz failed to uncover Elizabeth's ritual abuse. 'Elizabeth is very good – she will throw something out at you, and will look at you to see how you respond. It's like an adult. She gives you this look of, "Well, you're not going to get it," and then that's it. You won't get another word out of her.'

Veronica knows why Schwartz was reluctant to diagnose sexual abuse. She says there's a backlash going on about diagnosing child sexual abuse. 'On a national level, people are raising more and more concerns about over-diagnosing it.' And this backlash includes a note of caution to 'be very suspicious of parental reports'. Veronica goes on. 'The research is still holding pretty strong to the notion that most of these reports are probably accurate allegations. But there is a sense among the courts … that what we have is parental hysteria and overreaction.'

Veronica explains how best to counter this backlash. 'Now, one of the first things that I do with parents – and I would keep this tape with you and not be distributing it around – is I say, "This is how the system works. If you want the system to work with you, there are certain things you have to be careful about.'"

Veronica tells Niki she thinks the system is working against her, because she has two reports – the Schwartz and Hegburg letters – that hurt her case for ritual abuse. 'You have the psychologist's report and the social worker's report ... Both professionals seem to have concluded that you were too involved. You were overreacting.'

Veronica is critical of Schwartz's assessment, since it was based on only three sessions. 'With ritual abuse ... these children, for all they know, I [the therapist] am part of the bad people. And the idea that they are going to spill their guts to me, either in indirect play or under direct questioning, is ludicrous.'

But she agrees Schwartz was right to wonder about contamination. 'Obviously you were very forthright and said to him, "I interact a lot with her. I have asked her questions. I have all these detailed notes". I mean, you couldn't have got them without interacting with her.'

Veronica tells Niki that switching around between therapists 'is used against you – like the Munchausen that goes from doctor to doctor, until they get someone that agrees with their opinion ... Because, I am here to tell you, the way that is interpreted is, you didn't get what you wanted so you went shopping for somebody who agrees with your opinion.'

Veronica then shifts focus from Schwartz to Hegburg. 'We have a child who, if you [Niki] are to be believed, has severe symptoms ... We have [Hegburg] who engages in maybe six sessions, and already begins to talk about improvement and resolution. I don't know how she reached her conclusions ... It almost seems like she wanted her problems to be taken care of.'

'That's what I was seeing!' Niki exclaims. 'She was acting out monster stuff nonstop at home and yet Faye was saying she was okay in sessions ... I thought, well, Elizabeth picks and chooses ... She does that with her dad ... She does not disclose to her father ...'

Veronica says this raises the question of suggestibility. 'I'm pretty familiar with suggestibility because of testifying in court. Children are suggestive, and you can contaminate, and I don't deny that. But I think we can suggest, lead and contaminate them a lot less than people would have you believe.'

Veronica elaborates on the theme of leading questioning. 'I am criticised in the courts, just to be real upfront with you. I get more information out of children than other people ... And I have searched my soul about why that is. Because the implication is, maybe I get more because I lead and suggest. And I am doing just really unethical things, and that's why I am getting some of the [ritual abuse] stories that I am getting. After really thinking this through, I really think that I make mistakes at times. And, yes, I do lead and suggest because, again, with children under five, sometimes to get information, you have to ask leading questions ...

'Now, the research is beginning to come out that says that this is a very critical part of therapy – to be very persistent in the questioning. So, I do get more information. I am also a lot more persistent than most ... I know that it makes children very anxious and uncomfortable. And it is painful. And I am not here to tell you it isn't.'

Veronica continues to discuss the therapeutic disclosure process for children. 'Now, what the child is doing with the therapist is ... trying to ascertain, "Does this person want to hear my story or not?" Now, I believe that because I am so persistent in questioning, children learn, "This is somebody who wants to hear the story; why does she keep asking me if she doesn't want to hear the story?" And I think, over time, they tell me.'

Veronica continues. 'I have observed therapists back off at the first sign of what I call avoidant strategies. Now that is something that both Paul [Schwartz] and Faye [Hegburg] are talking about in their reports. They are called avoidant strategies. They don't refer to them that way; they say she [Elizabeth] got distracted and disinterested. This child didn't get distracted and disinterested. This child was engaging in avoidant strategies. Which is a hallmark of a post-traumatic stress disorder. But the fact is, if we are dealing with avoidant strategies ... [they] do not respond to avoidant tactics by the therapist. What they [Schwartz and Hegburg] do is a collusion!'

Veronica says she finds avoidant strategies more common with ritually abused children. 'Well, see, ritual abuse really hasn't been researched. So I can only tell you clinical observations. And my guess is the child is overwhelmed with the emotion that is being generated by the memories ... Backing off is a psychological survival technique.'

Veronica has her own techniques to counter a ritually abused child's avoidant strategies. 'Now, the way I go about it is, I have a list of a hundred indirect techniques ... When they're in that avoidant kind of phase, I go heavy on my indirect techniques to move them. Sometimes it's a year in therapy!'

Veronica then reviews Niki's vast list of Elizabeth's symptoms and phobias. 'There are way too many that are not appropriate!' she says. Then warns Niki, 'You are going to have real problems.'

Niki mentions Elizabeth's upcoming forensic medical examination. Veronica is pleased. 'I sure hope you find something, because everybody is saying ... "maybe we have an over-involved, overreactive Mom". But once you get the physical evidence – and you usually do in ritual abuse cases ...'

I'm dismayed by Veronica's response. The desired outcome is a horribly abused child in order to vindicate a possibly overreactive mum. What an awful trade-off.

Veronica then hedges her bet regarding physical evidence. 'Well, they might do rape by instrumentation – that is one of their biggies. They stick the most awful instruments into these children ... They may train them from birth to be larger – so they won't scar, the way you and I might, if that was just suddenly done to us. They gradually use larger and larger things.'

The discussion then shifts to cults using drugs. 'Well,' Veronica says, 'of course, people who don't believe in ritual abuse say, "How convenient for you to come up with the idea they use drugs – and therefore these children are too confused." All the children I work with claim to have had drugs used on them.'

Niki is thrilled to hear this. 'Elizabeth has talked about it! She has talked about it!'

Veronica feeds off Niki's excitement. 'If she has been a victim of ritual abuse, then you are talking about two or three years of initial therapy, and then periodic therapy for the rest of her life. You need a therapist who believes in ritual abuse ...'

Veronica then bemoans how difficult it is to be a therapist who believes in ritual abuse. 'We have the backlash occurring, where some adult survivors [of ritual abuse] are being discredited … Probably some of them were making it up. And this throws questions on the children's stories as well …'

Niki wants to know how Veronica makes her ritual abuse diagnosis. 'How do you know for sure that it's happened, that you can believe them?'

'There are certain symptoms that are real typical of these [ritually abused] kids,' Veronica answers. 'These children are very confused about what I call opposites. They get confused about good being bad and bad being good. Right is wrong, wrong is right. Red is go, green is stop. They are confused about who their parents are. They are confused because the abusers give them other parents and convince them that these are their real parents and the parents they are going home to are fake parents, and, "Don't get attached to them, because they are not your real parents."'

Veronica goes on. 'They [ritually abused children] like to mark on themselves. See, when you talked about the lipstick and Elizabeth, I'm going, "That is real similar." Initially these kids mark themselves all over their clothes, their hands. I'm like, "What is this?" Well, the best I can make of it, the ritual abusers use paint a lot. They paint their faces and they paint their arms.

'And they love to confuse sexual identity. That is one of the core elements of the personality. I thought, 'How are they doing this?' Well, they use … paraphernalia … They have penises, they have vaginas and they switch them. They really do! They just totally disorientate these children.

'Now, from the little bit of what I've looked at [Elizabeth's symptoms] she appears to be more disorientated than most of my cases. But with most of the kids it's confusing at first. But then after six to eight months [of therapy], then it begins to make sense. You start to see the ritual abuse.'

Niki wants to talk about Elizabeth's interest to protect babies. 'Baby Jenny had a birthday, so I put her baby doll present out in the garage. And Elizabeth saw that, and she went hysterical on me …'

Veronica builds on this topic. 'One of the things they [the cults] do is they … get the child bonded to the baby that they then end up having to kill. "This is your baby." They get to feed the baby. They get to change the baby. They get to play with the baby. And then they make the child, with their help, kill the baby. And that's why they [ritually abused children] are so traumatised …'

As if participating in baby sacrifice isn't enough trauma for a one or two-year-old child, Veronica then says, 'It's not just watching it [the baby] being killed, although that could be extremely traumatic, in and of itself. But they [the cults] make it even more sadistic than that. They make the children do things to the grown-ups, to the other children, so that they convince them, "You are one of us – you've done all the things we've done, so if we're bad, you're bad." To keep them within the group … bonded to them as evil – as evil as them.'

Niki believes this preposterous nonsense, and has Rick as proof. 'He's the adult survivor [of ritual abuse],' she tells Veronica. 'Being cooked for dinner, he talked about that! And then Elizabeth popped up talking about it. And, of course, I hadn't brought it up. He talked about being put in an oven. She [Elizabeth] talks about being put in hot water and being cut up and cooked like soup!'

Veronica agrees. 'Yep, they [the cults] like to put them in water, sometimes cold water, then hot water. And hold them underwater until they almost drown.'

Veronica then talks about cult nonbelievers. 'Of course, people say, "Well, you know, if they're coached, they [the children] can come up with this." Well,' Veronica says with fanatic conviction, 'they couldn't come up with the emotional responses, such as the trances.'

Niki's ecstatic. 'She's [Elizabeth] been taught how to go into a trance! I'm sure of that. I've seen her do it.'

Veronica agrees. 'Well, to survive, they have to learn to dissociate.'

Niki's still excited, and interrupts. 'She turns into animals too!'

'Yep.' Veronica agrees. 'And when you dissociate, you're not really there. They [the cult] work hard to get them to develop that ability, because then they go through the rituals and they can cooperate without giving them a problem. Some of the adult survivors say … the children that ended up being sacrificed were kids that didn't learn how to dissociate.'

Veronica believes Niki will never be able to prove ritual abuse occurred. 'It's a million in one that … they [the cult] would ever admit it. It's also a million in one that you would ever come across the pornography that is often involved.'

Veronica moves on to the issue of contamination. 'Your husband raises real serious concerns about how the information was obtained. He feels like Elizabeth was led – things were suggested to her. And that really clouds the picture, because if someone believes that, then after a certain point, it's very hard to say what's the chicken and what's the egg? In other words, if there was a lot of contamination early on, it might be very hard to tease back …'

Veronica then says it's asking a lot of me to believe in ritual abuse, 'because this is unbelievable information … and I think, you know, he raises good questions about leading questions. I would reiterate what I said before – I do think you can lead a child to some degree …'

Finally, Veronica discusses brainwashing. 'A child will have good memories for what they actually experience. They do not have near as good a recall of things that are told to them. Because they experienced those things [ritual abuse], and they were highly traumatic, that tends to lock into the memory …

'Usually, if a parent is brainwashing a child … the child has real negative feelings toward that parent. But, at the same time that I say that, you have the cult situations where people were brainwashed. We know that in cults there is brainwashing … The question then becomes, is it possible for a parent to brainwash a child? And I would say, probably not. Unless they used terror tactics. And if you were using terror tactics, your child would not be coming to you. They would be distancing themselves from you. So that doesn't make a lot of sense.

'And what would be the motivation? In Munchausen's, they say the motivation is that the parent gets a lot of attention and so forth. But Munchausen's is a very rare disorder. The fact that Munchausen's exists – and is being diagnosed in some of these [ritual abuse] cases – leads me to mention it.

'So then the question becomes, what is your motivation? … In some of the cases I've handled, the issue has been, "Well, they're getting a divorce, so the motivation is retaliation." But in your situation, well, you're trying to keep your family together. And you're trying to come to some agreement …

'Now, your husband is saying, "Well, this is just a bunch of disjointed babblings of a two-to-three-year-old". And, you know, they do kind of sound like that. But, they're just so atypical for her age. I mean, if this is her type of fantasy, then we've got to be looking at, like, childhood schizophrenia.

'And he raises the question, "Can we drop this? Enough is enough." And on the one hand, I hear what he is saying. This can totally possess your life.'

twenty five

Tillman's Perspective

Monday April 5, 1993

Up to now, I've tried to see Niki's obsession as an expression of a mother's love and as the frantic anguish of a parent who believes her daughter was abused. Even though, to me, this belief is a hysterical overreaction, it fits with her family's overly dramatic response to any perceived crisis. I also wonder if, maybe, there are unresolved abuse issues in Niki's past. But, then, since the entire country's in collective hysteria about sexual abuse, multiple personality disorder and satanic ritual abuse, Niki's obsession sits squarely in the current hype. So I try to consider Niki's behaviour inside the boundary of extreme-but-normal. At least, that's the way the glass-half-full, hopeful side of my psyche has pigeonholed Niki's obsession.

For the sake of its survival, I keep the glass-half-empty, hopeless side of my psyche under wraps. Sometimes, however, the dungeon door creaks open and a voice screams up at me from the depths, 'Richard, this is nuts! And you know it!'

Today, it's Tillman's turn to scream at me. I see her alone, to learn about codependency. Tillman only wants to talk about Niki.

'I provided a consultant psychiatrist with the facts of Elizabeth's situation,' she tells me. 'The consultant's opinion is Niki is a hysterical overreacting mother. Richard, Niki has a pathology, maybe paranoid hysteria. I can't diagnose her, but there is a pathology.'

Tillman then tells me the consultant warned her to be cautious, because Niki might accuse her of abusing Elizabeth. 'Richard, I am concerned

Niki will find a way to accuse me of hurting Elizabeth. And she may also again accuse you of hurting Elizabeth.'

I'm stunned. Niki has a pathology? Tillman feels threatened? I feel like I've just had my face shoved into a pile of poo and I can't pretend it doesn't stink. I don't know how to respond to Tillman's pathology comment, so grab hold of her concern about Niki accusing her of hurting Elizabeth. 'I can't see that happening,' I say. Although Niki has, more or less, accused me of the same thing, so I should probably agree with her.

Tillman goes on. 'Niki has manufactured her ritual abuse obsession for reasons that aren't clear, either to me or to her. And she has an obsessive-compulsive need to be right – about everything. My opinion is she's projecting pain from her own past onto Elizabeth. She may be doing this subconsciously. It's likely impossible for her to admit to her past pain, or whatever abuse or trauma she experienced. Richard, I don't think Niki knows how much she's harming Elizabeth.'

'What's your diagnosis?' I ask. 'I think Elizabeth was traumatised by something.'

'Elizabeth was traumatised,' Tillman agrees, 'but not by sexual abuse or ritual abuse. With all the contamination, a diagnosis is impossible. The trauma was probably a combination of all the known stressors she experienced. The nucleus of a terror state for children can be something very small.'

Sometime during our meeting, I zone out, shut down, drift off into my own thoughts. Even though Barbara speaks, I don't really hear her, can't remember what she says. I leave her office wondering what I'm supposed to do with this information?

I feel helpless, stranded, afloat on a raft in a storm, along with Niki, Elizabeth and baby Jenny in diapers. Dr Schwartz sails by and shouts to me, 'Elizabeth is a wonderful, normal, bright young girl, but your wife is obsessed about ritual sexual abuse,' and sails on. Then Hegburg sails by and shouts to me, 'Niki should allow Elizabeth to recover according to her needs and at her pace. If Niki burdens her with her adult need to understand and "know", it will keep the trauma alive for her,' and sails on. And now Tillman sails by our raft and shouts to me, 'Your wife has a pathology, maybe paranoid hysteria, and her obsessive-compulsive need to be right about ritual sexual abuse is harming Elizabeth,' and sails on.

After all the shouting, these experts invoice me for their opinions, accept my money, wish me good luck on my journey, and sail away. I need some practical advice. I'm lost, drifting, trying to hold my family intact. What action can I take?

If I confront Niki, if I demand she stop what she's doing, I'm certain we'll quickly spiral into separation, divorce, court battles and a custody dispute, which I doubt I can win. In the current sexual abuse hype, and given Elizabeth's brainwashing, Niki could try to pin an abuse label on me. There's also the wealth and influence of her family to factor in. I doubt I'd stand a chance in a Bartlesville court. So I hang my hopes on getting the hell out of Bartlesville, getting the hell out of America. Stepping off our raft, stepping onto a plane and then stepping off in Australia. We need to stay afloat until July.

Tuesday April 6, 1993

Today, Niki and her mother take Elizabeth to see Veronica. This evening Niki tells me, 'Barbara called Veronica last night. It sounded to her as if Tillman wants all the credit for stabilising Elizabeth. Tillman said Elizabeth was out of control when their sessions began. Veronica wondered why didn't this concern Barbara from a ritual abuse viewpoint?'

Niki goes on. 'Veronica and Elizabeth spent time alone. Elizabeth was happy to talk to her. She told Veronica about her monsters and the naughty people, and no-one believing her. She wanted to talk more about it. She told Veronica, "I have more to tell you!"'

As Niki says this, I imagine the open conversation between Niki and her mother – with Elizabeth listening – during their three-hour car trip from Bartlesville to Oklahoma City; long tirades about ritual abuse and all the therapists not believing Niki, not believing Elizabeth. Niki and her mother are either breathtakingly ignorant, or breathtakingly shameless, in their interaction with Elizabeth.

Niki tells me Veronica conferred with a consultant who 'agrees we're likely dealing with ritual abuse. Richard, Veronica thinks we should terminate with Barbara, since she can't see ritual abuse.' Niki says Veronica won't see Elizabeth as a patient, since we're leaving for Australia, but suggests we seek ritual abuse therapy in Australia. 'But, Richard, my mother is very worried there won't be any ritual abuse therapists in Australia.'

Friday April 9 – Tuesday April 13, 1993

A beautiful, sunny Easter weekend. Elizabeth and I work in the garden and visit a neighbour, who has a three-year-old daughter. Elizabeth delights in playing with the girl. She's been isolated from other young children for around nine months. Her life has been therapy, videos, Niki and weekend play trips with me.

Over the weekend, Niki raises the possibility of her staying in Bartlesville while I transfer, alone, to Australia in July. 'Richard, this way Elizabeth can see Veronica for ritual abuse therapy.'

I feel panicked by this proposal. 'Niki, that idea doesn't feel good to me. I want the family to stay together. And it may stress Elizabeth if she develops a strong bond with Veronica, which later has to be broken.' I'm clutching at straws. I hold my breath. Niki agrees.

Wednesday April 14, 1993

Again I visit Tillman alone, to discuss codependency. Again Tillman only talks about her dilemma with Niki, and her conversation with Veronica, the evening of Monday April 5. 'I told her the best hope for Elizabeth would be for Veronica to support Niki in her belief about ritual abuse. But also to say it's best to let Elizabeth heal – to back off from therapy.'

Tillman tries to explain her strategy. 'Richard, I can't support Niki in her belief about ritual abuse, because Elizabeth's my patient, so it would have legal ramifications.' Barbara says that if Veronica supports Niki, it has no ramifications, and might help reduce Niki's anxiety. 'My aim is to help Elizabeth heal. But that won't happen while Niki's obsessed and stressed to find a therapist who supports her.'

I don't agree. 'Barbara, Veronica supporting Niki's belief about ritual abuse will only reinforce her obsession. And this will increase the pressure on Elizabeth.'

twenty six

The Veronica Tapes – Part Two

Friday April 16, 1993

Niki believes if I meet Veronica, I'll be convinced Elizabeth was ritually abused. So, today, we travel to Oklahoma City to talk to Veronica. I'd guess in her forties, Veronica is attractive and trim. She looks pumped, powerful, shoulder-padded, a confident professional at the top of her game.

We arrive just as a media photo shoot winds up. Veronica poses in her office for a picture to accompany a soon-to-be-published *Oklahoma Gazette* article on cult ritual abuse. The media remain fixated on cults and the ritual abuse of children. And Veronica – a therapist and true believer in cult abuse – is someone the newspaper is pleased to interview.

The article, when published, has the banner headline: *'Too terrifying to believe – Tales of ritual cult sacrifice make believer of veteran social worker'*. Don't be fooled, Veronica certainly believes. In the article, she explains how she came to believe the children's tales of human sacrifice and other unimaginable horrors. These lurid crimes are perpetrated on children by 'people who hold good jobs, work hard, do this secretly in the dark of night, get up and go to work the next day'. Veronica's statements are quoted without a hint of scepticism.

Niki and I talk with Veronica for a few hours and audiotape the session. Throughout the meeting, Veronica paints Elizabeth as damaged goods, with cult ritual abuse her only explanation. She begins by describing Elizabeth's behaviour when she saw her ten days ago. 'She was friendly,' Veronica says, adding that she didn't seem anxious about separation, which was unusual for her age. 'It might be that she's used to therapy,' Veronica admits.

Veronica then explains how she used a hand puppet, in the form of a turtle, to question Elizabeth. She told Elizabeth the turtle was scared of a secret that he couldn't talk about. Elizabeth said to the turtle, 'Well, I can help you, because I've been hurt like you,' and then added, 'I know why you're not talking – because they won't believe you're telling the truth.' Asked by Veronica why the puppet was scared, Elizabeth had said, 'Nobody wants to hear this – nobody will believe me.'

This is absurd, so I interrupt Veronica. 'It seems strange that she would say that – so many people have been listening to her and not telling her they don't believe her.'

Veronica slaps my wrist, telling me Elizabeth is genuinely worried she won't be believed. 'And I think she rightfully has reason to think that. And I think she's been told that.'

Veronica wants to get back to a replay of her turtle interrogation. She says she then asked Elizabeth, 'What's happened to the turtle?' Elizabeth told Veronica the monsters came. And then talked about her own abuse by the monsters. 'They threw me in the cold water and they tied me up and they tried to cut me.'

Veronica says Elizabeth then got up and looked out the window, saw a blue house and said, 'The monsters are in the blue house … in costumes. They hurt kids. They are cooking kids. They have to cut them first and then they cook them.' Then Elizabeth tells Veronica, 'The turtle has more he wants to say, but it would be very hard, because he knows that people don't believe him. He knows by the way they ask questions, by the look on their face.'

I hear the voices of Niki and her mother echoing down the corridor of this conversation.

'For her age,' Veronica says, 'that was a miracle session – in terms of how much talking she did. My experience is abused children do not want to talk.'

Veronica then tells us Elizabeth's gruesome disclosures must be believed. 'I know the question has been raised – "well, of course, Niki has talked to her so much, so, has she [Elizabeth] concocted this vast fantasy fuelled by videos and fuelled by being given attention to for talking about this?"'

Veronica discounts this possibility. Her clinical experience tells her it's hard to suggest and lead children into making up gruesome stories, although admits there were times when, 'I felt like I was able to suggest things to them. And, certainly, there is research by Elizabeth Loftus, who is a professional who is very determined to prove that children's reports aren't very reliable.'

Veronica expands on the topic of suggestibility, referring to an article in the latest edition of *Newsweek* entitled '*Rush to Judgement*'. An elderly couple were recently convicted of sexually abusing their grandchildren, based only on the children's testimony. The article claims the children's testimony is false, because of suggestive and leading questioning. This claim is supported by research which proves children make up stories under suggestive questioning, including the story of 'Chester the janitor'. In a series of experiments, children are questioned about Chester the janitor's actions while he's in a room with them. The children readily agree with suggestive questions about Chester's actions. However, what they readily agreed to is false. In the experiments, what they agree to never happened.

'Now, that is a slanted article,' Veronica says, scornfully. 'What they failed to mention is the extensive research that would refute the findings of the 'Chester the janitor' research.' Veronica tells us the research that children's accounts are believable and credible is 'the majority of the research'.

'Now,' Veronica continues, 'I go into that long spiel because that's really at the heart of what we have to look at with Elizabeth: how reliable and credible is she?' Veronica says she's looked at Niki's edited journal notes, with their hundreds of bizarre symptoms and phobias and statements by Elizabeth, and that, 'Number one, the child has clearly been traumatised. Number two, the content of what she is mentioning would have to suggest physical and/or sexual abuse. So,' Veronica goes on, 'then we're faced with, okay, do we believe [what] Elizabeth's reporting, or could it be that she has a wild imagination, or she watches too many videos, or whatever?'

After making these definite pronouncements, Veronica backtracks. She concedes Elizabeth incorporates aspects of things she's seen in videos into her play, and agrees that monster themes could have been imprinted in her mind, 'because of the attention they were given, and I

will not dispute that. I would have to say, with Elizabeth, that she's talked
a lot more [about monsters] than most. And the only way I can understand that is she did get a lot of attention for it? She was encouraged.'

After this brief caveat, Veronica gets back on course. 'Does that mean
she shouldn't be believed? No! I don't think so.' Veronica defends her
opinion based on Elizabeth's play in her office, where she was 'not contaminated. I never asked her, "Tell me your story about the monsters."'

That's bullshit. Veronica used the hand puppet to ask Elizabeth about
her monsters.

Even Veronica allows for a smidgen of doubt. 'Now, if she had been
influenced to say what adults wanted to hear – she might have said that.
I can't say that she didn't have it figured out, being a bright kid, that she
was seeing another counsellor.'

Veronica admits she's puzzled as to why Elizabeth was so determined
to tell her about the monsters, but 'did not report it to the psychologist
[Schwartz]. Why did she not report it to the social worker [Hegburg]?
Why is she not reporting it to her current therapist [Tillman]?'

I answer her last question. I tell Veronica that Elizabeth does talk
about the monsters, and does talk about tee-tees, to Tillman. However,
Tillman's interpretation is 'innocent – because we contaminated the
whole issue.'

So Veronica shifts topics to contamination. 'Barbara feels it's been
contaminated,' she agrees, 'and I'm here to tell you, it's been contaminated. There isn't a case in the world that isn't contaminated. I mean, any
time a parent asks a child, "Has somebody touched you?" – if you want
to get real strict about it – you know, that's contamination!' Then she
allows for an extra dose of contamination in Elizabeth's case. 'But there's
been more contamination in Elizabeth's case than many cases, I would
be the first to say.'

Veronica then unleashes a barrage of criticism against Tillman. She
and Tillman 'are not on the same wavelength', Veronica tells us. 'I have
a lot of training in developmental abilities of children. Like, I'm a consultant for the therapeutic nurseries statewide, okay! My specialty is
children under the age of six.' Veronica complains that when she talked
with Tillman, she detected 'a negative opinion, from day one, about the

possibility that there could be any serious trauma [for Elizabeth].'

Veronica thinks Tillman went into this case believing Elizabeth had been set up, by Niki, to act out monster stories. And that Tillman had discounted Niki's journal, which documents Elizabeth's monster talk. 'I want every piece of information,' Veronica stresses, 'if I'm going to do a thorough job. I might be inclined to want to dismiss it, but I can't.'

Did I just hear Veronica say she wants every piece of information? This contradicts what I heard her tell Niki and her mother a couple of weeks ago, in the tape, about the Schwartz and Hegburg reports damaging the case for ritual abuse, and that it would better to not have those reports. This doesn't jive. So I interrupt and ask, 'So you advocate, then, that you should review prior therapists' material?'

'Yes, everything!' Veronica replies enthusiastically. 'I mean we've got to look at everything. And we've got to try to keep an open mind in looking at everything.'

More bullshit, so I interrupt again. 'There was a comment you made in the previous session – not to look at prior therapists' material.'

Veronica realises she's contradicted herself and back-pedals. 'Yeah. Yeah. And I'll explain why I said that. Because that is how I feel about it. But I have a reason.'

But before she gives her reason, she wants to continue to criticise Tillman. 'She reported that Elizabeth took her dress off in her office and pulled her pants down and asked her, "Don't you want to see my tee-tee?" Barbara's comment was, "If this was any other child, I would immediately suspect sexual abuse."'

Veronica goes on. 'So I wrote that down, okay, that she would immediately suspect sexual abuse. But with Elizabeth, she doesn't want to do that? So I said, "Well, tell me more about that?"' Veronica says that Tillman told her, 'Elizabeth was questioned "relentlessly", was her term. And that she was "given no boundaries". And that, you know, "any child that was in total control of a house and was totally out of control would behave like she behaved."'

Veronica thinks Tillman's analysis is flawed. She tells us, 'Sexual acting out is the most definitive symptom of a child who's been sexually abused.' But Tillman wasn't going to see it that way because, 'Elizabeth was so out of control. And you, as parents, were so incapable of dealing with her. What she had to do was get the situation under control ... then Elizabeth improved one hundred per cent. And at that point there weren't any indicators of anything that was troubling.'

Veronica disagrees with Tillman's assessment. 'Common sense will tell you that to produce extreme reactions requires extreme trauma. And what we're seeing with Elizabeth is an extreme case, okay!' To illustrate just how severe, Veronica wants to focus on Elizabeth's confusion. 'What jumps out at me the most is the confusion about who key people are and their relationship to her.' Veronica tells us this confusion is 'a red flag, to me, about possible ritual abuse.'

I wondered when Veronica would pivot to ritual abuse. 'Any other options?' I ask.

Veronica admits brainwashing is another option, caused by 'people questioning her – so she begins to get confused in her own mind about, "What is happening?" "What have I experienced?" "What have people told me?" "What do I remember?"' Veronica goes on. 'It would be a brainwashing technique. If the family situation was totally chaotic – it is possible that she could get this confused. So brainwashing is possible.'

Veronica has the right answer, which is brainwashing – but she doesn't know it. I want to somehow tell her she's found the right answer, so interrupt and subtly ask, 'Okay, how would you get the answer?'

'Well, that's a difficult one,' she replies. 'With these very young children – over time it [ritual abuse] becomes real clear! Well, it becomes clear to me! Okay!'

Veronica thinks I meant reaching an answer about ritual abuse. I meant reaching an answer about brainwashing. So I try a new approach. I tell Veronica that Niki and I are compulsive journal keepers. That we both have detailed notes, and, 'I think the answers are in the detail.'

I'm being too subtle. What I should say is, Veronica, our unedited journals provide unequivocal proof of Elizabeth's brainwashing. But, of course, I don't say that.

Niki, of course, disagrees with my comment. She needs to deflect attention away from our journals. So she says, 'I think the interaction Veronica had with Elizabeth is more important than our journals.'

This spurs Veronica on to a generic discussion of journal keeping. 'If I'd been in your situation,' she says, 'I would have probably kept a journal. And, in fact, many attorneys would say, "Keep a journal!" I will tell you, my basic opinion is, you need to lose your journals. Because I have been in numerous court cases where, you know, they've taken journals and made people look like lunatics for what they wrote in their journals.'

We've drifted away from the point I'm trying to make about our journals. 'I'm not talking about a court situation,' I say, 'I'm talking about an answer.' I'm talking about the truth about brainwashing.

Veronica counters. 'I understand,' she says, 'but you have to understand they [the journals] biased your case for the people who've read the journals.' Veronica goes on. 'My impression of the journals, my impression of people who have had contact with you, they feel like the way you present, you were too focused on this child. And that was the problem. This child was under a microscope.'

Veronica elaborates. 'The way that comes across to professionals is – these people have let this child overtake their lives … And there is a lot of leading and suggesting and relentless pursuit of this child – making something out of everything.'

Veronica has nailed it. I look across at Niki. Her head is bent forward and swings from side to side. Her hands are locked together, fingers wrestling. She's agitated – threatened by this talk about parenting. She needs to end it, so lifts her head and shouts, 'In the last two days, Elizabeth started to go down again! And to say a lot more about monsters and sexuality. Barbara won't be open to seeing that!' Niki gets on a roll. 'I feel like we have both worked *very, very, very* hard. And it is irritating to me to have a professional think that because they did one little—'

Veronica interrupts Niki's tirade to support Tillman. 'Well, you know, she is giving credit to you for having changed things and set limits and so forth.'

'But we did that before all this started!' Niki shouts, lying.

Veronica stands her ground and explains structure and boundaries to Niki. 'I think that there was less structure than Elizabeth needed, okay. Now, I'm going to be honest with you – and some of it may be hard for you to take. I think she was too stirred up for too long about this stuff.

That's how she got your attention – she knew that you would listen and you would respond ... If you pick up any pamphlet on sexual abuse that's written for parents, one of the pieces of advice is, "Don't relentlessly question your child about the sexual abuse ..."'

Veronica goes on. 'The kid was in acute distress at the time that Barbara came into the situation. And I want to credit Barbara with getting the situation under control. I did ask Barbara, "What is it you are doing?" She kept saying, "I'm providing clear boundaries." And that's important. Setting clear boundaries and being consistent ... is a hard deal with this kid. Elizabeth needed somebody to say, "You can't hit me." "You can't spit at me." "You can't lick on me." And she needed you at home to say, "No, you can't run around naked. We don't do that in our house. We wear clothes. When we have dinner, you sit down to eat." She needed that because she was so out of control. She had lost all of her mechanisms for controlling her own behaviour.'

Wow! I'm awestruck. Veronica has perfectly scripted Elizabeth's behaviour and our home situation. I want to ask – can we go home now? There seems little more to talk about.

But, in a most impressive lateral arabesque, Veronica shifts the plot to ritual abuse. 'I think her mechanism for controlling her own behaviour broke down because of the intensity of the ritual abuse she suffered.'

Whoa! So it wasn't the absence of boundaries or lack of structure in our home. It wasn't Elizabeth's out-of-control behaviour. It wasn't the relentless questioning about the naughty people and the monsters. It wasn't the obsessive search for answers. It wasn't the brainwashing. It was Elizabeth's ritual abuse. So there's more to talk about. We can't go home.

Veronica continues. She says Elizabeth makes too many comments about the people at day care, so, 'I would be concerned at what happened at Miss Mabel's.' She thinks Mikee and Alan may well have done things to Elizabeth, 'but I would be more inclined to think that they were forced to do things to each other. And that's what brought in the trauma – when adults get in there and make kids perpetrate on each other.'

I want Veronica to spell it out. 'So, you're suggesting – there was ritual abuse at day care?'

'Well, I'm suggesting that that's what she's [Elizabeth] suggesting,' Veronica replies.

Veronica now shows her true colours. Rather than explain why Elizabeth's statements suggest ritual abuse at day care, she delivers a dialogue dump from the ritual abuse swamp in her own mind. She says ritual abuse victims at day care 'come up with something like, "Let's cook these babies." "Well, where are you going to cook them?" "Well, you have to have a special oven." "Well, why do we want to cook the babies?" "Well, first you have to cut them and then you have to bleed them and then you cook them." Now this is a three-year-old!'

This is absurd. I have to interrupt. I ask Veronica if she looks into the possibility of other sources of these strange statements by a three-year-old, like scary videos, or, 'Have they been sitting with a babysitter watching a Dracula movie?'

'Well, you do ask,' Veronica replies. 'This is a good question. There are things on TV that are very questionable … about what they might be conveying to children.'

I want to expand on the issue of scary and grizzly images implanted into the minds of two- and three-year-olds. I give the example of reading *Snow White* to Elizabeth. I say that when I got to the part when the Witch talks about coming back for Snow White at sixteen, 'I'm thinking, I shouldn't be reading this.' Then the Witch 'is stirring this big cooking pot and makes a poisoned apple. And Elizabeth says, "Why does she do that?" And I'm thinking, "That's a good question, why does she want to poison this little girl?" And I'm saying, "Well, Elizabeth, there are some bad people in this world." And she says, "There are? And they give poison to babies?"'

I ask Veronica, 'Can you see the confusion?'

I get on a roll, citing other episodes when Elizabeth was terrified by scary images. 'I took her to *Beauty and the Beast*, her first time in a big movie theatre. She's sitting on my lap. And what is the preview for the next movie? *Dracula*. This Dracula head comes on, and blood flows down the screen and she was like, "Dad, I've got to get out of here." She tried to tear herself out of my lap.

'And then *Beauty and the Beast* comes on. Great movie, but scary as hell.

She was literally trying to tear herself out of my hands to get out of the movie theatre. And I was holding her and keeping her there … I should have left, because the kid was terrified.'

Veronica agrees, then disagrees. 'Those are good questions,' she says, 'and you do have to consider it.' Then she argues that ninety per cent of American kids are exposed to the same material, so why are a small handful of kids coming up with ritual abuse disclosures? Veronica goes on, 'You're raising an issue … aren't they taking this [ritual abuse disclosures] from things they're reading, things they're hearing, things they're seeing? And my response would be, probably not …'

Veronica has discounted my concern, so I ask, 'How do you know how they internalise things? It could be scaring the living daylights out of them, but we're not recognising it.'

Veronica, at last, agrees. 'Right. That's right. I know Elizabeth has watched a lot of videos and I know Barbara's opinion is that all her fantasies are from videos.' However, Veronica still wants to discount the influence of videos, so switches to the sexual component of Elizabeth's statements, and says that Niki and I are not 'exposing her to things that would give her sexual ideas'. Veronica says sexual ideas are integrated into all of Elizabeth's statements.

After Veronica says this, Niki's excited and jumps to the conclusion, 'So that means ritual abuse has happened to her! Based on your professional experience?'

Veronica hedges her bet. 'It's suggestive this is something she's experienced,' she says. 'If it was just the videos and just scary stuff, then she would be talking scary stuff, scary stuff, scary stuff. She wouldn't be putting in the sexual stuff.'

I think Veronica's sexual stuff slant is wrong, so ask, 'Okay, what is the sexual stuff?'

'Oh, the monsters touching her tee-tee,' Veronica replies, 'and French-kissing.'

This is a huge stretch. I tell Veronica Elizabeth's watched a lot of videos 'where at the end of the video, they kiss – a mouth-to-mouth kiss. And she wanted to know what that was. It was explained as a French-kiss. And then she wanted to do that.'

'She was wanting to do that before!' Niki shouts, then immediately contradicts herself. 'She asked me what that was called and I said, "That's called a French-kiss." And I asked her where she got it from and she said, "From *Beauty and the Beast*".'

Veronica defends her position. She says she's had other kids come to the attention of the authorities, and it was the French-kissing. 'There's some kid around that's French-kissing that has not been sexually abused. But I'm here to tell you, that was the tip-off in a number of [sexual abuse] cases I know of. It was French-kissing. Nine out of ten kids will never do that ... Why be persistent about French-kissing?'

'But why not?' I ask. 'Elizabeth is curious about all the kissing in all the videos.'

Veronica plays her psychology trump card. 'Because it's not developmentally typical.' But then she agrees. 'If we took French-kissing by itself [as proof of ritual abuse], I would have to say, well, gee, that's kind of weak.'

Veronica finally agrees that Elizabeth's fascination with French-kissing, by itself, is not proof of ritual abuse, so I interrupt. 'Okay, so beyond French-kissing, what are the other—'

Veronica interrupts back. 'Well, she's got the repeated talk about being touched on the tee-tee. And she strips off and shows Barbara—'

I don't agree with this point either, so interrupt to ask how Elizabeth's preoccupation with her tee-tee links to ritual abuse, 'as opposed to just, say, molestation by older boys or constant questioning about, "Has someone touched her tee-tee?"'

'Well, it doesn't for sure,' Veronica answers, defensive, then retreats to her argument that, developmentally, children don't perceive their tee-tee is 'something so unusual and bad that they're, like, obsessed with it!' Veronica qualifies her statement with a reference to probabilities. 'The probability is she wouldn't be as sexualised as she is from just experimental play with other children. And she's not reporting, unless I've missed something, she's not reporting Alan and Mikee have done something?'

Veronica has definitely missed something. Niki provides the bad news. 'They touched her tee-tee. They boinked her in the tee-tee,' she says.

Veronica realises Elizabeth's fascination with French-kissing and fascination with her tee-tee are insufficient proof she was ritually abused. After a moment's consideration, she grasps at the straw that three-year-old Elizabeth has made 'certain statements that are real unusual, like, being put in the cold water.'

Veronica then wades into the significance of cold water. She tells us her ritually abused children all talk about their fear of being put into cold water. 'I know you've [Niki] done a lot of reading … about ritual abuse. You might be introducing ideas to her – that has to be noted. But the cold water? When the [ritually abused] kids started introducing this to me – "hey, what is this about?" – I'm wondering if it's something the cults do in this particular area.'

Veronica believes Elizabeth's statements about cold water imply 'nuances to her account that ring true to me, having treated ritual abuse victims. And they ring true in certain ways that I don't think you could even pick up from reading material in the field.'

Veronica wants to end this debate about evidence of Elizabeth's ritual abuse. She admits to me, 'You are right to question this, because we don't have clear-cut disclosures from Elizabeth. You know, you asked me a question and I don't think I answered it – can we get to the bottom of this?'

Veronica believes we can get to the bottom of this, but it might take forty years. 'There is a theory that dissociation occurs – splitting off – which protects the child from the memories. The memories are in the unconscious, they're in the bank, the memory bank, and they're sometimes difficult to draw out. But they're in the memory bank. And so they're not lost.' Veronica believes that young children repress memories of sexual abuse, which 'might stay buried for forty years'.

Until the memories come out of the bank, Veronica can't diagnose Elizabeth's ritual abuse. But in the meantime, she can't offer any other explanation. 'She shows the symptoms,' Veronica says. 'She shows the confusion. The characterising of the people involved as monsters is very prevalent in young ritually abused children. But she doesn't fit it together sufficiently for me to say, gee whiz, it's ritual abuse. But I can't give you any other explanation that makes sense.'

Niki commiserates. 'Well, we don't expect that of you today. But just to know if it's reasonable to be concerned about ritual abuse is all I want to know at this point.'

Veronica agrees it's reasonable to be concerned about ritual abuse, because Elizabeth shows, 'a repetitive, consistent reporting of key ritual abuse themes, and nothing else I know of. She has the characteristic elements [of ritual abuse] that run in the nineteth percentile! I've done sexual abuse for twenty years.'

Veronica then tells us that out of the one thousand sexually abused kids she's seen, 'about eight were ritually abused, and probably a few that I've missed. But still, eight out of one thousand – we are talking a small number.'

I sense Veronica is proud of her scorecard – the eight notches of cult ritual abuse in her diagnostic belt. Those eight notches represent real children. Real lives. Real families. I wonder about the consequences of Veronica's diagnoses for those lives? Those families? What a horrible badge of victimhood for those children to wear for the rest of their lives. And what a tragedy if it was all nonsense.

Niki wants to shift the focus back to Elizabeth. 'Okay, Veronica,' she says, 'so you see the red flags for ritual abuse for Elizabeth. And I'm not saying that you're diagnosing it, you're just saying that you see some red flags? Right?'

Veronica's stamp of approval would mean a professional supports her belief in ritual abuse. This would prove Niki is not a hysterical, overreacting mother. Veronica hesitates in her response, and then stumbles over an answer. 'Well, what I would do … there's just … you know … again, if you can believe what she's saying here, there's a, I can't quite tell you what other explanation I can give, but …'

Veronica's stumbling continues until she comes up with the idea to throw the question of a ritual abuse diagnosis, like a long ball, like a Hail Mary pass, out into the future. 'I recommend that when you move, you take your doctor's report that thought it was sexual abuse. And if you get anything from the forensic exam that's suggestive of sexual abuse, I'd certainly take that—'

Niki interrupts for clarification. 'If that [exam] doesn't conclude anything, just don't take it?'

'Probably not,' Veronica answers.

I'm stunned by this collaboration about cherry-picking evidence to achieve a ritual abuse diagnosis. What about the truth? What about the horrendous implications of this diagnosis for Elizabeth? What about Veronica proclaiming she wants all the evidence? I'm in the presence of fanatics.

'Why is that?' I interrupt. 'From a scientist's point of view, you want all the evidence.'

'Okay,' Veronica answers, 'well, I will tell you that if you take all the material you have now, that no-one will believe anything has happened to Elizabeth, except that you have made mistakes in parenting. You've got professional reports that imply you were over-involved, you were over-focused – you're suggesting, you're leading, you're relentlessly pursuing this child. And it's coded, but if you're a professional, you know what it means. You know what they're trying to say without them being really ugly. There are certain words that are damning ...'

But it's the truth! I shout to myself. And because it works against your ritual abuse paradigm, you want to censor it. So I interrupt again. 'The prior clinician's interpretations,' I ask, 'are you saying not to give that?' I want to hear Veronica say it. I want to hear Veronica condemn herself as a fanatic.

Veronica senses the trap and changes her recommendation. 'The journal. If I were to say only keep out one thing, I'd say, keep out the journal!'

Veronica has only seen Niki's highly edited journal notes – lists of Elizabeth's bizarre statements and supposed phobias, without context. If Veronica read Niki's unedited journal, which detail her constant questioning of Elizabeth, she'd throw in the towel.

Veronica goes on. 'I told Niki I would be willing to write a letter to try to summarise [Elizabeth's case]. I'm not going to say I absolutely believe it to be ritual abuse. But I will suggest she's been severely traumatised. That some of the abuse appears to have been of a sexual nature. And there may be multiple perpetrators.'

It's hard to believe I'm hearing this. 'But, from my perspective,' I say, 'if someone came to me for a diagnosis of an oil well to be drilled, I would want all of the evidence. And all the input from somebody who was a professional.'

Niki jumps to Veronica's defence. 'What Veronica's saying, Richard, is we presented ourselves very poorly in the beginning. We were very confused. We were very upset. We didn't know what was going on, and we've gotten off base with these professionals, Richard. And all those reports just document our disturbance.'

Veronica then suggests how we should approach a new therapist. We should tell the therapist Elizabeth mentions, 'The monsters hurt me, and Alan and Mikee boinked me. You know, this kind of thing. I don't know how helpful it is to even mention that first [Schwartz] evaluation.'

This feels, to me, like withholding evidence, obstruction of justice. The truth about this ritual abuse fantasy, this obsession, is documented in the detail; in Niki's unedited journal, in my unedited journal, in the Schwartz and Hegburg reports. Any reasonable professional who reviewed the hundreds of pages of this material would see that Elizabeth has been brainwashed.

'Veronica,' I say, 'to me the answers are in the detail.'

'Oh, the answers are in the detail,' Veronica agrees.

'Okay,' I say, 'so that's where the detail is. It's in the journals.'

Veronica wants to work around the journals. 'Okay. Well, once she gets into therapy, they've got my letter, they've got their general interview with you. And if they ask you, "Well, do you have any (other) details …?" I would say, "Well, yes, we did keep some notes. And maybe if we summarised them and brought them to you once we've uncovered them? We moved and everything's packed away." Are you following me here?'

Yes, I'm following you, Veronica. You want us to hide the journals. You know the journals are toxic to your ritual abuse case.

Veronica continues to tell us how to get the truth from a future therapist. 'You are interested in them taking plenty of time. You are willing to pay for that. You understand that it could be costly. And since the other therapy was short-term, they have not arrived there yet. That way they go into it thinking, "This is a longer-term case. I don't have any rush."'

Niki needs a ritual abuse caveat to this approach. 'As long as we are open-minded about the ritualistic aspect,' she says. 'To at least have Veronica say [in her letter], as a professional, she sees red flags. That makes me feel like I've been saved from being a hysterical mother.'

Veronica then shifts the discussion to our family life. She says she usually invites parents to be more involved. 'In your case, I would say, back out of it. Try to get things as normal as you can … I don't want anybody saying, "I asked her this."'

We've received this same advice from all the therapists – the same advice Niki has ignored in the past, and will continue to ignore.

Another expert, Veronica Oliver-Bell, sails by our raft and shouts to me, 'Your eldest daughter has likely been ritually abused and your wife is the victim of biased therapists. Ignore them. I know the truth. I'll write a letter explaining it,' and sails on.

Saturday April 17, 1993

The next day, Niki's agitated and needs to talk continuously about ritual abuse. 'Richard, why don't you believe Elizabeth was ritually abused after talking with Veronica?'

'Niki, my interpretation is different to Veronica's,' I answer.

'You don't think I'm responsible for Elizabeth's behaviour, do you?' Niki asks with a nervous, worried and defensive tone, which shifts to aggression. 'How can my parenting have been so bad? Richard, we need to go back to Veronica for input about how you not believing Elizabeth was ritually abused might harm her.'

Later, Elizabeth wants me to help her find the bird with a broken wing from *Little House on the Prairie*. So we walk together along a riverside pathway. It's rained, and she notices foam on a puddle, and asks, 'Dad, is that ice?'

'No,' I reply, then ask, 'Elizabeth, have you ever been in cold water? Water with ice?'

'No,' she answers.

'Then why do you say you've been thrown into cold water?' I ask.

'It's just something I tell Mommy,' she replies.

Sunday April 18, 1993

Niki's agitation continues. 'I'm very upset with Barbara,' she tells me today. 'I want to confront her and tell her how wrong she is about me. And how poorly she's treated Elizabeth. She missed the obvious ritual abuse diagnosis. All because she was biased against me!

'Richard, surely you don't believe I'm harming Elizabeth?' Niki asks, nervously, again and again. 'All the therapists missed the ritual abuse diagnosis. No-one helped us parent Elizabeth. Don't you see we need Veronica's help to find out who the abuse perpetrators are?'

Niki's obsession is undiminished.

twenty seven

The Tulsa Justice Center
And The American Endgame

Monday April 19, 1993

Niki must have Elizabeth forensically examined for physical evidence of sexual abuse. Her first attempt at the Tulsa Justice Center was unsuccessful. The 'scary table' frightened Elizabeth. She refused to go into the examination room, let alone get up onto the examination table. Since that event, Niki's taken Elizabeth to the Justice Center numerous times, to calm her fears. Finally, this morning, Niki and Dr Doyle will take Elizabeth to Tulsa for her examination.

'Won't it be great if we finally get some physical evidence of sexual abuse?' Niki tells me.

'Niki, it would be terrible if she was so abused there are scars,' I answer. 'I hope there's nothing.'

Niki then tells Elizabeth, 'Today we're taking you to the teddy bear place. You said the monsters hurt your tee-tee. We want to make sure your tee-tee is okay.'

Niki calls early afternoon, despondent. 'There's no evidence of sexual abuse,' she says. Then she shifts to an assertive tone, 'But this doesn't mean sexual abuse didn't occur. Just that there hasn't been vaginal or anal penile penetration. There still could've been oral sexual abuse, fondling and masturbation.'

'Niki,' I reply, 'I'm relieved Elizabeth went through the examination without upset.'

Although I do wonder what message was sent to Elizabeth. Lying on a table, a doctor in a white lab coat peering at her tee-tee and bottom with a magnifying glass, under bright lights, with a camera recording the action.

I arrive home around dusk to a strangely quiet house. The girls entertain themselves on the family room floor. Where's Niki? I walk through the house to find her. She's not here. Then a silhouette catches my eye through our bedroom window. I watch as Niki wanders aimlessly around our backyard, hands locked together as if in prayerful meditation. Then she halts under our clothesline, head among a scattering of clothes pegs, frozen, staring at our side fence, just a few feet away.

I go outside. Niki looks dazed. 'What's wrong?' I ask.

'I'm stuck,' she answers.

I try to sound positive. 'Isn't it good news there's no sign Elizabeth was harmed?'

'No,' Niki says. 'No, it's not good news. I'm stuck. It didn't provide any answers about her ritual abuse. They must have used small objects, like pens, to put into her vagina, so it didn't leave marks.'

I can't respond to that comment, so leave Niki standing in the dark.

Tuesday April 20, 1993

The day after the Justice Center examination, Rick returns to Bartlesville from Albuquerque – to attend his grandmother's funeral – and tonight he visits Niki. His manner is assertive and animated, in contrast to the vacant, placid monotone he exhibited in Albuquerque. He sits on our couch and holds court, proclaiming confidently to Niki and me, 'Elizabeth would have been used as a prize. Men would have been enticed to join the cult by the promise of having her for sexual intercourse.'

I want this idiot out of our house. 'Rick,' I reply, 'she hasn't suffered vaginal or anal penetration.'

Rick counters, 'Well, they would've had intercourse ephemerally, without penetration.'

Rick and Niki then talk privately for hours about ritual abuse. Later, Niki tells me, 'I learned a lot from Rick tonight. He said, "Of course Elizabeth was out of control. She was taught to act out of control and demand attention, to please her abusers." Richard, her out-of-control behaviour was programmed by the cult to cause us problems. It wasn't our parenting.'

Tuesday April 27, 1993

Today I'm in New Orleans for an oil exploration conference and tonight Niki calls my hotel, in distress. 'Richard, you have to avoid travelling. Elizabeth's having a bad reaction to you being gone. She's disclosing really bad stuff.'

Niki then speaks to me as if lost in a dream, and keeps repeating the same thing, over and over. 'Richard, it's bad, really bad. It's bad. It's gross stuff. I swear to God, it's just awful. It's bad. She talked about really bad stuff. About being married to another family for real. That Kimberley's parents were bad monsters. That Kimberley's parents were the ones who were bad. She said it was just a dream, but I think that's a cover and it really happened. It was bad. It was really, really bad. I swear to God it was bad. Her ritual abuse is finally bubbling to the surface.' Then she sobs uncontrollably on the phone and I try to comfort and calm her.

Thursday April 29, 1993

This evening I return from the conference with presents for the girls. One is a fossil, the skeletal outline of an ancient fish in siltstone. Elizabeth asks, 'Dad, how did the fish get into the rock?'

I try to explain. 'The fish lived in a lake a long, long time ago. When it became old and sick, it died and left an impression in the fine silt on the bottom of the lake. And then it went to heaven.' I have to go over and over the concept of the fish being born, getting old, dying and going to heaven.

Elizabeth's sad the fish died. 'Where were its mommy and daddy?' she asks.

'Even though the fish was dead, it lived on in its mummy and daddy's hearts,' I reply.

Friday April 30, 1993

Niki and the girls have a great day. They pick spring flowers at her mother's house, then deliver flowers to my office. I'm thrilled they're happy. But when I arrive home, Niki sits by the bathtub, distressed, with notepad and pen. Elizabeth's in the bath, smiling. 'Dad! Dad, I'm Mermaid Ariel.'

'You are?' I reply, laughing. Elizabeth laughs back.

Niki then talks to me until two in the morning about Elizabeth's dissociation. 'Richard, she only discloses to me, not to you. You don't respond to her in a way that encourages disclosure. You shouldn't laugh when she says she's Mermaid Ariel. She's dissociating.'

During this marathon outpouring, Niki weeps and sobs. 'Richard, our honeymoon with Elizabeth is over. I was so relieved when she clamped down on her ritual abuse disclosures. Now she wants to disclose again. I don't know how to handle it. Veronica told me not to dwell on ritual abuse with her, but I can't not respond to her when she wants to disclose. She needs at least two years of ritual abuse therapy, or she'll have to be institutionalised.'

'Niki, that's a bit exaggerated,' I reply, without editing my words. I'm exhausted.

'I am not an overreacting mother!' Niki shouts. 'Elizabeth's been ritually abused and she's dissociating!'

Saturday May 1, 1993

This morning Niki remains distressed, and shows me her notes from Elizabeth's bathtub disclosures:

> I'm Ariel the mermaid. Elizabeth is in heaven and she's never coming back. She got old and sick … She stays in your heart. She's never coming back … It'll take a long time. When we go to Australia. I'm Ariel. Elizabeth is in heaven for a long time. My real name is Ariel.

'Niki,' I say, 'Elizabeth's statements relate to my fossil fish story. I told her about a fish that got old and sick and died and went to heaven but lived on in its mummy and daddy's heart.'

Niki ignores my explanation. 'I have a call in to Veronica,' she tells me, distressed.

Niki has called Veronica on a Saturday morning, distressed that Elizabeth wants to be Mermaid Ariel? Niki can't reach Veronica, so calls her sister Carmen. Niki then puts three-year-old Elizabeth on the phone so Carmen can ask her, 'Why are you Mermaid Ariel and not Elizabeth?'

Young girls in America are besotted by Ariel, from the Disney classic *The Little Mermaid*. Elizabeth has Ariel bedsheets, Ariel pillows, Ariel bathers, Ariel towels, Ariel T-shirts, Ariel panties and Ariel dolls. She even wears green pantyhose in the bath, both legs shoved tightly into one pantyhose leg, to emulate Ariel's green flipper.

Monday May 3, 1993

Today Niki and her mother meet Penny Blake. They've concocted a plan whereby Blake will work with the FBI to uncover the Bartlesville ritual abuse cult. Niki's mother will fund the investigation. After the meeting, Niki feels let down. 'Blake wasn't keen. Richard, we'll have to hire our own private investigator.'

Niki then takes Jennifer to Dr Doyle. Niki now worries that babysitter Kimberley ritually abused Jenny. Linda agrees to an examination of twenty-month-old Jenny, who would have been less than six months old when any abuse could have occurred. The examination shows the vagina and anus are normal, with no signs of trauma.

Tuesday May 4, 1993

Tonight Elizabeth tells us she's pregnant and has to go to the hospital to have her babies. Her being pregnant started after an episode of *Little House on the Prairie*, in which the mother's pregnant. 'I'm distressed by Elizabeth always saying she's pregnant,' Niki tells me. 'I don't know how to handle it. I have a call in to Veronica.'

I need some fresh air, so take Elizabeth out to our backyard swing. She laughs and sings in rhythm with the pendulum motion, 'Nobody believes me! Oh no, they just don't! Nobody believes me! Oh no, they just don't! Nobody believes me! Oh no, they don't!'

'Elizabeth, why do you sing those words?' I ask.

'I don't know, I just do!' she shouts, in a silly, high-pitched tone.

Thursday May 6, 1993

Today Niki sees Tillman for her 'Goodbye, Tillman' meeting, and later tells me, 'We're like two ships passing in the night. She gave benign explanations for Elizabeth being Ariel. She talked about fantasy and videos.'

Niki again tells me Elizabeth's obviously dissociating when she says she's Ariel the mermaid.

Tonight, Veronica finally returns Niki's numerous calls. 'Thank God for Veronica!' Niki exclaims after their conversation. 'We really click. She hears what I'm saying. I told her about Elizabeth's reaction at seeing a cooked chicken at my mother's and asking if it was a cooked baby. Richard, Veronica agrees with me – this behaviour is too consistent a theme. It must relate to ritual abuse and cooked babies.' Niki's now happy and bubbly, her anxiety gone. Cooked babies worked a treat.

Wednesday May 12, 1993

Today Elizabeth and Jenny attend Tiny Tots day care so Niki can have time for herself. I make a surprise visit to Tiny Tots. Both girls are happy, playing with the other children. Elizabeth tells me, 'Dad! Dad, I'm playing with Robert.' Then, at home this evening, Elizabeth says, 'Dad, Dad, I'm married to Robert.'

Niki begins crying. 'Richard, this is related to ritual abuse. We have to get her into therapy soon.' Then says, 'I'm afraid to leave Bartlesville with you. I'll be away from the support of my mother. Richard, Elizabeth will probably need to live close by me as well, all her life.'

Monday June 21, 1993

Today Niki and her mother travel to Oklahoma City to see Veronica, who is still crafting The Letter, to provide the correct background for a future therapist. This evening, Niki is strangely subdued. Her obsession seems threatened. She tells me Veronica warned her the other therapists' letters could be used to take Elizabeth away from her. 'Veronica said I could be accused of Munchausen's by proxy,' she says.

Niki goes on. 'I begged Veronica to state in her letter the possibility of ritual abuse. If she does that, I can close the book. I can surrender involvement. I'm exhausted. I've done all that's humanly possible.'

Tuesday June 22, 1993

This morning, Niki talks for hours with Penny Blake, and her friends Sandra and Rick, about The Letter. She asks them, over and over, to, 'Please, please speak to Veronica, and support me.' Niki is strangely bereft.

By this evening she's defensive and withdrawn, struggling mightily with whatever arose to challenge her obsession during yesterday's meeting with Veronica. So, again, Niki calls Sandra and Rick for support. 'Surely Elizabeth was ritually abused. Don't you think Elizabeth was ritually abused? I think Elizabeth was ritually abused.' The same statements are repeated, over and over and over. After these long phone conversations, Niki seeks my reassurance, telling me over and over, 'Richard, I'm a good mother. There's no way I'm responsible for Elizabeth's behaviour. Richard, I did not cause Elizabeth's problems.'

Niki feels immensely threatened. Something happened at yesterday's meeting with Veronica to shake her certainty. I try to reassure her. I want calm until we can get on the plane and get the hell out of Bartlesville, away from the influence of Niki's mother and sister and Penny Blake and Rick and Sandra and Veronica and all the other nut jobs. 'Niki, you're a wonderful mother!'

I do wonder, however, why my wonderful wife, who tries so very hard to be a loving mother for our children and a supportive partner for me, became obsessed? When we married, Niki told me she was eccentric and dramatic, with wildly fluctuating enthusiasms and religious and spiritual beliefs. It all felt harmless at the time. It doesn't feel harmless anymore.

Wednesday June 23 – Tuesday July 6, 1993

Work obligations and preparations for our transfer to Australia consume most of my time. Meanwhile, crafting The Letter becomes bigger than Ben Hur. Niki must have a letter that points to the possibility of ritual abuse, and says nothing negative about parenting. Numerous drafts travel back and forth between Bartlesville and Oklahoma City. Niki sometimes holds up, and waves, the latest draft, exclaiming, 'This letter is great. Veronica is great. Veronica gets it. Thank God for Veronica!'

I wonder about Niki's reaction if I'd behaved in the same manner with the letters we received from Schwartz or Hegburg? Or if I were now crafting a letter with Tillman, to support my perspective, and waved drafts of Tillman's letter in front of Niki with similar exclamations? I'm pretty sure we would not be travelling together to Australia.

Wednesday July 7, 1993

Today Niki finally receives The Letter (Appendix 3). Despite conceding that there are likely some elements of fantasy in Elizabeth's abuse disclosures, Veronica completely dismisses the idea of contamination through questioning. She believes Elizabeth has been abused because, 'children of her age rarely fantasize about being powerless and victimized,' and 'do not tend to fantasize outside of their experience'. She concludes:

> I saw Elizabeth on 04/06/93 [April 6, 1993] ... She spontaneously disclosed that monsters threw her in bad water, tied her up and tried to cut her. She said they hurt her tee tee and bottom ... The monsters have knives and cut up bodies and cook them ...
> It is my opinion ... that Elizabeth has been seriously traumatized. Due to her sexual acting out I believe the trauma was at least in part due to sexual abuse. It is highly unlikely that her story could have been maintained over time as vividly as it has if it was not based on personal experience. The bizarre nature of her disclosures are consistent with documented disclosures of alleged ritual or sadistic abuse cases involving multiple perpetrators and multiple victims. Thus, it is important to explore the possibility of ritual abuse and try to reach some determination regarding its validity.

Monday July 12, 1993

Niki ended Elizabeth's sessions with Tillman in mid-May. Niki did not want Barbara to write a report, in spite of four months of twice-weekly therapy with Elizabeth. I did request a report (Appendix 4):

> By the time the parents came to me, the mother was convinced that her child was a victim of ritualistic abuse ... She suspected ... baby-sitters, day care providers ... even the natural father at times. The more she read the more the symptomatic behavior she identified and was compelled to find out from the child ... [who] was allowed to be in the house in winter nude or came to the office twice a week in summer plastic shoes or barefoot even in the ice and snow in a summer dress.
> I indicated to both Mr. and Mrs. Vos that information that Elizabeth

could share would be highly contaminated by the questioning, investigative approach that the mother took ... The mother ... wanted desperately to have her theory supported and I could not do so.

In summary, my evaluation of Elizabeth is that she is a bright 4 year old who has experienced trauma: successive ear infections, yeast infections, being put to sleep to put her tubes in, experiencing the mother's difficult pregnancy and birth when she was 2 years 4 months. The traumas, compiled with being 2 1/2, caused aggressive, demanding behavior. This was then interpreted by the mother ... in light of ritualistic abuse, which fed her anxieties with no boundaries on her demands or actions her behavior became more and more out of control. With reinforcement of the boundaries first in the office and then at home, normalcy returned to this happy bright 4 year old.

Part Two

Australia:
July 22, 1993 – August 12, 2010

twenty eight

The Obsession Travels

Thursday July 22, 1993

On Tuesday evening July 20, 1993, Niki, Elizabeth, Jennifer and I board a plane in Tulsa, Oklahoma, to begin a journey toward a new life as a family in Australia. We cross the International Date Line and arrive in Perth at midday on Thursday July 22.

Perth, a beautiful, young, open, clean city. Isolated in the south-west corner of an almost empty island continent, pinched between a wild Indian Ocean and eucalyptus forests, full of barefoot memories and unimaginably blue skies. I'm home. I left in 1968 with my parents and sister. I return today with my wife and two daughters, to offer them the gift of a very lucky country, Australia.

I'm here as Phillips Petroleum's Exploration Manager, to lead geologists and geophysicists in the search for oil and gas along the north-west Australian coastline. My work plate is full. Niki's also busy; before the week is out, her search for a new therapist begins.

Monday August 16, 1993

Today we see Elaine Albertson, a therapist recommended to Niki by the agency hired by my company to relocate executives. During the session we express our beliefs about what may have traumatised Elizabeth. Tonight Niki's distraught. She cries, sobs and accuses me, over and over, of not letting therapists see the obvious diagnosis of ritual sexual abuse. Then she talks for hour upon hour about ritual abuse being the only logical diagnosis for Elizabeth. I listen patiently, and gently express my differing beliefs.

Tuesday August 17, 1993

This morning, Niki remains distraught. 'I couldn't sleep last night,' she tells me, crying. 'I'm worried a new therapist will be like Tillman – accuse me of being the problem, and take my children from me.' Niki says Albertson knew nothing about ritual abuse, and wonders if any Perth therapist does. 'And even if they did, Richard, you wouldn't let them diagnose ritual abuse.'

Niki's crying upsets Elizabeth. 'Daddy, what's wrong? Why is Mommy crying?' I do my best to calm and reassure Niki and Elizabeth before I have to leave for work.

By evening, Niki's mood has morphed to steely determination. 'I'll take responsibility for Elizabeth's therapy from now on!' she exclaims as I walk through the door, then tells me Elizabeth started her monster talk again today. Niki says she asked her if the monsters were a dream, or did they really happen? Elizabeth said they were a dream. 'So, Richard, I told her, "All I want is the truth and that you live to be an old lady and die a natural death."'

In answer to that bizarre comment, Elizabeth asked Niki if she'd live to be an old lady if she didn't talk about her monsters, then said, 'Well, the monsters did happen.'

After relaying this narrative, Niki's steely posture dissolves to weeping distress. 'Richard, I won't find a therapist in Australia to diagnose ritual abuse,' she cries. 'I'll have to work with her myself.'

Niki's anxiety is back through the roof. We have to talk until early morning about ritual abuse. 'Niki,' I say, 'trying to be Elizabeth's therapist will cause you distress, and this will stress Elizabeth.'

'She's already anxious!' Niki shouts. 'She needs me to do this. I won't abandon her.'

Friday August 20, 1993

Today, Elizabeth develops a cough and sore throat. Late afternoon we take her to Princess Margaret Hospital for Children. As the doctor begins his examination, Elizabeth emits a choked cough. Niki tells the doctor, 'Elizabeth's always talked about being choked during her ritual abuse.'

I'm dumbfounded. The doctor, a young man with a caring manner, is also stunned. He looks suspiciously at Niki, then quizzically at me, as if asking, 'Is your wife nuts?'

After the consult, script in hand, we prepare to leave. Niki walks ahead with the girls, toward the exit. Before I can follow, the doctor pulls me aside. 'What was that ritual abuse about?' he asks.

'It's complicated,' I answer. I don't know what else to say. I wonder if he'll pursue Niki's comment. He seems lost in his own thoughts for a few moments, then leaves it at that. We all head home.

Late January 1994

Fast-forward five months. Exploration work consumes most of my time.

Saturday is my day to take the girls on trips to the beach, zoo, parks, playgrounds and other Perth attractions, and give Niki a break from parenting.

On some weekends we take family trips to Margaret River, 300 kilometres south of Perth. Margaret River owes its existence to an act of geological serendipity. About 130 million years ago, when the Gondwanaland supercontinent began breaking apart, a 150-kilometre long and 30-kilometre wide sliver of ancient crust, which had begun to leave Australia and drift off with India, suddenly refused to leave. This fragment of ancient rock now sits proud on the south-west Australian continent as a magnificent stretch of granitic coastline, graced with pounding surf, scenic rolling hills, vineyards, forests and farms. I camped and surfed in Margaret River as a teenager and the pristine environment seeped into my spirit, leaving me forever drawn to this stretch of coastal paradise. We look at real estate and purchase a small farm. We now plan to retire in Margaret River.

Following our debacle with Albertson, I bowed out of the search for a therapist. Niki engaged Dr Geoff Dixon, a child psychiatrist at Princess Margaret Hospital for Children. Niki provided Dixon with Veronica's letter as background information. 'I won't allow the other therapists' letters to bias a new therapist against me,' she tells me. I assumed an Australian psychiatrist would see through the ritual abuse hysteria and reach his own conclusions. Niki rolled the therapy dice exactly the way she wanted, and I waited on the outcome.

After a few sessions, Dr Dixon requests a parent conference. Middle-aged and greying, Dixon struck me as busy, and something of an absent-minded professor, confident in his assessments, with no time for nonsense. 'Elizabeth is a bright, normal, very assertive four-and-a-half-year-old,' he says, 'although somewhat controlling and manipulative.'

He wraps up his assessment of Elizabeth in about five minutes, because he wants to talk about Jenny, who had accompanied Niki to the sessions. 'I'm more concerned about Jenny,' Dixon says. 'At two-and-a-half years of age, she's not talking.' He wonders about arrested development and suggests a psychological assessment.

Niki pleads with Dixon for a few more sessions with Elizabeth. After these sessions he concludes, 'Elizabeth's normal. Her occasionally unusual comments are attention-seeking behaviour. She does not exhibit psychosis or reality distortion and has a strong, assertive personality. However, if you want to pursue further therapy, I'll refer you to Helen Davidson, a child psychologist at Princess Margaret Hospital.'

Niki wants to pursue further therapy, and I attend an initial parent session with Davidson. Somewhere in her thirties, she presents as lean and neat, with a precise, clinical, competent, grounded, professional manner. I sense she'd be a great poker player – would not reveal her feelings, would not be swayed to make reckless decisions. A mix of cautious but candid.

We tell Davidson we want to bring closure to the subject of Elizabeth's trauma when she was two years old, and ask her to assess Elizabeth's current psychological status. We say we don't want to get stuck in a diagnosis rut about what happened. At least, that's what we say. Davidson receives Veronica's letter as background information. I withdraw to my work.

After about six sessions, Davidson requests a parent conference. 'Elizabeth's delightful to work with,' she tells us. 'She's bright and normal, but I am concerned about her anxiety. I think she experienced a trauma of some kind. She's hyper-vigilant about family illness and there was major upset with the introduction of a sibling.' Helen says further sessions will be beneficial.

Meanwhile, life at home since August 1993 has been wonderfully calm, with lots of outside play. But now, suddenly, in late January 1994, Niki's anxious again, and continually questions Elizabeth about the monsters: 'What did they do to you?' 'Where did they do it?' 'What did they look like?' 'Let's draw pictures of the monsters.' And, again, she talks to me all evening about ritual abuse and Elizabeth's disclosures. 'Richard, don't you see Elizabeth must have been ritually abused?'

I don't. What Elizabeth says and does are re-enactments of the latest stories and videos she's locked into, as well as learned, paraphrased responses to Niki's questions. The same questions she's asked Elizabeth for the past eighteen months.

Finally, it happens. 'Richard, I want a ritual abuse diagnosis of Elizabeth,' Niki says.

If we pursue a diagnosis, Niki and I will descend into conflict. Any discussion with a therapist regarding a diagnosis will draw out my beliefs, and other therapists' beliefs, about contamination, and then Niki will accuse me of sabotage. It also means more probing therapy for Elizabeth. This will not help her grow into a normal, happy young girl. It will keep her stuck and anxious.

Niki is again all-embracing, all-consuming of her abused daughter. I sense an unhealthy partnership developing against the non-believer, against me. And what about Jenny? Her first two-and-a-half years of life have been in a family consumed by stress and conflict, with most of the attention flowing to Elizabeth. Maybe that's why she's still not talking?

I want to scream, Niki, let's please move on and let Elizabeth and Jenny live normal lives, for heaven's sake! But, of course, I say nothing. I feel ill. I'm not sleeping. I'm writing again.

Tuesday February 1, 1994

'I discussed the stress I'm under with my hormone doctor,' Niki tells me this morning. 'She referred me to a counsellor who's an expert in sexual abuse. I'm seeing her today. Richard, I need to cry with someone over Elizabeth's suffering.' Tonight, Niki says the counsellor wasn't the sort of person who could support her. 'She said to just focus on moving ahead.'

Tuesday February 15, 1994

After her failure with the counsellor, Niki began sessions with psychologist Liz Riley. 'I need her emotional support,' Niki says. 'I no longer have my mother and my sister for support. I've found the support I need with Liz.'

After a couple of weeks, for some unknown reason, I'm invited to meet Liz Riley. I accept the invitation, happy to support Niki's efforts to feel supported. While we're riding the elevator to her office, I learn why I'm invited. 'Richard,' Niki says with a look of superficial concern, but underlying satisfaction, 'Liz believes Elizabeth's obviously been sexually abused.'

Riley, middle-aged, has a matronly manner and clearly enjoys the science and the art of psychology, delving into the mysteries of the mind and the foibles of human behaviour. I also sense she can assert herself – put down strong boundaries. Riley tells me that, based on Niki's account of Elizabeth's statements and behaviour, and Veronica's letter, she must have suffered a sexual trauma. So I ask Riley, 'What kind of sexual trauma do you think occurred?'

'What was the extent of her injuries?' Riley replies. She's surprised to learn a forensic medical examination revealed none.

'Could molestation or rough play by older boys at day care cause trauma?' I ask.

'What was the age difference?' Riley responds. Told they were five years old while Elizabeth was two, she states, 'Elizabeth would have been terrorised by a sense of powerlessness,' then adds, 'You should only tell her about her molestation when she's much older. And only if she acts unsure of herself. Discussing her trauma with her now will only keep her traumatised and anxious.'

Wednesday March 9, 1994

Today Elizabeth slices a finger while cutting paper. She calmly and proudly shows Niki the cut. Niki tells me, 'I gasped with shock and then Elizabeth had one of her fall-down fits. Nothing comforted her until I talked to her about her ritual abuse. I said, "Elizabeth, this reminds me of when you would get upset and talk about the monsters cutting you."'

I'm stunned. Angry. 'Niki, why would you say that? That comment plants a memory. We know it never happened. She was never cut. You shouldn't say such things!'

Niki flares back, 'I am perfectly comfortable with the way I parent Elizabeth!'

'But, Niki, it's obviously contaminating.'

'Richard, it's the only way Elizabeth copes with her fall-down fits.'

'I wonder what Helen Davidson would think of your approach?' I reply, grasping at the straw thought that Davidson might help talk sense into Niki.

'I'm sure Helen would agree with me – why don't you ask her,' Niki fires back, then adds, 'Richard, in the past I've censored my dialogue with Elizabeth in deference to your concerns about contamination. But from now on, I'm parenting Elizabeth as a victim of ritual abuse.'

Wednesday March 16, 1994

A week later we attend a parent conference with Davidson. 'Elizabeth's doing well,' she tells us, 'but she's very tuned in to the topics of sickness and hurt babies and the upheaval and conflict the family experienced around her trauma, whatever it was.'

I want to raise the issue of Niki implanting abuse memories. Trying to be subtle, I ask, 'I presume we shouldn't talk about Elizabeth being abused, or introduce ideas which suggest she was abused?' Helen, of course, agrees. So I turn toward Niki and ask, 'What's your opinion on the issue, given our disagreement of a week ago, when Elizabeth cut herself?'

Niki becomes flustered. Hands together, her interlocking fingers begin to wrestle. Then her head tilts forward and swings from side to side. She mumbles, 'I didn't sleep well. I can't remember what my point was. I've been so busy lately. I really can't remember. Everything's a bit confused.' Her mumbling trails off while her fingers continue to wrestle.

I feel sorry for her, so don't dredge up what I remember perfectly well. I let it slide.

Sunday March 21, 1994

Today I travel to Sydney on business and call home in the evening. Niki talks for hours about Elizabeth's ritual abuse and the need for a diagnosis. Then she shifts topics to Jenny. 'Her speech therapist thought she might be suffering selective mutism, and another therapist I've just talked to said babies can stop talking, or not even start talking, if they've had penises put into their mouth. Richard, I've been freaking out ever since she said that. I wonder if Jenny was also ritually abused?'

'Niki,' I say, as firmly and as calmly as I can, 'Jenny's speech therapist changed her mind, remember? She thinks it's just developmental speech delay and not selective mutism. And there's no evidence Jenny was abused.'

Niki agrees, but says she's trying to arrange for Jenny to start therapy. 'She's two-and-a-half years old and isn't speaking.'

Friday March 25, 1994

I return from Sydney early evening and Niki talks about ritual abuse until the sun rises, repeating the same lines of reasoning. 'Richard, you have abused Elizabeth and you have abused me, by not believing us. Elizabeth feels abandoned by you for not believing her.'

I wonder what Elizabeth tells me that I don't believe? Why does she say I don't believe her? Why would she feel abandoned by me? We don't talk about the monsters. I don't question her about the monsters. Then the answer arrives. Elizabeth doesn't say, 'Daddy doesn't believe me.' Niki tells Elizabeth, 'Daddy doesn't believe us.' Niki's weaving a psychologically incestuous partnership with Elizabeth as a united defence against those who don't agree with Niki; don't believe Niki; don't tell Niki she's right; don't tell Niki she's a wonderful mother. Niki is cocooning Elizabeth into her obsession web.

Sunday March 27, 1994

Sexual abuse is all around us. 'Richard,' Niki tells me today. 'I think the neighbour's children have been sexually abused. They're saying and doing things that indicate sexual abuse.' And she keeps asking me, 'Could we be such bad parents? Could we have caused Elizabeth's breakdown?'

Niki's anxiety is reaching some sort of climax.

Monday March 28, 1994

Which happens tonight. Niki announces, 'Richard, if you agree Elizabeth suffered a major trauma and I didn't cause it, I can let it go. I won't need a diagnosis.'

I agree a major trauma occurred for Elizabeth and reassure Niki she has been a most loving and caring mother. And we agree Elizabeth's doing really well with Helen.

'And, Richard,' Niki adds with emphasis, 'you agree I worked my butt off to reach this point.'

I agree. And hope we can now move on.

Tuesday March 29, 1994

The next day we see Liz Riley, Niki's support psychologist. It's six weeks since my first visit, and, again, I'm not sure why I'm invited. I figure it out pretty quickly. 'Richard,' Riley tells me, 'your reactions to Elizabeth's monster talk should be more supportive. You should acknowledge she's telling you she suffered a trauma. Don't take her comments literally, just accept she's trying to tell you she suffered something.'

I nod agreement, even though Elizabeth and I don't engage in monster talk, and Riley has no idea of the context of her monster talk. It feels pointless to enlighten her.

Then Riley stuns me. She turns to Niki and says, 'I keep hearing information from you that makes me think either Elizabeth has suffered a very major abusive event, as you describe, or that you are a neurotic, overreacting, hysterical mother. I want a chronology of what happened to Elizabeth, and what evidence you have.'

Whoa! How will Niki react?

'I absolutely believe Elizabeth was ritually sexually abused,' Niki replies, 'and either that is the truth, or I've driven Elizabeth crazy. And I'm crazy myself.'

'Well, Niki,' Riley says, 'based on your accounts of Elizabeth's statements and behaviour, she suffered a major sexual trauma. I would like to see the evidence.'

We leave the session in silence and stand, facing each other, on the street corner outside my office building, about a hundred metres from Riley's office building. I remember standing with Niki on the pavement outside lawyer David King's office building, in Bartlesville, nearly two years ago. I feel as lost now as I did then.

It's midday and a late-summer heatwave envelops us in furnace-hot air. Niki's in torment, struggling with her thoughts, trying to reach a decision. I stand fixed to the pavement, silent, waiting. We've stepped from office light into bright sunlight. It feels like a cosmic spotlight is shining down on our drama. Niki makes up her mind. 'Richard, I must have a diagnosis of ritual abuse so the girls know they don't have a crazy mother. I need a diagnosis to prove I did not cause this crisis.'

'Niki,' I plead, 'don't be so hard on yourself. We're not perfect parents. Don't back yourself into a corner over a ritual abuse diagnosis.' But Niki needs proof she did not harm Elizabeth. She needs to be right about ritual abuse.

The spotlight turns off and the curtain falls on this act, but the drama continues. I walk back into my office, unable to work.

Tuesday April 12, 1994

Two weeks later we again see Riley, and, again, I don't know why I'm invited. Niki has continued to see Riley – I assume to provide evidence of sexual trauma. As we walk toward her office I wonder when the penny will drop? When will Riley realise Niki's obsessed with a fantasy?

I soon find out. As the session begins, Riley acts coolly toward Niki and tries to engage with me in rational, friendly discussion. I give clipped answers or just nod my head. My heart races. I know exactly how Niki will react if I engage with Riley. I'll have sabotaged her with Riley, just as I sabotaged her with all the other therapists. A monologue rolls on in my head: Liz, stop talking to me. Stop it! Talk to Niki instead.

The session becomes surreal. There's an elephant sitting here with us.

Niki points at the elephant. 'I feel like you're trying to bond with Richard,' she tells Riley. 'I feel like there's been a power shift, away from me and toward Richard, and that makes me feel very uncomfortable.'

I'm impressed by Niki's honesty. She's admits she wants a therapist to bond with her and oppose me, that she wants an ally in her obsession. I'm pretty sure if Riley were beating up on me, Niki would sit here, enjoy the spectacle and shout, 'Hit him again!'

Riley, without hesitation or preamble, replies, 'Niki, I want to begin therapy with you to treat your anxiety. You keep asking me to be a judge. You keep asking me to tell you that you've done all the right things. You keep asking me to tell you that you've been a good mother. And you keep asking me to provide a sexual abuse diagnosis. I think you have a major anxiety disorder.'

I'm stunned. American therapists trod cautiously around Niki. They certainly never confronted her so forcefully. The rest of the session is a blur. Niki vehemently disagrees. Riley ends by saying, 'The best thing for Elizabeth is to keep the family situation calm.'

This evening, Niki weeps and sobs. She's been abandoned. Again. Niki's abject distress upsets me. No-one should suffer like this. I hold her and do my best to comfort her. 'Richard,' Niki pleads, head against my shoulder, 'you have to give up some of your personal power to me. Men, by their working and appearing professional and responsible, are automatically awarded power. You have to share your power with me. You have to defend me against the therapists.'

Here's my dilemma. If I state my beliefs, to Niki or to therapists, I'm sabotaging her, abandoning her, and Elizabeth. To not abandon Niki, I have to abandon myself. Although it's really a simpler dilemma than that: Niki's obsessed with a fantasy – that's my dilemma. This whole God-awful nightmare is an insane fantasy, driven by some crazy pathology that Niki, God bless her, has no idea she has. A pathology that needs Elizabeth to be a victim, an abnormal abused child.

Tuesday April 19, 1994

Niki, of course, fires Riley. A week later I'm invited to the 'Goodbye, Riley' session. Again, I don't know why. The session is polite, superficial and brief – Niki and Riley simply close the book. Then I learn why I'm here. Niki wants to make an announcement. 'Today I'm putting closure to the question of ritual abuse. The ritual abuse question is over with.'

Thursday April 28, 1994

Elizabeth has been in weekly therapy with Helen Davidson for six months. Today, at a parent conference, Helen tells us, 'Elizabeth is a wonderful, bright, assertive, normal young girl who's experienced anxiety around issues to do with illness, pregnancy, sibling rivalry and parental conflict, as well as talk about adults hurting children. It's time for you to stop focusing on themes of her having been harmed and hurt.'

Davidson also prepares a written report (Appendix 5):

Elizabeth presents as a very friendly, warm child who relates enthusiastically and confidently to adults. Her verbal skills reflect a capable child ...
Elizabeth ... has clear and definite ideas about the way she wishes anyone playing with her to be involved. She is very assertive ... but is also able to negotiate ... treating the adult in an instrumental way ...

The themes of Elizabeth's play centre around children becoming sick, mother's giving birth, mother's nurturing, sibling competing for their mother's attention, father being at work or dead, and animals being lost or buried in snow or sand. Some of these themes do relate to some of Elizabeth's own experiences, particularly the [mother's] illness and the birth of a sibling and the rivalry and sense of displacement she may have experienced at the time.

Elizabeth has made reference on a couple of occasions to children being hurt or harmed by adults, but ... generally retracted the statements, claiming they were 'just an expression'

Elizabeth is hypervigilant around the content of adults' conversations and will anxiously attend to words such as 'cut' or 'hurt', although seemily [sic] occupied in play ...

In the near future, I feel it also could be appropriate to help Elizabeth bring a sense of closure to whatever she has experienced in the past, in some sort of symbolic age appropriate way, as discussed previously with her parents.

twenty nine

The Lull Before School

Monday June 27, 1994

After April, a period of joy. Niki's parents visit from Oklahoma during May, and we play. Ritual abuse disappears from the radar and Jenny's speech improves.

During the Easter holiday, Niki sleeps over at a religious conference, then joins the local Catholic church. She asks to convert from Anglicanism to Catholicism, but it all gets too hard, and the conversion idea fades, to be replaced by her desire to pursue studies leading to ordination as an Anglican priest. She joins the governing body of her Anglican church and develops close, wonderful friendships with many of the elderly parishioners.

Elizabeth remains in therapy with Helen Davidson, and today we attend a parent conference. 'I don't think Elizabeth needs further therapy,' Helen tells us.

Tuesday June 28, 1994

The next day, Niki's anxiety spikes. 'Richard,' she says, 'Elizabeth's making traps with yarn wrapped around a baby stroller. She's protecting the baby from being taken away and eaten.' Niki tells me Elizabeth will be anxious and will have special needs when she starts primary school next year, so, 'She needs to stay in therapy.'

So Elizabeth stays in therapy. Niki also begins counselling sessions with Helen, 'for emotional support. Sometimes I cry with her for an hour.'

Friday November 25, 1994

Then more months of wonderful calm, until, suddenly, this evening, Niki tells me, 'Today Elizabeth talked about the blue house in Bartlesville. She said adults pointed a gun at her.' Niki thinks we should take Elizabeth back to Bartlesville so she can tell the police what happened, 'and, Richard, they can track down the perpetrators.'

I'm stunned by this stupidity and snap, 'Niki, that's absurd!'

'I swear on my grandmother's grave I didn't bring this up,' Niki replies. 'It's all Elizabeth!' But with her next breath, she admits, 'Well, I did ask Elizabeth about the blue house. She looked pale and worried after her visit today with Helen.'

Something has raised Niki's anxiety.

Monday November 28, 1994

Today I figure it out. A sexual abuse trial in Western Australia attracts huge media attention. Two sisters, in recovered memory therapy, have accused their father of ritual sexual abuse. Newspaper reports provide lurid details of depraved rituals. Even though the accusations are proven false, with the concept of recovered memory therapy painted as fraudulent by the media, news about the trial rekindles Niki's obsession. 'Richard,' Niki says, 'the ritual sexual abuse suffered by these women is similar to Elizabeth's.'

Tuesday November 29, 1994

Today, Niki calls my office, in distress. 'Richard, I asked Elizabeth if our trips to Margaret River upset her. I think she was ritually abused in a forest. She said our forest does scare her.'

Elizabeth is happy on our farm, so Niki's statement surprises me. Her next comment seems stupid beyond belief. 'Richard, Elizabeth also told me the monsters wore a mask with my face stitched onto theirs. But she knew it was a mask because she could see the stitch stripes.' Niki goes on. 'She said the monsters pretended to burn her. They put her in a cardboard box and used pretend flames. She said they made flame-shaped cardboard cut-outs, painted red, and moved them up and down like burning flames next to the box.'

This is why I'm incredulous: we'd just attended an end-of-year pantomime at Elizabeth's kindergarten. Elizabeth sat in a cardboard box. There were pretend flames on either side of the box, created by flame-shaped cardboard cut-outs, painted red, moved up and down.

'Niki, are you questioning Elizabeth?' I ask.

'Richard, I trust my instincts as a mother,' Niki answers, then tells me Elizabeth's abuse must have occurred before she was two years old, because if she could talk, she would have spoken out. 'So, Richard, First Christian Mother's Day Out must have been where she was handed over for abuse. Then she was taken into the forest around Bartlesville.'

Tuesday December 20, 1994

Today we see Helen Davidson. 'Elizabeth's not interested in further therapy,' she tells us. 'You need to put closure to the monsters. On the few occasions I've asked her about the monsters, she says, "That happened a long time ago and I can't remember."'

Davidson goes on. 'I've reviewed Elizabeth's case with paediatric specialists.' Helen says they made two comments. 'First, they were pleased there was no physical evidence of trauma. It's easier for children to recover from emotional trauma if no physical abuse is involved. Second, they were pleased I'd taken a reflective approach and not questioned Elizabeth, which is dangerously contaminating in such a young child.'

Davidson pleads with us to put closure to the monster issue. 'Allow Elizabeth to grow normally without it forever clouding her life and your life,' she says.

'What problems might arise for Elizabeth at puberty?' Niki asks.

'Elizabeth will have no memory of events when she was two years old,' Davidson answers. 'If she's allowed to move on and grow normally there should be no problems.'

This evening Niki says she feels like celebrating. 'This stage of Elizabeth's life is finally over,' she announces. 'And now I know what happened. Elizabeth was ritually sexually abused at First Christian Mother's Day Out.

thirty

School Starts

February 1995

In February 1995, Elizabeth enters Grade 1 at Dalkeith Primary. Niki requests Helen Davidson prepare a letter for Elizabeth's teacher, Mrs Bradbury, stating, 'Elizabeth may present as a child with separation anxiety with over-involved and anxious parents …' Helen ends her letter with, 'A query concerning her ability to test reality has been raised in the past, but no evidence of any distortion or deficit in this area was apparent in my work with her.'

After her first week of school Mrs Bradbury reassures us, 'Elizabeth is bright, happy and full of confidence. Mr and Mrs Vos, Elizabeth is certainly not anxious.'

Sunday February 12, 1995

But Niki's anxious. 'Richard, I think Elizabeth's behaviour with the boys at school is sexually inappropriate,' she says this evening. 'And I think she's anxious. She was rough with Jenny today, hitting her. I told her, "That's what you said the monsters did to you."'

Niki then turns and asks Elizabeth, 'Do you want to talk more about the monsters?' Elizabeth looks uncertain, but nods. So they retreat for a long private talk about the monsters. Later, Niki tells me, 'Elizabeth needed that. She's feeling so much better now.'

Friday February 17, 1995

This morning Niki says Elizabeth's anxious because, 'She was frightened by a man with a turban at the school swimming carnival yesterday.' So Niki keeps her home from school. Tonight she tells me, 'We crawled into bed and talked about the monsters most of the day. Richard, it's strange, her memory of the monsters is confused. Some things are consistent, some things are different.'

Elizabeth, who stands nearby, interrupts Niki and asks, 'Dad, do you believe me and Mommy about my monsters?'

'Elizabeth, I believe you have feelings about them,' I answer.

February – July 1995

Then five months of wonderful calm. Elizabeth enjoys school and makes friends. Niki is busy with church and community activities, and I'm very busy at work. In January 1995, our Bayu-1 exploration well in the Timor Sea discovered the Bayu-Undan gas-condensate field, with the energy equivalent of over one billion barrels of oil.

Wednesday July 19, 1995

Three years have passed since questions about ritual abuse and the monsters erupted into our lives. This evening, six-year-old Elizabeth walks to our bedroom doorway, and, with a serious, assertive look, announces, 'Mommy and Daddy, I want to tell you something. You know what I told you about the monsters? Well, I made all that up. When you asked me things, I would make it up.'

I'm stunned. We've had months of calm and I want to keep it that way. 'We've put all that behind us, Elizabeth,' I say. 'We can forget about all that.'

Niki says nothing.

Wednesday November 1, 1995

Four more months of wonderful calm follow that event. I begin to believe our family nightmare is finally over.

Then, today, Niki tells me, 'Richard, I'm concerned Elizabeth's having brain seizures, blanking out, going into an altered state. I wonder if she needs a brain scan?'

What?

thirty one

Would I Be Normal If
It Wasn't For The Monsters?

Tuesday January 23, 1996

Even though the obsession travelled, in Australia we've had wonderful periods of respite from ritual abuse. Then, from December 1995 through January 1996, Niki and the girls visit her family in America. When they return, Niki's hysterical. She tells me Elizabeth wanted to talk about the monsters during their trip. 'Richard, she brought the subject up, I promise!'

Elizabeth told Niki that both she and Jenny were with the monsters. 'So it must have been Kacey or Kimberley, since they babysat both girls. Richard, I felt schizophrenic talking to her. I tried not to question her, but I had to allow disclosure.' Elizabeth disclosed the monsters took her and Jenny to a cottage in the forest and threw them into cold water. 'So this means Jenny was abused as well. Richard, we need to talk to Jenny's doctor. If Jenny was anally abused, it might explain why she's always constipated.'

'Niki,' I say, 'if Jenny was anally abused, Dr Doyle would have seen the trauma. She examined Jenny, remember? And Jenny was less than six months old when this could have happened.'

Niki's adamant. 'Richard, the abusers torture babies with small instruments!'

'Niki, if you tell Jenny's doctor she was anally abused with small instruments at less than six months of age, and suggest this explains her constipation, he'll think you're nuts.'

Tuesday February 6, 1996

Elizabeth starts Grade 2 at Dalkeith Primary. Niki thinks she's anxious, and talks continually with her about her monsters. Today she tells me Elizabeth remembers being thrown into cold water, and, since it's summer and she's swimming more lately, 'Maybe the extra swimming increases her anxiety?' Niki turns and asks Elizabeth, 'Are you feeling more afraid because of all your swimming?'

Elizabeth looks uncertain, but answers, 'Yes.'

This makes no sense. Elizabeth took to swimming like a duck to water. She shrieks with joy when we play together in our backyard pool, and loves our trips to the beach. As I begin to say this, Niki interrupts. 'Richard, today Elizabeth asked me, "Mommy, would I be normal if it wasn't for the monsters?"'

'Niki, that's awful! That's wrong!' The words fly from my mouth unscripted. Niki isn't upset at all. In fact, she looks pleased Elizabeth's acknowledged the impact of the monsters on her normality.

Friday February 9, 1996

'Richard, Elizabeth's anxious,' is now Niki's mantra. After each such proclamation, Niki and Elizabeth spend hours huddled together, usually in bed, talking about the monsters, the bad people who hurt her. 'Niki, dwelling endlessly on the monsters is not helping Elizabeth at all,' I protest.

Niki disagrees. 'Richard, she has to tell her story. She now says I took her to the bad people's houses, but, then, other people, including me, took her to other bad people's houses. The story is getting really confused.'

Elizabeth stands nearby and interrupts, asking, 'Mommy, Daddy, maybe I'd be normal if the bad people hadn't taken me away?'

Panic grips me. How do I neutralise this poison in her mind? Unscripted words again fly out, and I shout, 'You are normal, Elizabeth! You are wonderful!'

Niki sits rigid, silent, a vacant stare into the void, no trace of emotion. She says not a single word. Job done. Mission accomplished. Vindication. I feel disgusted.

A little while later, driving alone with Elizabeth on an errand, she says,

'Daddy, you don't want to believe Mommy and me about the monsters and bad people, do you?'

I'm numb. 'Elizabeth, it was a long time ago,' I reply. I don't know what else to say. I don't know how to explain fantasy, obsession and brainwashing to a six-year-old. I don't know how to explain insanity to a six-year-old.

'But, you know, Dad,' Elizabeth responds, 'I do get anxious when people look sexually at me.'

May 1996

After the summer spike, Niki's anxiety calms. I'm not sure why. Maybe because her spiritual quest goes up a notch. She moves on from Anglicanism to the Baha'i faith. A group of enthusiastic Baha'i followers live in our neighbourhood, and Niki spends days and evenings attending meetings. She likes their concept of a 'spiritual unity of all humankind'. Niki even tells me, enthusiastically, 'Richard, Elizabeth told me she can't remember anything anymore about the monsters and the bad people.'

And Elizabeth's happy at school. She turned seven on May 19, and it's almost four years since our crisis erupted. Have we finally turned the corner?

September 1996

We move happily through winter and into spring, when the school calendar fills with sports carnivals and end-of-year events. Sadly, Niki's anxiety returns. She thinks Elizabeth's anxious about her sports carnival, so begs Helen Davidson to see Elizabeth for three sessions. Her last session with Helen was almost two years ago, in December 1994.

At a follow-up meeting, Helen tells us, 'Elizabeth's doing great,' then unleashes some frustration. 'You must stop attributing her behaviour to the monsters, and stop questioning her about the monsters. Her cognition skills are not sufficiently developed for you to talk with her about what might have happened when she was two years old.'

Thursday September 12, 1996

Then I erupt.

We're seated at the dinner table when Niki casually tells me, 'I ferried

Elizabeth and her school friends in the car today. I told them Elizabeth gets anxious sometimes because of her monsters. So she can't do all the things her friends do.'

Elizabeth was in the car, and heard this? And sits here now, at the dinner table, listening to this? Something inside me 'pops'. I begin vibrating. Slowly and angrily I growl, 'Niki, you are crippling Elizabeth. You should not bring up the monsters with her and her friends. You should not say things to paint her as a victim. Niki, that is so wrong!'

Niki bolts out of her chair. Standing upright, knuckles pressed down into the tabletop, elbows locked, she stares down at me, and shouts, 'You don't support me! You don't support Elizabeth! You just sabotage me!'

Anger, Niki's and mine, sends me into adrenaline shock. Niki rages, but I can't hear much. Elizabeth and Jenny, audience to this rage, start crying, then screaming. This jolts me to my senses. This is like my childhood. We have to make them feel safe. I stand up and take both girls into the living room and talk calmly to them. I say they're okay. Niki joins me and we reassure them they are safe, and Mummy and Daddy are okay. Eventually they stop crying. We didn't handle that episode at all well.

Sunday September 15, 1996

A few days later I collect Elizabeth from a Sunday afternoon play visit with her good friend James. His mother wants to talk to me. A well-to-do, well-connected, wealthy western suburbs housewife – not shy with her opinions. Her son James is disappointed Elizabeth will not be going to the school camp and sports carnival with all the other children.

'I'm concerned about Elizabeth,' James's mother says. 'Does your wife suffer anxiety? She holds Elizabeth back from school events, saying Elizabeth's anxious. I think it's Niki who's anxious.'

Monday September 23, 1996

Finally, Elizabeth's teacher, Mrs Danforth, confronts Niki. 'You're over-protecting Elizabeth. Have you considered parental separation anxiety?' Niki's response is defensive. 'That teacher doesn't know what Elizabeth and I have been through.'

October 1996

In October Niki tells me, 'Elizabeth refuses to go to school. Her teacher always shouts. This plays right into Elizabeth's post-traumatic stress disorder.' Niki requests Helen Davidson recommence therapy with Elizabeth.

Other children, and other parents, also complain about the teacher's loud manner. So, in October, we switch Elizabeth from Dalkeith Primary to Loreto Nedlands Primary, a local private school.

thirty two

Epilepsy

Monday December 9, 1996

In September, ritual abuse fades as Niki's major concern, to be replaced by brain seizures. 'Richard, Elizabeth's right eye drifts, and she has blank periods.' So Elizabeth undergoes an electroencephalogram, and today the doctor sees possible benign temporal lobe spikes, which, he says, 'Elizabeth will grow out of'. When I arrive home, Niki is ecstatic. 'Richard, I'm beside myself happy. The doctor diagnosed possible brain seizures. We have to go to McDonald's to celebrate.'

We need to celebrate because Elizabeth has possible brain seizures?

The earliest appointment we can arrange with a specialist neurologist, Dr Silberstein, is in March next year. Meanwhile, Niki's now convinced Elizabeth has epilepsy, and joins an epilepsy support group. A CAT scan reveals no brain abnormalities.

March 1997

In December 1996, Elizabeth was prescribed 'harmless seizure medication', and developed a hand tremor, concentration problems and occasional blurred vision. I suggest to Niki that she reduce the seizure medication. 'I tried that,' Niki replies, 'but Elizabeth gets anxious.'

Niki's new friend, Zita, from her Baha'i group, is a general practitioner. Based on Niki's description of symptoms, Zita thinks, 'Elizabeth's probably having seizures, but there's no way of proving it. It's an opinion thing. It could be schizophrenia or psychosis.'

Whatever it is, Niki knows Elizabeth's not normal. 'Richard, her teacher needs to make allowance for her anxiety.' So Niki speaks to her Grade 3 teacher, Mrs Jenkins, who tells Niki, 'Elizabeth's normal in class. Her unusual comments to me about being anxious were obviously planted by an adult.'

'That teacher's not sympathetic toward me,' Niki says. 'She won't listen to me.'

I feel sad for Elizabeth; new school, new class, new group of cliquey girls. And now, as well as monsters, she has brain seizures. And has to tell her teacher she's anxious. What a burden for a seven-year-old.

Monday March 17, 1997

This evening Niki tells me Elizabeth said she'd been on vacation for two weeks and had just returned. 'I wonder if it's psychotic episodes?' Niki says, then leaves for an evening Baha'i meeting.

I ask Elizabeth why she told Mummy she'd been away on vacation. 'Mom keeps asking me things,' she replies, 'so I just tell her things. She keeps asking me, "What's going on?" And I only said I was away for two minutes, not two weeks.' When I ask why she said that, Elizabeth wriggles her shoulders in a childish manner and replies, 'I don't know.'

Wednesday March 19, 1997

Today we have our long-awaited appointment with neurologist Dr Silberstein. Niki's excited. 'I think Elizabeth's suffering seizures and absent spells,' she tells him.

Silberstein, middle-aged, has a gentle, caring and calm manner. He asks our permission to examine Elizabeth. They stand close, facing each other, and commence a five-minute conversation about her interests, her activities, her classes. Elizabeth responds in her usual bright and confident manner. Silberstein then flips through pages of Elizabeth's test data, notes and charts. Then, after a minute or so of silence, he turns to face us and smiles.

'There's little likelihood Elizabeth's suffering seizures,' he says. 'Migraine might be a problem, but I see no organic basis for absence spells. She may be daydreaming. She's obviously very intelligent and should cope well at school.'

Great news?

Niki looks in shock, frozen. She's turned pale and seems unable to speak. Finally, she blurts out, 'Elizabeth's always thirsty and going to the toilet.'

Huh? Where did that come from?

Silberstein asks if Elizabeth's been tested for diabetes.

'No,' Niki says.

Has Niki lost the plot? Elizabeth's been subjected to endless medical tests – I'm sure a test for diabetes is in there somewhere. And I haven't noticed she's always thirsty and going to the toilet. Silberstein orders an immediate blood test. Niki has to take Jenny home, so I take Elizabeth across the road to Princess Margaret Hospital.

Elizabeth and I walk toward the hospital for another medical test. Just seven years old, she has a courageous spirit and keeps up an adult pace, focused ahead, holding tight to my right hand with her left. Then she slows, turns, and looks up at me. 'Dad, I wish I was normal,' she says, with sad, pleading eyes.

'You are normal, sweetheart. You're a great, normal kid,' I reply, trying to sound positive.

At that moment my heart breaks. My precious daughter thinks she's not normal. I have not protected her enough. I have not done enough. I have completely failed Elizabeth. This is the worst moment of my life.

We walk on and Elizabeth's subjected to another medical test, another nail in the coffin of her normality.

I feel crushed by sadness. On top of the sadness is a mountain of guilt and shame. All I see is Elizabeth's sad young face, full of intelligence, looking up at me, her father, pleading, 'Dad, I wish I was normal.' I want to scream at the universe for allowing this injustice to happen. But I allowed it to happen. I'm the one who did nothing while madness rained down on this bright, courageous, innocent young life.

Thursday March 20, 1997

This morning, Niki calls my office, excited. 'Richard, I just visited the Perth Epilepsy Foundation and, from my description of Elizabeth's symptoms, the lady at the foundation thinks Elizabeth definitely fits the diagnosis of temporal lobe seizures.'

Niki is desperate for an epilepsy diagnosis. As with the therapists who would not diagnose ritual abuse, Niki disagrees with Silberstein. 'Richard, we need to pursue further epilepsy testing for Elizabeth,' she tells me.

'Niki, Elizabeth was very upset yesterday,' I reply, begging. 'She told me she wished she was normal. Niki, please, I don't want to bring more medical drama into her life.'

As if I'm ignorant of the facts, Niki slowly and calmly explains, 'Richard, well, yes, of course Elizabeth thinks she's not normal, based on all the medical attention and therapy. But, Richard, if the medical attention and therapy is justified, well, then, we just have to pursue it.'

I sit dazed, distressed, depressed, and talk to myself. 'This will never end. I have failed Elizabeth. But what should I have done? I assumed things would get better. I didn't want to lose my children. Okay, but I have to do something. I have to save Elizabeth from epilepsy.'

Helen Davidson? Niki will see Helen today or tomorrow for personal counselling. I call her private number. 'Helen,' I say, 'Niki's moved on from ritual abuse to epilepsy. I'm worried about Elizabeth's mental health. Niki now sees all of Elizabeth's behaviour as fitting epilepsy, but the neurologist isn't concerned. I'm desperately worried for Elizabeth.'

Davidson listens, but all she says is, 'Yes, I understand.' I do pick up a hint of concern in her voice, but she offers no opinion, no advice.

Niki does see Davidson this afternoon and, this evening, she mentions their session with a dismissive comment. 'Helen just doesn't get it,' Niki tells me. 'I won't be seeing her again.'

Helen must have confronted Niki. Today is 'Goodbye, Helen Davidson' day.

Friday March 21, 1997

Today, Niki calls my office midmorning, excited. 'Richard, I bet ten to one, based on my reading of the epilepsy literature, Elizabeth is suffering temporal lobe seizures. We'll just have to adjust our parenting.'

After this call, Niki somehow arranges an urgent follow-up appointment with Silberstein to review his diagnosis. When I arrive home from work Niki tells me, 'I had a complete fall-apart, crying. I explained all of

Elizabeth's symptoms. How she hadn't displayed any of her symptoms when he saw her. And how desperate I am.'

Niki walked out of Silberstein's office with a prescription for Tegretol. Tonight, Niki's elated – Elizabeth is taking epilepsy medication.

thirty three

The Move To Margaret River

March 1997 – November 1997

Epilepsy is the next chapter in Elizabeth's abnormal life. Niki's new mantra, to one and all – family, friends, acquaintances, strangers – is, 'Elizabeth has epilepsy.' This is also Niki's go-to statement for withholding Elizabeth from activities deemed anxiety-producing.

I suppose if I had to make a choice between epilepsy or cult ritual abuse, I'd choose epilepsy. But epilepsy also seems crazy. I haven't seen Elizabeth absent. I've never seen her right eye drift. She's never had seizures. And the neurologist saw nothing of concern.

There is, however, a silver lining: when Elizabeth commenced epilepsy medication, Niki's anxiety vanished. Medication proved Elizabeth's abnormal status, and proved Niki was not a hysterical, overreacting mother, was not the cause of Elizabeth's problems. It was epilepsy.

We enjoy eight months of calm. Family life is relaxed, playful, joyful. Jenny starts school, also at Loreto Nedlands Primary, and just loves it. By sheer chance, her first-grade teacher, Jennie Deering, is an old and close family friend. I named Jenny with Jennie in mind.

However, a few niggling issues persist. The girls in our neighbourhood, and in Elizabeth's class, remain cliquey. For Elizabeth, making friends is a challenge. And Niki clashes with the Loreto teachers and the other mothers. 'They just treat me like an anxious mother. They don't understand Elizabeth's situation.' So Niki suggests relocating with the girls to our farm in Margaret River.

Saturday November 15, 1997

Today, Niki and the girls move into the cottage on our farm. Elizabeth is eight years old and Jenny is six. I'm happy to be one step closer to retiring to our farm. I begin commuting to Margaret River Friday evening, returning to Perth late Sunday evening.

The girls are happy. They enrol in Margaret River Primary and make close friends. Niki's also happy. She makes friends through the Anglican church, and with mothers of the girls' school friends. A few of these mothers are also American expatriates. We enjoy a further four months of calm.

Thursday March 12, 1998

Today the calm ends. I don't know why. Niki calls my office from Margaret River, distressed. 'Richard, Elizabeth's Barbie dolls were undressed. I asked her why they were undressed.' Niki tells me Elizabeth used the Barbies to demonstrate sexual positions. 'And she's been kissing Jenny,' Niki adds. 'She has sexual urges. She wants to see a therapist. I think it's because she was involved in child pornography.'

Friday March 13, 1998

When I arrive at the cottage this evening, Niki's distraught. She wants me to watch Elizabeth's Barbie doll play. I go to Elizabeth, who flips the dolls around in her hands to demonstrate kissing, sexual intercourse and oral sex, in a mechanistic, learned way. It takes about four seconds. She seems bored demonstrating Barbie sex, yet again. 'Mom said this is what the monsters and bad people did to me when I was little,' Elizabeth tells me.

I feel numb with despair. 'Do you remember anything about that?' I ask.

'No,' she replies, 'but I've played kissing with other girls and one boy.'

Six years of Niki's brainwashing about sexual abuse has, in a way, sexualised Elizabeth. It doesn't surprise me that she plays kissing and possibly sexual games with other children, including Jenny.

'I played kissing with girls in my neighbourhood when I was your age,' I tell her. 'Don't feel bad about playing kissing, because most kids do that. But don't do it if you don't want to. And don't believe monsters and bad people did this to you if you can't remember it.'

Then Jenny, who sits at the dining room table, needs to speak to me. She wants to tell me something important, which is unusual for Jenny, who normally listens, observes and says little. I sit down next to her. 'Dad,' she says, 'when you're away, all Mommy does is talk with Elizabeth about the monsters.' Jenny then performs an amazing pantomime. She tilts her head from side to side, like a metronome, and begins a verbal repetition of, 'monsters, monsters, monsters, monsters, monsters,' for about ten seconds, her head moving from one side to the other with each 'monster' utterance.

While Elizabeth and Jenny talk to me, Niki is close by in the kitchen. She hears our conversations. After Jenny completes her metronome impersonation, I turn and look at Niki. It takes a few moments to absorb what I see. She's walking in circles around the kitchen emitting a strange, tuneless whistle. Her hands are locked together in front of her waist, fingers wrestling, and she stares at the walls.

I stand up. 'Niki I'm very concerned you're telling Elizabeth the monsters did these things to her when she can't remember anything herself. We don't know that happened. You shouldn't tell her she's been sexually abused.'

Niki snaps back to the present. 'I did not say that to Elizabeth!' she shouts. 'She put it all together for herself. She figured it all out for herself. Richard, I want Elizabeth back in therapy for ritual sexual abuse.'

I wonder, do we look in the Margaret River phone directory under Ritual Abuse Therapy? 'Niki, I can't go through another family crisis trying to reach a diagnosis of ritual abuse.'

Niki won't be deterred. 'Richard, Elizabeth has sexual urges. She said she kissed boys and girls in Perth. And James wanted to have sex with her. And I caught Elizabeth kissing Jenny.'

Then she ups the ante. 'I want to contact Interpol. Richard, I want a worldwide search of child pornography images to find a picture of Elizabeth. That would prove I'm right. That would prove she was used for pornography.' Niki tells me that pornography abuse is the only thing that explains Elizabeth's behaviour. 'I was hoping epilepsy would explain everything, but now I see it can't. It has to be ritual sexual abuse, as well as epilepsy.'

Thursday April 2, 1998

Today Niki brings the girls to Perth for medical check-ups; Jenny for ear infections and Elizabeth sees Dr Silberstein about epilepsy. I can't attend the meeting with Silberstein. Later, Niki calls my office to tell me she asked Silberstein if epilepsy caused sexual urges. 'He said it was rare, and only in sexually mature people.'

When I arrive home, Niki greets me in the driveway, agitated. As I step out of the car door, she says, 'Richard, we need a referral to a therapist for Elizabeth's sexual urges.'

The steps leading into our house are right in front of me. I can't move. I can't talk. I feel trapped inside a bubble. Outside the bubble is the rest of the world. Our garden. Our street. But they're blurry because I'm inside the bubble. I'm in a bubble of madness. The first thought I have inside this bubble is that I want to be dead. I want to be dead and done with madness. I want the peace of death. The next thought I have is of Elizabeth and Jennifer. If I'm dead, I won't see them again. They will be hurt by the loss of their father. They will be at the mercy of madness. This can't happen. By an act of will, I step through the bubble, walk up the stairs and into our house.

The thought of death, the peace of death, recurs for days – along with thoughts about my weakness for not acting to end this madness; not telling Niki she's obsessed, delusional, hysterical and abusing Elizabeth. And that, 'This must stop!'

Or what? I feel helpless to stop Niki. If I challenge her, she'll return to America with the girls. Elizabeth is almost nine and Jenny only seven. The thought, the image, of losing them, not having their arms around my neck when I kneel down to greet them, is unbearable, unacceptable. It can't happen.

But my life also feels unbearable. I see Elizabeth, my amazing little girl with a big courageous heart and a big, bright mind, being worn down, beaten down, made to feel less and less normal, less and less okay, more and more convinced she's been abused. If this goes on and on, what will be the outcome? Will she self-destruct? Will she disappear into the same mad fog that Niki lives in? And how is all this craziness impacting Jenny?

For Niki, Elizabeth's abuse and epilepsy are fundamental truths. So her actions are entirely reasonable and proper.

Niki is a loving mother and a loving wife in so many ways. On most family issues we work well together. We reach easy agreement on common goals. But over the question of Elizabeth's abuse and medical abnormality, we are completely at odds. Niki's obsession to have Elizabeth branded abnormal feels like madness. To brainwash Elizabeth to believe she's been sexually abused, when we don't know that to be the truth, feels incredibly damaging. It feels like abuse.

But then, I think, Elizabeth is courageous, assertive and very intelligent. When she's older, she'll figure it out for herself. She'll be okay. So, even if I failed to save her from Niki's obsession, she'll save herself. The weak part of me abdicates from the role of protector, thinking the child can, one day, protect herself, save herself, because I, the adult, the father, for sure haven't done that.

thirty four

Retirement

April 1998 – July 2006

After April 1998, the obsession fades away or goes underground. Either way, the family wound, bleeding since July 1992, heals over. There's a scar, but we don't look at it, don't touch it – or, at least, I don't. Occasionally, a shadow from our crazy past flits across my path, but when I turn to look, whatever cast the shadow has gone.

My stress subsides, and eight years pass without a diary entry. Epilepsy also ends. Elizabeth just stops taking her medication.

In September 1999, at fifty years of age, I retire from corporate life to our farm in Margaret River, to pursue other creative interests and be at home with Niki and the girls. Elizabeth is ten years old and Jenny eight. I can now be close by as they grow into adulthood – and clear decades of corporate cobwebs out of my system. I set up a furniture workshop and learn woodworking; help build a new family home; enjoy the dirt, sawdust, sweat and exhaustion of selling firewood; help run an amateur swimming club; join the local volunteer bushfire brigade and the local Rotary Club; rekindle an interest in surfing; and make new friends.

Niki showers the girls with motherly love and supports my furniture and farm work. She initiates successful community programs: a children's church and a high school mentoring program. Niki also pursues her religious and spiritual interests, moving from the Baha'i faith back to the Anglican Church, and applies to become an Anglican priest. This hits a roadblock and she moves on to the Uniting Church.

The euphoric first few weeks of retirement are spent tutoring

Elizabeth. Both girls are changing school, from Margaret River Primary to St Thomas More Primary. Elizabeth feels behind in her subjects, especially maths. It's wonderful to see her courage and determination as we review the basics. She's bright and learns quickly.

I become assistant coach of the Margaret River Amateur Swimming Club, so early morning, before school, it's swim club training, which the girls enjoy, I think, mostly. They become confident swimmers. In summer we swim at our local beach, Redgate Beach. I show them how to survive the dangers of heavy surf and rip currents.

In the evenings, during school, it's help with homework and interesting discussions about whatever comes to mind. The girls are inquisitive and love to explore ideas. We also laugh and talk and hug and play. And explore the Australian bush together, learning about the vegetation and the wildlife in and around our farm, and Margaret River. On school holidays we take road trips, just Elizabeth, Jenny and me. We drive north, south and east, exploring wide swaths of Western Australia. Thousands of kilometres of bitumen flow beneath us while we listen to music, debate and philosophise, joke and laugh. We're close. They grow into beautiful, wonderful teenage girls who love their dad. I'm a very happy father.

Apart from the usual problems of everyday life, we flourish. Elizabeth and Jenny make close friends, although being isolated on a farm has its challenges – we're about ten minutes' drive from town. Niki and I go out of our way to taxi the girls to their friends and their activities.

The girls do well at school. They top their classes in many subjects and receive numerous academic awards and positions on student council. Jenny becomes Head Girl of St Thomas More Primary. She feels unsettled at Margaret River High School and asks to transfer to Bunbury Cathedral Grammar, a private school about an hour's drive north of Margaret River. She boards in 2006, her Year 10, and has the time of her life. She travels to school Monday morning, returning Friday afternoon, makes wonderful friends, matures and develops independent self-confidence.

In 2005, Elizabeth develops chronic fatigue, probably from chemical exposure while dusting her pet chickens for mites. She begins homeschooling with Student Independent and Distance Education. She splits

her final Year 12 into two years of study, so is scheduled to finish high
school in 2007. During this period, she struggles with self-image and
feels isolated at home. Niki shows me a couple of letters she's written,
to herself and to her friends, saying how very upset and very sad she is
about her appearance and social and romantic isolation. Reading her letters is gut-wrenching.

I try to help her take up exercise. She jogs with me, slowly at first – a
walk and jog. I try not to push her. At the end of each run, we have a ritual
of sorts. She thanks me for encouraging her and I take her pulse. Then
we walk and talk. She shares what's on her mind – typical teenage stuff.

During these eight years, Niki and Elizabeth talk privately, between
themselves, about her sexual abuse at two years of age, and with a psychic they visit together. And maybe also with some close friends. They
develop the joint understanding that she was sexually abused by adults
when she was two years old. They know this happened, even if the rest
of the world doesn't know it. They keep this part of their reality and their
relationship to themselves. I'm left out of the loop. I know nothing about
these conversations, or about Niki and Elizabeth's shared reality. I learn
about it later.

Later is about to happen.

thirty five

The Obsession Returns

Sunday July 9, 2006

After eight wonderful years of calm, the obsession returns. If there were warning signs, I missed them. I thought our family was happy and thriving. I thought Niki's obsession over Elizabeth's sexual abuse had faded away, had died. I was wrong. Today, almost exactly fourteen years to the day since the nightmare was born, it's resurrected. The coffin lid opens and the obsession comes screaming out.

Niki tells me, 'Richard, over the last couple of weeks, Elizabeth's been dreaming of sexual activity, like one of her teachers making sexual advances. And being tied up and made to watch other people being sexually abused.' Niki says Elizabeth wants therapy, but is worried this will cause a family crisis.

I try to calm Elizabeth's concerns. 'In the past, Mum and I were on different mountaintops,' I say, 'with different viewpoints. This issue was a huge ball of confusion when you were young. Elizabeth, if you want therapy now, I support that.'

Elizabeth has just turned seventeen. I imagine she holds her own ball of confused thoughts and emotions. She was just three years old when the crisis erupted, and it dragged on for six long years. She knew her parents were in terrible conflict over something to do with her being hurt by the monsters and the bad people. So I appreciate her request for therapy. I'm sure there are local counsellors to help her process her confusion.

That's not what Niki has in mind. After our conversation, Niki picks up the phone and calls an emergency sexual assault counselling service in

Bunbury, 100 kilometres north of Margaret River.

'Niki, is calling an emergency rape hotline on Sunday night really necessary?' I ask, diplomatically.

'It's time to get the show on the road!' Niki replies, excited.

Thursday July 13, 2006

Today, on the fourteenth anniversary of our crisis, Elizabeth sees Angie at the Waratah Sexual Abuse Counselling Centre in Bunbury. Elizabeth provides Angie with Veronica's letter, written thirteen years ago, as background information. Angie apparently tells Elizabeth, 'Yes, you could've been sexually abused when you were two years old.'

Tonight, Niki's ecstatic. 'Finally!' she exclaims, 'After all these years, vindication!' Niki and Elizabeth then review Niki's journal and speculate about abuse perpetrators based on the content of her dreams. They zero in on Kacey's father.

What do I do now? If I tell Elizabeth I believe she was brainwashed about sexual abuse as a child, it would push our family back into conflict, into the nightmare of 'Dad's opinion versus Mum's opinion' and 'This therapist's view versus that therapist's view'. I'm also afraid of the rage it would initiate in Niki, who now exclaims vindication.

Conflicting thoughts bounce around in my head. Elizabeth deserves validation of her unusual childhood, with all the therapy and confusion and conflict. Therapy could help her heal and grow. But if she believes, as truth, that she suffered childhood sexual abuse, and for the rest of her life carries the baggage of that belief, then I struggle to accept that. Do I tell her what I believe? Or trust she can heal without my interference? If I raise my beliefs, it could shift the focus away from Elizabeth's healing and reignite conflict between Niki and me. That is my nightmare. I want to hold tight to the illusion that we're not going back into this nightmare, not going back into family conflict.

Thursday July 20, 2006

Today Elizabeth has a second session with Angie in Bunbury. When she returns there's an air of despondency. Niki is subdued. Elizabeth withdraws to her room.

Friday July 21, 2006

Late this morning, as usual, I take a coffee break from furniture work. Seated at the dining room table, I sip my coffee. Then I overhear Niki on the phone with her mother in America. They agree the content of Elizabeth's dreams tie back to specific people and places in Bartlesville linked to her sexual abuse. They discuss men's clothing, facial looks and house colours. As I hear this, I look up and I see the nightmare. It's right there, right in front of me. A black wave of conflict, cresting, coming straight toward me. I can't survive another wave of family conflict and madness. I can't swim through it again.

Niki then comes to the dining room and asks, 'Richard, don't you think it's amazing Elizabeth's dreams have such clear details about the people and places I suspected were involved in her sexual abuse? Her descriptions are a perfect fit for Kacey and her father. Don't you see that?'

I stretch out my arms, place both hands flat on the tabletop, look up and growl, 'Niki, no I do not. I was there. I lived through this nightmare. I saw the contamination.' My words tell Niki I will not be a party to any more madness.

I'm stunned. Niki's also stunned. Right at that moment, the girls enter the house and Niki leaves the dining room. And it hits me – I've re-lit the fuse of the bomb in our marriage.

Saturday July 22, 2006

This morning, Niki's upset and calls a family meeting. We sit together at the dining room table and she opens proceedings. 'No-one in this family has hurt Elizabeth,' she says. 'The people who sexually abused Elizabeth are the ones who caused all this trouble. I am not going to accept the blame.'

Elizabeth picks up the narrative. 'Angie at the Waratah Centre queried my relationship with Mom. She wondered if Mom had influenced my memories about sexual abuse.'

Jenny then astonishes me. 'And what about all the monster talk I remember when we were young?' she says. Out of the mouths of babes.

After Jenny's comment, Niki drops her chin to her chest and sobs, 'I did the best I could.'

Jenny, embarrassed and mortified, jumps out of her chair, rushes around the table and embraces her mother. Niki then leans forward, head over the table top, weeping.

While Niki weeps, Elizabeth looks coolly at me, and asks, 'What do you believe happened to me, Dad?' She looks ready to pounce if I say I don't believe she was sexually abused. While Elizabeth speaks, Niki lifts her head, turns, and sobs into Jenny's shoulder. Jenny's still embracing her mother.

'Elizabeth,' I reply, 'I don't want to discuss my opinion now. It brings the focus back onto the different opinions between Mum and me. The focus should be on you and your healing, not the conflict between Mum and me.' A cop-out, I know, but how do I summarise this nightmare, here and now, sitting at this table, with Niki weeping?

Then I go upstairs to my office, pull open a filing cabinet drawer and take out a white three-ring binder. My diary. The entries begin on July 13, 1992. I flip through hundreds of pages of entry notes. I feel nauseous. I can't return to this nightmare. I put back the file binder and shut the drawer.

I decide to jog, to release stress. Elizabeth waits for me on our gravel track, at our western boundary gate. She wants to talk. 'Elizabeth,' I say, 'I don't want to go back into conflict with Mum about sexual abuse. But if I have to, it will mean divorce. Because this time I'll be forceful.' I get dramatic. 'I've kept a diary. I have all the information. Up to now I haven't pushed my opinions. I've just wanted things to be calm. I don't want to attack Mum.' I tell Elizabeth that, if I have to, I could resurrect a whole lot of information, and really make my case.

Instead of telling Elizabeth, calmly, what I believe and why I believe it, I tell her how passive I've been, but how tough I could be. It's an act, expressing false bravado, saying what I could have done in the past, but had not done. It's a rant, driven by pent-up shame over my own inaction. And a veiled threat of mutually assured destruction aimed at keeping the conflict genie in the bottle, avoiding a final, open showdown with Niki.

Then I cry. Why? Stress? The awful thought of going back into the nightmare? To show Elizabeth how much pain I feel? To manipulate her? I feel pathetic.

My crying upsets Elizabeth and she hugs me. I calm down, apologise, and say, 'Elizabeth, I support your therapy. There has been trauma, family trauma, for you. So therapy for trauma is valid. But nobody can ever know what happened when you were two years old. What I really want is for you to move on with your own life.'

'Angie told me just having all the therapy I've had was a trauma,' Elizabeth replies. We laugh. 'Angie's really nice, Dad. You'd like her – very matter-of-fact and no-nonsense.'

I then state flatly, 'Elizabeth, I witnessed lots of events in your young life when Mum contaminated you regarding sexual abuse. And you learned to manipulate Mum by saying you would tell her about the monsters if she did what you wanted.'

'Dad, I want to resolve my issues without getting lots of input from either you or Mom,' she replies. I'm proud of her. We walk back to the house, arm in arm.

Thursday July 27, 2006

Elizabeth, of course, stops seeing Angie – without even a 'Goodbye, Angie' session. Niki then initiates therapy for Elizabeth in Margaret River, with a sexual abuse counselling service called Bravehearts. She tells me, 'The counsellor, Lisa, was really nice, very friendly and supportive.'

Thursday August 10, 2006

Over the next two weeks, I withdraw, close down, shrink into my shell. Niki and I don't discuss Elizabeth's issue, but I feel the tension between us increasing. It's just there, just beneath the surface.

Today I travel to Perth to stay overnight with an old friend, Peter, so I can attend a woodworking exhibition. Just after I arrive, Niki calls to tell me, 'Richard, there's no easy way to say this, so I'll just say it. Our marriage is over. I'm divorcing you and returning to America with the girls. I called you now so you can get support from Peter. I suggest you stay in Perth for a while.'

Niki goes on. 'Richard, I can't trust you. You tried to sabotage me with Elizabeth. She told me what you said about me contaminating her when she was young.' Niki says that because I won't believe Elizabeth, and because I won't believe her about Elizabeth's sexual abuse, our marriage is over.

'Niki, the girls should decide for themselves about leaving Australia,' I reply. I'm not upset at the thought of Niki leaving, only the girls.

'Okay,' Niki agrees, 'the girls can decide where they want to live.' We both know Elizabeth will leave with Niki. 'I'll meet Jenny when she returns from boarding school tomorrow and explain what's happening,' she says.

It didn't take long for our nightmare to reach a climax. My one, short conversation with Elizabeth was too threatening. Niki needs to flee.

Friday August 11, 2006

I don't sleep. This morning I call Angie in Bunbury and identify myself as Elizabeth's father. I'm grateful she'll speak with me. 'What's your assessment of Elizabeth?' I ask.

'I was surprised her visits stopped,' Angie replies. 'I told her we can't know what happened. Dreams aren't conclusive. She should focus on moving on, develop coping skills, and not look back into her mother's journal. More therapy could be a black hole for her. I think her relationship with her mother influences what she does.'

Then I drive home. To not return home feels wrong, like I'm abandoning the girls. The highway to Margaret River goes through Bunbury. Beside Jenny's school, I stop. She loves this school. I pray she decides to stay. She's thriving in Australia. I worry she'll be swallowed up by the madness if she returns to America. I wonder if I should go into the school to talk to her before she catches the bus home, before Niki can speak to her. But that feels treacherous. I drive on.

As I arrive at the house, Niki backs out of the carport to take Elizabeth to stay overnight with a friend. Elizabeth sits in the front passenger seat. She doesn't look at me, just stares ahead, with the aura of a tortured spirit.

My first action is to go upstairs to my filing cabinet. I worry my diary will be gone. I pull open a cabinet drawer. It's all here: my diary, a copy of Niki's journal, the therapists' reports, the Veronica audiotapes. This material feels like my lifeline to sanity. My evidence and explanation for what happened. My own pile of obsession. The product of my own avoidant, furtive dysfunction. I box it all up and lock it away in my furniture workshop, and move some clothes into our granny flat.

Then I see a poem Elizabeth's written and left on the dining room table.

The people who love me are in charge
Look after me
Take over
Carry the burden I shouldn't have carried

I wonder about her state of mind, trapped, with Niki, in a prison of belief about childhood sexual abuse. Niki probably thinks she's freeing Elizabeth, unlocking the prison door to the truth of her abuse. I think it's the opposite. Niki is locking Elizabeth away, with herself, inside a prison of victimhood, inside her obsession.

Niki drives Jenny home and shares her plans. I meet Jenny when she walks through the door from the carport. She's distraught, crying. I hold and comfort her. We hold together for a long, long while in the hallway. 'It's your choice where you decide to live,' I tell her.

'No it isn't!' Niki exclaims. 'I've changed my mind. I'm taking both girls back to America. I know the court will be the final arbiter. But I'll take it to court.'

Jenny and I look at each other. We both know Elizabeth will return to America. I think Jenny wants to stay here. She loves her school and her friends. After a few moments I say, 'Niki, the girls should decide for themselves.'

'The girls should be with their mother!' she fires back. 'I know what's best for them.'

I retreat to the granny flat and consider how my actions over the past fourteen years led to where I sit now, shut off from my wife and children, in a room beside my house. If I'd agreed with Niki about sexual abuse, all would be fine with the family. But I didn't believe it. Over the years I tried to inject some sanity. What did I accomplish? Not much, by the look of it.

Jenny interrupts my tumbling train of thought. She opens the granny flat door, walks in and starts a conversation. I'm touched she wants to be with me. Thank you, Jenny. 'Dad, why can't Mom trust you?' Jenny asks. 'Mom says she can't trust you.'

How do I tell Jenny what I believe without seeming to attack Niki? I try to be low-key. 'Jenny, there was confusion, and some therapists believed Mum's reaction was a hysterical overreaction. I don't think we can ever really know what happened to Elizabeth.' I'm not sure Jenny understands the small picture I paint. How do you condense a fourteen-year nightmare into a couple of sentences? The devil and the truth are in the detail.

'Dad, I don't like America that much,' Jenny then says, 'especially being around all Mom's family dramas. And I'm worried about American schools. But I won't tell anyone, until required by a court, where I want to live. Otherwise I'll have to suffer through all the lobbying.'

Jenny then tells me how hard it is to be home on weekends. 'I feel like I'm drowning in all the tension surrounding Elizabeth, her moods and her problems.' She says it's nice to get back to her school and her friends on Monday.

I think about Jenny's life in our family. Elizabeth's issues have used up most of the family oxygen. Jenny harbours no bitterness, but I think she now feels a comforting degree of separation from The Family Drama at her boarding school. If she sustains this, I think she'll escape the madness.

Saturday August 12, 2006

Jenny and I have a Saturday morning ritual. While Niki and Elizabeth usually sleep in, I make her 'Daddy Eggs', light and fluffy scrambled eggs on pita bread. And we talk. It's our thing. This morning, for the first time I can recall, Niki rises early to make Jenny breakfast. Her campaign to win over Jenny has begun.

When Elizabeth arrives home from her sleepover, I go to her room. 'Elizabeth, don't blame yourself for the divorce. You're not responsible.' She looks tired, fed up.

'Dad, all my life I've felt like I've had to carry you,' she says, raising her hands above her head, like a weightlifter pushing up a barbell, or Atlas holding up the earth. 'I've had to be calm and normal, to keep you happy. I've only shared my fall-apart emotions and my abused side with Mom. I've had to be two people. Dad, you can't cope dealing with my bad stuff.' She says she knows I don't believe anything really bad happened to her. 'And I've always known you and Mom had massive tension over this. But you wanted calm and no arguments. I've felt suffocated under the burden of avoiding upsets. And I've felt bad about myself growing up. I want to confront all this crap and be a well-adjusted woman.'

'You're right,' I reply, 'I don't cope well with conflict. I probably need my own therapy.'

'Dad,' she says, 'I dream that I witness some strange and abusive stuff around a babysitter. I'm not abused myself but I witness abuse.'

It's good to talk with Elizabeth. I don't want to lose her. I don't want Elizabeth and Jenny to leave for America. 'Let's talk together about this as a family,' I say.

Elizabeth calls Niki and Jenny, and we all sit at the dining room table. 'Elizabeth,' I say, 'I'm sorry I haven't been available to listen to you about your bad feelings. I support you getting therapy. I believe you about your dreams of sexual abuse. I don't think a divorce and you leaving is the right thing. I know I don't cope well with upset and conflict over your issues, and I always just want things to be calm. I have my own childhood stuff.'

At which point I get tearful. Niki then passes me a tissue box, like I'm in therapy, but I recover my composure. I'm trying to walk a fine line. I want to acknowledge Elizabeth's truths and my own dysfunction, but not betray my beliefs.

Niki enters the conversation. 'Richard, I'm happy to take the divorce off the table. But I'm not convinced you believe Elizabeth was sexually abused. I want to hear you say that. I want to hear you say you agree Elizabeth was sexually abused. And I want you to admit how wrong you've been about me.'

I'm not being humble enough for Niki. But I refuse to grovel, so she starts a tirade. 'You sabotaged me all along! You aren't really admitting what you've done to me. You aren't really admitting what you've done to Elizabeth. You've got to say that you now believe Elizabeth was sexually abused!' Niki's harangue goes on and on.

If I react, it's all over. How long can I sit here and stay quiet? Finally, fourteen-year-old Jenny comes to the rescue. 'Mom, that's enough!'

Monday August 14, 2006

The divorce is shelved. Niki attributes this to a miracle of enlightenment on my part. But the focus is now on me: my dysfunction and my bad behaviour. All I hear from Niki is the word 'sabotage'. I sabotaged her when I spoke to anyone about my opinions, especially the therapists. I was the persuasive communicator – the tall and believable man – able to convince people I was right and make Niki look like a hysterical mother. Niki was helpless. She was defeated by me in her efforts to have the therapists diagnose Elizabeth's sexual abuse.

Voltaire suggested, 'God is a comedian playing to an audience that's too afraid to laugh.' If that's true, I think the devil stole the laughter and hell is a life without humour. I'm not laughing anymore. Nothing is funny anymore. I feel lost in despair, in sadness, in defeat. My lights slowly switch off. My life goes dark.

I need some time out with my cheerful sister. Niki's happy for me to, 'Go and get some support for your dysfunction.'

thirty six

Cape Town

Wednesday August 16 – Sunday September 3, 2006

Cape Town lies on the flank of Table Mountain, surrounded by beautiful headlands and bays. My sister's house is adjacent to the University of Cape Town, on the picturesque lower slopes of Table Mountain. I arrive at her house late Wednesday night.

Suzanne has lived an amazing life. She began a career in journalism in Perth, which she continued in South Africa, then shifted to black liberation politics. In 1994, she was elected a member of the first black-majority national parliament of South Africa. The parliament then elected her to serve in the Pan-African Parliament, a construct of the African Union. This work involved courageous forays into Zimbabwe, Libya, Nigeria and other challenging African countries. She was later appointed by the South African president to the board of directors of the South African Broadcasting Corporation. Suzanne has led an exemplary life of fearless political and intellectual involvement in the complex issues facing South Africa as it crawled out from beneath the burden of apartheid.

After a few days in Cape Town, Suzanne takes me to Doctor Ron. Ron is a family friend. He helped nurse our cancer-ridden mother prior to her death. I can talk with him. 'Ron, I can't eat, and the thought of leaping off a cliff is appealing.' Ron diagnoses depression.

Then I see Trevor, a clinical psychologist. Trevor wonders if Niki's suffered some sort of abuse. He thinks the outlook is grim. 'She will never, ever change her beliefs.' And we talk about dreams. 'Dreams are not reality. Elizabeth's dreams are not a recollection of what happened to her at two years of age. That's impossible.' And as for me, 'It sounds like you're pathologically avoidant.'

Wednesday August 23, 2006

I'd sent Niki an email that included a comment about Suzanne and I talking about our family of origin, to make conversation. Today I receive her reply:

> I'll tell you again, Richard: If I can't trust you with my life, to keep me safe and protect me ... then I cannot remain here ... If you can't face the truth of the pain and abuse Elizabeth experienced ... then I WILL NOT be able to trust you.
>
> I WILL NOT stay here and be abused like that again ... So my bottom line is ... my own safety. This is exactly why I thought there was no hope for us – because even in the therapeutic situation, I could not trust you to support and protect me against the therapists. So our future depends upon you taking care of your problems.

Monday August 28, 2006

The days are cool, overcast and short. Rainclouds swirl over Table Mountain. My sister is busy with parliamentary duties, and I take long strolls through the university campus, and, each afternoon, jog around one of their sports ovals. I have time to reflect.

Niki and I have parented Elizabeth with different paradigms. I parented her as a normal, courageous, bright girl who could grow beyond whatever impacted her as a two-year-old. Niki parented her as a victim of sexual abuse who needed lifelong therapy. From age three onwards, Niki wove Elizabeth into her fantasy of ritual sexual abuse, monsters and naughty people. Sitting together inside the fantasy, inside the obsession, Niki convinced Elizabeth: 'Your father doesn't believe me. Your father doesn't believe you. Your father doesn't believe us.' Elizabeth tried to negotiate these parental paradigms, doing normal stuff with me, talking about sexual abuse, monsters and the naughty people with Niki. Walking the tightrope between these two realities was not sustainable.

For years I silently screamed, 'Niki, this is nuts! It's crippling Elizabeth!' My silence avoided conflict and anger and anxiety. And it avoided the loss of my children. Even low-key disagreement was considered sabotage by Niki. She could not abide any threats to her obsession.

Therapists recognised Niki's obsession and told me, 'Elizabeth would be normal, if Niki would allow it.' But opinions were all they provided. After that, I was on my own.

So we arrive at the present. Niki believes Elizabeth's dreams vindicate the obsession, and for the family to remain together I must accept her paradigm, keep her safe, protect her from the therapists and take care of my problems.

Ironically, Niki chose all the therapists. I didn't pursue therapists to get a diagnosis to support my paradigm – that Elizabeth was normal and Niki was obsessed. My doing so would have instantly shattered our family. I just wanted the nightmare to end. The obsession to end. When therapists did not support Niki's paradigm, I almost felt sorry for her. I took no pleasure in her grief and frustration. I never gloated. I never claimed vindication. Instead, I walked on eggshells and agreed to move on to the next therapist.

I told myself the nightmare would end when Elizabeth grew up and claimed her own life as a normal and independent adult. I hung onto the raft, survived the storms and enjoyed the calm periods. I swallowed my truth, thinking time was on my side. Well, now I realise time was not on my side. Time worked against me. The longer truth is hidden, the longer fraud rules, the more the damage done.

Is it too late for the truth to be retrieved, to be revealed, to be understood, to have influence? Tragically, I sense Elizabeth is lost to truth, inside the cocoon of the obsession.

Throughout this crisis, Niki had the courage of her convictions to take whatever action she thought necessary to defend her paradigm. She spoke her truth freely with me, with family, with friends, with therapists, and especially with Elizabeth. From Niki's perspective, she was crusading for Elizabeth's wellbeing.

I didn't have the same courage. I did not speak my truth freely with Niki, with family, with friends, or with therapists. Especially, I did not speak my truth freely with Elizabeth. And I did not seek therapists to vindicate my beliefs. To do any of this would have meant attacking Niki, crucifying her on the altar of her obsession. And that would have shattered my family.

I'm faced with the same dilemma again, probably for the last time.

thirty seven

Back Into The Fray

September – November 2006

I return home in early September intent to try to make my marriage work. To find a way to engage with Niki that is supportive and loving, but acknowledges our different paradigms regarding Elizabeth. I'm not sure this lofty goal is achievable, but I want to try.

I visit my GP, Graham, who prescribes an antidepressant and books me into therapy with Jodie, a clinical psychologist. Jodie's job is to treat my pathological avoidance.

Elizabeth moves on from Bravehearts to therapy with a private counsellor, Michele, and continues study toward high school graduation. Jenny continues at Bunbury Cathedral Grammar, happy to be back in the rhythm of her boarding school life.

After a month of therapy with Michele, Elizabeth requests Niki and I attend a session with her. Somewhere in her fifties, Michele looks like a gypsy therapist; bangled forearms and flowing white gown. She seems confident and experienced, with a quick intellect and the courage to stand up to Niki. She praises Elizabeth as a wonderful girl with a keen mind. When Niki tries to paint Elizabeth as handicapped by sexual abuse, Michele disagrees. 'Elizabeth's okay,' Michele says. 'She has all the usual teenage issues, and we'll never know what happened to her when she was two years old.'

During the session, Elizabeth raises a number of resentments she feels toward me. She talks in an honest way, and I don't feel under attack. She mentions the episode of my crying with her, and how much it upset her. Elizabeth also feels I've grown apart from her. 'Dad, you talk to the dogs more than you talk to me.' She also says she has self-harming urges. 'Dad, where do you think they come from?'

I assure Elizabeth I love her. I agree I didn't handle myself at all well during the crying episode. I say my dog-talk is a nervous reaction at not knowing how welcome I am in my own home. And I suggest, 'Hurting yourself would be a distraction from bad feelings, but, Elizabeth, I don't know for sure.'

During the session, Niki challenges Michele on numerous points of therapeutic interpretation, which Michele handles tactfully, standing her ground. After the session, Niki says, 'Michele just doesn't get it about Elizabeth's sexual abuse. I need to make sure she's read Veronica's letter.'

Elizabeth and I become close again. We resume our habit of humorous banter. We debate movie plots and news stories. We take farm walks. I ferry her to town and to her friends. She hugs me, and I treasure each hug.

Jenny's also happy, boarding at Bunbury Cathedral Grammar. I sense she feels like a visitor when she returns home. And Niki now devotes more attention to her: cooks her breakfasts, takes her on drives and, occasionally, even to the school bus stop early Monday morning.

What doesn't recover is the love between Niki and me. She feels vindicated. 'Richard, I was right about Elizabeth's sexual abuse. Her dreams have revealed the truth. All the therapists not agreeing with me dented my confidence. But now I've regained my confidence. So watch out!'

I receive long lectures about my betrayal for not supporting Niki, for not believing her, for sabotaging her with the therapists. I'm constantly reminded of my flaws and failures as a husband and a father. These lectures conclude with Niki wondering why I don't apologise to her. Why I don't beg for her forgiveness. Why I don't praise her. 'Richard, if our marriage is to work, we have to resolve this. I pray that one day you'll come home from therapy and say, "Oh, my God! Niki! Now I understand how right you were and how wrong I was. I am so sorry." And tell me how amazing my perceptions were and fall at my feet and tell me how wonderful I am. And then beg on your knees for my forgiveness.'

I didn't think I'd ever hear another person actually speak like this. Maybe in the movies – in some psychodrama thriller – but not for real. I stay calm. I reassure Niki I'm working hard on myself in therapy, a veiled promise that, maybe soon, I'll wake up to the errors of my ways. But that's a lie to avoid the final confrontation and end the façade.

Then one morning during a workshop coffee break, Niki walks to the side of the dining room table to announce, 'Richard, I hate being naked around you. I hate the way you put your arm around me. I hate your betrayal. I hate your sabotaging. I hate your lack of trust in my insights. I want no further intimacy with you until you beg for my forgiveness. And that I know you really mean it!'

I'm speechless. It feels like the final curtain fall of a long and painful drama. Niki has just extinguished whatever hope I had we might rebuild our marriage. We had no intimacy in our marriage anyway, for almost years at a time. Niki has just announced our marriage is dead.

'Richard, you don't have to agree with me,' she says.

Not agree with what? Her list of hates? I revert to my old mainstay of avoidance cloaked in calm and logic. 'Niki, our focus for the next year should be on the girls, on being here for them. They'll soon have finished high school and flown the coop. Let's focus on holding the family together for them.'

Niki agrees, and demands a family meeting to tell the girls our plan. 'And when we talk with the girls,' she says, 'there must be no reference to me being the problem. The girls must be told that you are the problem, that it's your depression causing our marriage problems.'

Then Niki withdraws. Her days are spent watching television or on the phone with her mother and sister in America. She tells them she wishes she was back with them, in America, and complains about my mental illnesses. 'Mamma, I think Richard has multiple personality disorder as well as depression.' She hides in her art room to avoid visitors. Her church friends call me privately, asking if they've done something to offend her. If we're invited out, Niki refuses to leave Elizabeth home alone.

It's Niki's turn to be depressed. And angry. Angry that I don't praise her, tell her she was right, and beg for her forgiveness. Angry that Australia doesn't celebrate Christmas properly, 'like they do in America'. Angry with Margaret River because, 'It's poverty-stricken and everyone's depressed.'

Niki also researches options for in-house, institutional abuse therapy for Elizabeth. One option is Mayumarri, an organisation founded in New South Wales by Liz Mullinar, who recovered memories of sexual abuse by her grandfather. I don't want Elizabeth attending in-house therapy with Mayumarri if it's run by nut jobs, so tell Niki I'll test-run the organisation myself. Niki agrees.

A week-long Mayumarri retreat in November provides insight into the neurology of childhood trauma and the impact of trauma on anxiety and avoidance. They are well-intentioned people working in the complex arena of childhood abuse and childhood memories of abuse.

This retreat complements my therapy with Jodie, which is mostly about my learning to be assertive. Which, I'm sure, wouldn't go down too well with Niki, so I don't discuss my therapy with her. Which, according to Jodie, I have the right not to do. Working with Jodie I'm surprised to learn what my rights are. She gives me a list of my rights and tells me, 'These are only some of your rights, you have lots more':

> You have the right to express your feelings, opinions and beliefs. To make choices and accept responsibility for them. To say 'yes' and 'no', without explanation or apology. To change your mind. To say, 'I don't understand'. To make reasonable requests of others. To set your own priorities. To make mistakes, and feel comfortable admitting to them. To be illogical in making decisions. To say, 'I don't care'. To be cheerful or miserable. To decline responsibility for other people's problems. To provide for your own safety and happiness and fulfilment. To spoil yourself and do something just for you. To rest and relax.

When I first read Jodie's list of rights, I wonder why I hadn't been told all this before.

Friday November 29, 2006

Today, Niki's angrier than usual. 'Richard, you're not sharing what's happening for you in therapy. Don't you know I can help you? Why don't you communicate with me?'

Last August, when I told Elizabeth I believed she was contaminated by Niki about sexual abuse – I avoided the word 'brainwashed' – Niki's response was, 'I cannot trust you,' followed by the threat of divorce. By my ledger, that adds up to about fourteen years of brainwashing dialogue by Niki, and about five minutes of honesty by me. I tolerated Niki's fourteen years of obsessive brainwashing to preserve our family. My five minutes of honesty earned me a divorce threat. And Niki wonders why I don't communicate with her.

Tuesday December 5, 2006

Today we have visitors who compliment me on my work with the local volunteer bushfire brigade. After they leave, Niki rages, 'I just want to get on a plane and go back to where I'm appreciated. Where I am known as someone capable. Where people trust my opinions. If I could just get on a plane, I would just go home today. All this attention on you! What about me?! What about my incredible efforts with Elizabeth after her sexual abuse?!'

Tonight the girls and I lay on sleeping swags in front of our house, looking up at a clear, moonless, star-filled sky. We talk and joke and sing and look for satellites and shooting stars. It's wonderful. They sleep under the stars.

Wednesday December 27, 2006

Late this evening, Elizabeth and I are alone in the living room. Looking sad, she says, 'Dad, I had a bad day.' When I ask her to tell me about it, the surface issue is, 'All my girlfriends have boyfriends.' She feels alone and unloved. We talk about the exquisitely painful task of being a teenager, how love and attraction can work differently for boys and girls, how we invite love by being loving, and sometimes all it takes is a smile. That chasing after something can drive it away.

Then comes the underlying issue, 'Dad, I don't feel beautiful. Boys want the slim girl. I know I haven't helped myself by gaining weight. I've done this because of sexual abuse. It's textbook stuff. You gain weight to project a non-sexual image. I've been reading about it.'

How sad. This is all so unnecessary. Elizabeth has swum upstream, as hard as she possibly can, almost all her life. Niki has built one surging rapid after another for her to swim through. Now she struggles through another. What could have been, what should have been, a wonderful life journey for this gifted and beautiful girl, is an endless upstream struggle. Niki has stolen a normal young life from Elizabeth. And like the millions of crimes of dysfunction committed against children, this theft, too, will go unpunished.

Sunday December 31, 2006

Today Niki suggests we take up Buddhism together. I'm happy for Niki to become a Buddhist, but I'm not interested. Then she says she wants to devote the rest of her life to writing 'guides for living', starting with a book about crises in marriage. 'Richard, we can work on my book together. We can share how we overcame adversity with my counselling and therapy insights regarding Elizabeth's sexual abuse.'

I wonder – a bestseller?

Later, we watch the sun set on 2006 on the north side of Redgate Beach. A family of five walk past in the afterglow of sunset: parents, a son and two daughters. I recognise Alex, Jenny's current beau. An instant later Jenny lets out the sweetest 'Oh hi!' and skips to Alex to give him a hug. A wonderful, natural gesture. I introduce myself to Alex's parents and engage in conversation. Niki joins us and immediately lists her illnesses: chronic fatigue syndrome, fibromyalgia, allergies and on and on, and why her illnesses make her a victim, unable to live her life.

Alex's parents listen patiently.

thirty eight

India

January 2007

Over the years I've entertained the girls with stories about my three months backpacking around India, at twenty-one years of age, in 1970–1971. At the end of each story I'd announce, 'Girls, one day I'll take you to India.' Well, that day has come – we're off for an Indian adventure.

India is profoundly alive – the squeeze of humanity makes the juice of life flow. In spite of hardship, people try to live joyfully. Maybe it's the richness of their lives, the raw intensity of taste and smell and colour and noise and close human contact. Or maybe it's their genius for acceptance.

We start in Kolkata and tour the city, beginning and ending at Howrah Bridge – to watch the morning tide of humanity wash into the city, and then ebb away at dusk. We're shuffled and jostled, chewed up and swallowed, added to the masticated mass of humanity that thrives and swells by the gravitational pull of twenty million people.

We travel by first-class sleeper train, first from Kolkata to Varanasi. The people we meet are delightful and helpful. The experience of morning 'chai-chai-chai' and 'coffee-coffee-coffee' wallahs patrolling train corridors is unforgettable.

Sunday January 7, 2007

Varanasi is an unholy mess of a city, yet still very holy. At Sarnath, to the north, Buddha gave his first sermon in about 550BC. Varanasi's old city merges with the ghats along the Ganges. Steps lead down to the river where Hindus bathe or are cremated. As we walk to the river, we pass a fabric store, in which a large cow lies peacefully against an inside counter.

We stay at the palatial Taj Ganges hotel. Today, Niki tells me she feels a spiritual awakening. 'Richard, I'm excited to come back to India and go deeper. And Elizabeth would love to come back to live and study at the Hindu university in Varanasi.'

This afternoon, we walk along crowded, garbage-strewn, smelly, pot-holed pavements outside the gates of our five-star hotel, deafened by the din of cars, motorcycles and people on bicycles. Past roadside stalls, beggars, pedlars and poverty. Elizabeth wants to go back inside the hotel. How would she cope boarding alone in the chaos and poverty at the university in Varanasi? Is Niki on drugs?

She ups the ante. 'Richard, I now want to live in India. I want to be cremated and have my ashes scattered in the Ganges. I'll write my book, *The Millennium Matrix*, about humanity living together in peace. We could be rich if I write my book. The girls can help me write my book. You can help me write my book. We'll have money to come back, become Hindu and help the poor people.'

I realise Niki is on drugs. She's chomping prescription doses of codeine.

Sunday January 14, 2007

We're now in Dharamsala, home in exile of the Dalai Lama. Upper Dharamsala is perched on a mountaintop. What started as a sanctuary for the Dalai Lama has become the Tibetan government in exile, with library, museum, university and medical centre, along with markets, trinket shops, tourist hotels and meditation retreats. The city has fresh air, beautiful scenery and lots of red-robed Buddhist monks. We visit shrines, temples, the university, and watch the Dalai Lama pass by in a motorcade.

Unfortunately, Niki has progressed from happy high to hypochondria. Hour after hour I hear about her illnesses and allergies and fatigue and back problems and stomach problems and wheat intolerance, and, and … And I'm hypnotised. But if I say anything to indicate I haven't paid attention, the lecture starts over. 'You don't understand and appreciate my health problems. It's not like I want health problems!' I'm on alert.

Thursday January 18, 2007

Today's a doozy. In the afternoon it's The Walk Catastrophe. Usually the girls and I walk through the surrounding hills while Niki rests. This afternoon they want Niki to 'come and see the scenery'. After one strenuous hill she rages, "I might have a heart attack! You know I have asthma and allergies. Richard, I might have a chronic fatigue relapse.'"

In the evening it's The Meal Catastrophe. There's nothing on the menu she's not allergic to. She can't tolerate gluten, tea, red meat and salicylates – whatever the heck they are. Whatever I suggest on the menu, she rages, 'Don't you know I'm allergic to that too! The allergist in America was amazed at how allergic I am. My allergist in Australia says I have no allergies. The allergy doctors in Australia are stupid!'

After dinner it's 'The Spiritual Catastrophe'. Over the last few evenings I've taught the girls to play poker, while I enjoy a whisky and water. Jenny tries a sip and tells me, 'Dad, this tastes like an old man's musty coat.' Great description, Jenny. Then Elizabeth and I begin bantering, playing with words – rhyming Indian names and imitating the Indian-English accent. We randomly select names like Swami Rama. It's wordplay.

Niki thinks we're insulting Indian spirituality and is angry at me for being disrespectful. 'Niki, time out,' I say. 'We're not making fun of spiritual leaders, just rhyming words.'

'And I'm getting my own back at Indian men who leer at me,' Elizabeth adds.

Then, finally, it's The Toilet Catastrophe. Niki retreats to the bathroom with an upset tummy, to significant acoustic effect. I had the same problem a few nights ago, which I'd laughed about. Tonight, I make the mistake of joking about operatic intestines, and ask the girls, 'Who's going to conduct this time?'

Unfortunately, Niki hears my joke and comes out of the toilet swinging verbal punches. 'You are rude and hurtful! How could you say such a thing!' I apologise, but Niki's fuse is lit. 'You have never supported me spiritually or supported the girls spiritually. Science might be all very well and good, but spirituality is just as important, and you have not supported the girls' spiritual growth.' Niki's on a roll. 'And Australian humour is disgusting and hurtful. I hate Australian humour. And I hate

Australian cartoons in Australian newspapers.'

'Niki,' I interrupt. 'Wait a minute, Australians are down-to-earth. It's an Australian cultural characteristic to be self-deprecating.'

To my surprise, Elizabeth and Jenny jump into the conversation. 'Mom, we enjoy the friendly, sarcastic banter at school.'

'Well, I'm an American!' Niki shouts, 'and I hate that type of humour. And I won't stand for it. It's a form of bullying. And I hate your sister's sense of humour.' Then starts weeping. 'And Richard, you just paint me as a hysterical, neurotic mother.'

I've been dobbed in. Yesterday, when Elizabeth and I walked along a narrow track on a steep hillside, along with other tourists, I foolishly said, 'Mum would be nervous here.' Niki constantly complains about her fear of heights and fear of steep slopes.

'My worrying about the girls is good!' Niki shouts. 'Where were you when Elizabeth was being sexually abused? You were obviously not worrying enough, were you? What sort of protecting father were you to let that happen? Well, I'm not going to put up with your put-downs any longer, so you better get your act together. I hope your therapist does a good job of fixing you.'

I chew on my tongue. This trip is for the girls. I won't spoil it by reacting. I manage to keep my cool. But now Elizabeth's upset. 'You and Mom always argue through me. You've done this all my life!' She wants to go to her room, so Niki and Elizabeth disappear for an hour.

Jenny wants to stay with me and talk about philosophy. She seems oblivious to the drama that just unfolded in front of her. Maybe she's learned to zone out when Niki goes on about sexual abuse? Or maybe she doesn't want to listen to Niki and Elizabeth talk for an hour about sexual abuse and would rather spend time with her dad.

When Niki finally returns, it's all sweetness and light.

Monday January 22, 2007

Our last morning in India and we're in Delhi – in the lobby of a luxury hotel, waiting for a taxi to the airport. I'm tired, eyes closed, head back on a comfortable sofa. Niki and the girls sit in separate chairs, some distance away. I overhear Niki say, 'Your father's on probation. I wish he wasn't so cute. It would be easier to leave him if he doesn't get himself worked out.'

Elizabeth's silent. Niki and Elizabeth have no doubt discussed returning to America. But, bless her, Jenny reacts, shocked and surprised, with, 'What do you mean?!' Niki ignores her.

On our flight back to Australia, Niki tells me she wants to write 'books about the world's spiritual leaders, maybe for children, maybe for fathers, because, you know, fathers need so much help. They're doing such a poor job.' She hopes that after I've recovered, 'We can write these books together. Will you help me write my books? We can use the experience of Elizabeth's abuse and our recovery to show how families can thrive spiritually.'

Niki wants to rebuild the bridge back to me, using the only materials her mind can grasp: childhood abuse and spirituality. I feel sad because, from my side of the ravine, the bridge is broken beyond repair.

thirty nine

On Borrowed Time

Friday February 2, 2007

Niki's in torment. Vindicated about Elizabeth's sexual abuse, she's desperate for me to fix myself so I can appreciate the error of my ways. But it's not happening. I don't get better. I don't beg for her forgiveness. I don't praise her. I just keep the peace. I deflect her jibes and slingshots. I walk on hot coals and breathe in burning embers. I want desperately for the girls to finish high school in Australia. If they do that, there's a chance they will stay here for university studies. That's my hope. That's my plan. But I wonder when Niki's patience will run out.

Mine too. After some of Niki's tirades about all my failures, I stand on the edge of the precipice and consider stepping out into the void. 'Niki, it's not about me, it's about you, because you are nuts.' Armageddon. And the end of my hopes and plans. I always step back from the precipice.

Saturday February 3, 2007

Tonight I taxi Elizabeth home from a party. She's inebriated and pours out her drunken soul. She hates her life because she doesn't have a boyfriend. 'The guy I like leaves for uni in three weeks and isn't interested in romance. He let me down in the nicest way. If I lived in Arkansas, I'd have a boyfriend. In Margaret River, the guys just want skinny girls.'

It must be awful being a teenage girl who doesn't feel attractive to boys. I tell her she's a beautiful, smart, interesting, amazing girl. But all the crap in her head about sexual abuse, on top of the weight she carries, has her feeling down on herself. One day I hope she realises how beautiful she is.

Friday February 9, 2007

Niki's favourite television program is *Law & Order*. There's now a *Law & Order* re-run marathon on Foxtel and she sits glued to the TV, day and night. Diet Coke in one hand, popcorn in the other. Tonight I sit with Niki to watch an episode. Turns out it's about sexual abuse. A father has sexually abused his teenage daughter. Niki's rapt. But wait, there's more. The daughter recovers memories of her father raping her, along with all manner of ghastly ritual abuse. Freshen up my Diet Coke. Pass the popcorn.

Then her Coke bubble bursts. The girl is medically examined. There's no evidence of physical trauma and she's a virgin. Oh no! Her therapist had implanted false memories through suggestive recovered memory therapy, and the girl 'remembered' things that never happened. The father is innocent. The therapist is guilty. Niki chokes on her popcorn.

When the program ends I sit quietly and wait curiously for Niki's response. 'Gee, wasn't that interesting,' she says, with an excruciating grimace.

Thursday February 22, 2007

Niki wants a showdown. She wants to return to her mother and sister in America. She would prefer that I said or did something to precipitate the split, but I don't buy into her torment. I've done my torment. I'm calm and cooperative. This morning we have to run an errand together. Niki suggests coffee. Then it starts. 'Why do we stay married? How could I have been so wrong about you? Haven't I spent our marriage showing you how much I love you?'

Legitimate questions, but the only answer allowed is, 'Yes, Niki, you're right and I'm wrong, about everything.'

'I just want the truth on the table,' Niki goes on. 'If we lay our cards on the table, we can grow and move on. I know I'll cope. Why are you afraid to share your truth with me?'

Another legitimate question. But if I lay my cards on the table, Niki will leave with Elizabeth for Arkansas. And there might be fireworks. I still fear a high-voltage, raging fight. So I sit here, silent and frustrated, faced with irreconcilable options: tell my truth, lose my children and cope with anger, or withhold my truth and cope with tirades.

As I contemplate this option, Niki stares at me, intently, then blurts out, 'Richard, you have multiple personality disorder! You have this high-functioning adult who attracts praise and responsibility and this frightened, abused boy who is shut down and can't function. I can only go forward in our marriage on the basis that you have multiple personality disorder. I must be considered blameless in all this. I will not accept any accusation of having done anything wrong.' Niki's excitement grows. 'Richard, I've got you figured out. You're mentally ill!'

It worked, I'm angry. 'Niki, last August was a break point for me,' I say bluntly. 'When I spoke my truth, your immediate response was divorce. The truth I expressed was reflected back as, "You're sabotaging me." The stress of going back into the sexual abuse nightmare and your threat to leave with the girls was huge. It brought back the conflict trauma of 1992. I couldn't go through that again.'

Niki pounces. 'There you go again, Richard, playing the victim. You always portray me as the aggressor and you as the victim. Well, I won't stand for that anymore. Poor Elizabeth suffered terrible sexual abuse. But all through our marriage you manoeuvred against me with the girls, and you sabotaged me with the therapists. You poisoned them against me.'

The irony is amazing. Niki has forever vocally portrayed herself as the sick, tired, hard-done-by victim of dumb doctors, lousy therapists and me. Leaning forward across the table, I growl, 'Niki, that's just not true. I've never tried to poison the therapists or the girls against you. The one and only time I spoke with Elizabeth about my beliefs was last August.'

'Yes!' Niki shoots back, 'and Elizabeth said you told her you don't love her mother and only stayed with me because of Elizabeth and Jenny. This traumatised her.'

'Niki,' I reply, 'I don't remember saying that.'

'Richard, Elizabeth does not lie. You must have said that.' Then she gets on a roll. 'Throughout our marriage you have belittled and ridiculed me. Our Dharamsala evening drove home how abusive you are. You try to form an alliance with the girls to exclude me. To sabotage me!'

Niki conjuring up the Dharamsala fiasco riles me. 'Wait a minute!' I say angrily and crisply. 'I belittled you in Dharamsala? Niki, you bagged me. My sense of humour was crap. I had not protected my own daughter from sexual abuse. What sort of father was I to allow that to happen? I was a failed father.'

As I say this, I begin to feel light, agile, articulate, in control, unafraid. I don't care how Niki reacts. A tirade of my own is on the tip of my tongue: Niki, you are a bully and a hysteric. The whole ritual abuse saga was total bullshit. You abused the crap out of Elizabeth. She remembers images and stories of abuse that you planted into her memory from three years of age. I will never get down on my knees and beg you for forgiveness. I will never do that.

My tirade is stillborn. As I'm about to unleash, Niki jumps up from her chair. 'I have to leave,' she says, and goes. Then she flips. For the rest of the day she's gushy, friendly and pleasant. She cooks an amazing dinner, and compliments me, with 'okay, babe' this and 'okay, babe' that.

I try to figure this out. I think my short burst of honest feedback told Niki she doesn't need any more of my cards on the table. She saw enough cards. She now knows I'll never be fixed by therapy. She knows I'll never acknowledge she was right and beg for her forgiveness. She knows we've reached the end of the road together.

Niki's greatest fear is the threat that I, or a therapist, or any credible entity, will accuse her of being a bad mother and say her obsession is a fantasy. If her obsession is threatened, she bolts. She'll bolt now. She'll keep the peace and plan her exit.

Had I agreed with Niki's truth and begged her forgiveness, my marriage could have continued along the yellow brick road to Oz, and Elizabeth and Jenny could have stayed in Australia, where their lives would likely be less corrupted by obsession. But I'm worn out. Like Alice in Wonderland, 'I don't want to go among mad people.'

fourty

Divorce and Departure

Saturday March 3, 2007

A surreal calm lasts for a week before Niki bolts, her plans in place. 'Richard, I'm divorcing you and returning to Arkansas,' she announces today, in front of the girls. 'I need the emotional support of my mother and my sister.' Then follows a cooperative family discussion. As easy as that.

Niki will leave in December, as soon as the school year ends. Elizabeth, of course, knew the plan, but not so Jenny, who says, 'If I finish Year 11 here, I want to finish Year 12 here as well.' Niki grimaces.

Elizabeth, on the other hand, can't wait to leave. I tell her I'm glad she'll finish high school here. 'Well, I'm depressed about it,' she replies. 'I want to start a new social life in America.'

Sunday March 4, 2007

Niki and I respect each other's privacy. I continue with farm work and household chores, finances and paperwork, Niki the evening cooking and laundry. We occupy different parts of our large house. Niki tells the girls to, 'Respect Dad's space and do your best over the year ahead.' It's 'Team Girls' helping 'Crippled Dad'. Niki is the purveyor of wisdom and kindness.

Jenny's devastated. She would love to keep living her wonderful life at her boarding school and with her friends in Bunbury. All her life she's had to navigate around the storm of The Family Drama. She asks me, 'Dad, could you move into the old cottage to recover from your illness, and then, maybe, you'll be acceptable to Mom? Are you for sure getting a divorce?'

Niki focuses even more attention onto Jenny. This morning she rises early, prepares a pancake mix, and when Jenny gets up, she 'ooohhs' and 'aaahhs' over her, shows her the mix, and suggests they make pancakes together. I couldn't do that with a straight face. Surely Jenny sees through this? Do I get into a parental tug of war? That would feel abusive.

Thursday March 8, 2007

Niki's frenetic, rushing hither and thither, talking loudly and effusively to all and sundry. When someone calls, she answers with an exaggerated, 'Oooooohhh! Hiiiiiiiiiiiiii!' She's energised by the thought of returning to her mother and sister. This plan can't last.

Saturday March 10, 2007

The plan lasts a week. Today Niki tells me, 'Richard, I was only staying until year-end because I thought it would take that long to get a divorce. But once a financial settlement's reached, we can leave, and then the girls can get their American lives up and running.'

A local lawyer, Mary Wylie, gave Niki the good news. She goes on, 'I have no interest to retain any assets in Australia. I want a clean, final financial settlement, with no maintenance. I'll pay for the girls' education in America.' Niki states her dollar estimate of our total assets, and asks for a cash settlement of half. 'Mary said she could get me more, but I'll accept half.'

Our substantial assets include investments I accumulated during twenty years of work prior to our marriage, and a recent inheritance. But I don't argue. All I'm worried about is Jenny. 'Niki,' I reply, 'if she wants, Jenny must be able to finish her schooling in Bunbury. I'll pay.'

'I'm the girls' primary caregiver!' Niki shouts. 'The three of us are a natural unit. I do all the looking after of the girls. It's right and proper that we stay together. I will not leave Jenny behind. A court always awards custody to the mother.'

'Niki,' I reply, calmly, 'I'll agree to whatever Jenny decides. But if she wants to stay in Australia, I'm sure a custody court will consent to her wishes.'

Niki disagrees. 'My lawyer said a court always awards custody to the mother. And there are great high schools in Arkansas.'

'Niki, we have to respect Jenny's wishes.'

We're seated at the dining table. Niki's posture shifts to battle mode. Shoulders back, chin up, lips pursed, she rapid-fire taps her right forefinger on the tabletop. Then jabs her right forefinger at me, spouting another blast of burning embers. 'You're just twisting the issue to make me look inflexible. You never act in the girls' interests. You're selfish. You never understand where I'm coming from. I always act as the girls' protector. You've never understood that. You've never taken on the role of protector. Look how you failed Elizabeth. You let her get abused! You always just attack me and put pressure on the girls to think I'm wrong. You just sabotage me. That's why we're getting a divorce. You never support me!'

This exchange is our dilemma in a nutshell. If I express a different opinion, if I disagree with Niki, then I'm not protecting the girls and I'm attacking her. I calmly repeat my statement. 'Niki, Jenny should decide where she wants to live.'

* * *

Later this afternoon, I pick up a notepad from the dining table and open to a random page. It's Elizabeth's journal. I scan some of the pages and learn how awful I am. I'm an invalid who crumples when she gives me the silent treatment. I wasn't there for her when she was sexually abused. I manipulated the therapists to sabotage her mother. Like I'm probably manipulating my own therapist right now.

Elizabeth paraphrases Niki's mantra and writes of things impossible for her to have any memory of. Her writing is a replayed mental tape recording of Niki's brainwashing. It's Elizabeth writing, but Niki talking. As I scan the pages, I sense evil hovering.

As Elizabeth grew up, I tried to instil reason. I hoped she would emerge as a normal adult on the other side of Niki's obsession. I failed. Elizabeth's now fully invested in Niki's paradigm as a victim. She went through the obsession meat grinder, so she has a right to be angry and confused. I feel no less love for her. I love Elizabeth with all my heart. But after glancing at her written words I feel exhausted. Further struggle feels pointless. Hand me the surrender document to sign. The struggle is over for me, for now.

This afternoon, Niki takes Jenny to the movies in Busselton, a town fifty kilometres north of Margaret River. The sales pitch continues. Immediately after they return, Jenny tells me, 'Dad, I've decided to move to America with Mom.'

With smug condescension, Niki says, 'I lobbied Jenny to come to America. Richard, you have the same right to express your opinions and lobby for your viewpoint. I told Jenny she can be domiciled in either America or Australia, that it's her choice.' As Niki speaks, I sense evil hovering, again.

Sunday March 11, 2007

This morning, Elizabeth returns from an overnight party and complains, 'Dad, it was a crap party – some of the group have already left for uni, so it's just not the same anymore. I want to leave now for Arkansas, to make new friends and build a new social life.'

I'm surprised she feels the need to ask me. 'Elizabeth, go and start your life in America,' I reply. Then, as an afterthought, I add, 'Maybe try to get the paperwork done so you can go straight into university in August, rather than repeating your final year of high school?'

Elizabeth's excited by that prospect and perks up. Then Jenny says, 'I want to go too!' Niki has given her glowing accounts of great high schools in Arkansas. So now, Elizabeth flies out in a week or so, and Niki and Jenny will leave in April. I'm numb.

Tuesday March 13, 2007

The house is half packed and Niki talks constantly about 'getting the show on the road' and 'cosmic rhythms' and 'being vindicated.' These outbursts usually end with the declaration that, 'I'm never again, ever again, giving in to anyone else regarding my opinions. When I get home, I'm never going to be pushed around again. People just better watch out!' She's also bubbly and gushy and constantly proclaims, 'Isn't life great? Isn't it fabulous we're going home? This is going to make everything so great. Isn't life wonderful!'

I think Niki's on drugs again. I want some.

Sunday March 25, 2007

Elizabeth's less angry, and even speaks nicely to me. But Jenny's world has collapsed. The Family Drama has crushed her. She told me she burst into torrents of grief with her friends on a recent school excursion, and that her friends comforted her. I'll miss her deeply. I think she's making an enormous mistake. But, of course, I don't tell her that.

Tuesday March 27, 2007

Elizabeth flies out late this evening: Perth–Tokyo–Dallas–Tulsa. Niki asks her, 'Is it okay for Dad to drive you to the airport? I'm busy packing.' So I drive her to Perth – our last road trip.

It's nice to have this time alone with Elizabeth. I've imagined what I might say in a farewell conversation, but nothing goes to script. We don't talk about The Family Drama. We just talk. We've always had easy conversations, Elizabeth and I. Our sense of humour is similar and we blabber on effortlessly about politics, history, movies and books – whatever comes to mind. She has a sparkling intellect and comes up with wonderfully original, insightful and humorous thoughts.

We talk about Australian versus American vegetation, her love of lush green American oak trees and how it took her ages to get used to the harsher Australian eucalypts, how she feels half-American and her hope of finally getting a social life, new friends, hopefully a boyfriend. I tell her I hope with all my heart it works out well for her. That being half-Australian will be attractive to Americans, who are so welcoming of foreigners, especially Australians. At least that was my experience.

In Perth, I drive past 9 Donar Street, the house I grew up in. My house of horrors looks old and tired. Then we collect Jarrad, Elizabeth's close high school friend, and go for dinner at Bibik Chan's, a restaurant with a lot of wonderful family memories. It was close by our Perth house, and we ate there often when the girls were young. Jarrad has just started a geoscience degree at the University of Western Australia. A nice young man. I understand why Elizabeth likes him.

We take Jarrad home, then head to the airport. Elizabeth wants to talk about boys. She's happy she met a few nice boys, like Fred and Jarrad. I give her some fatherly advice about self-respect, and being respected. I lavish praise on her. 'Elizabeth, you look really beautiful.' She likes hearing that. 'Do I really?' she asks with the hint she'd like to hear me say it again. So I repeat the compliment, even more enthusiastically.

Then I mention an incident that occurred when I flew out of Durban, in December 1972. I was leaving South Africa for Morocco to commence geological fieldwork for my PhD studies. I'd said goodbye to my family, and half turned to walk toward the plane, when my father burst out crying. It shocked and upset me. He rarely showed strong emotion. I tell Elizabeth, 'I won't do that to you.'

'But how do you feel?' Elizabeth asks.

'Very sad, at times,' I reply. 'But, today, I've thought about our good times, weekends when I took you and Jenny to parks and zoos and playgrounds, vacation road trips, our talks about homework and movies and books, afternoons at Redgate Beach. I feel butterflies. I feel sad you're leaving. But I'm happy you can get on with your life. I'm sad but hopeful. Elizabeth, I hope you remember the good times we had. All the laughs we had.'

Elizabeth then talks about returning to Australia next year, in the winter of 2008, during her American summer vacation. And promises to send me emails and photos.

We reach the airport feeling connected. She hasn't closed me out. We'll communicate and we'll see each other again. This is all I wish for. I give her headphones as a gift. She's thrilled. Then we look for a Paul Simon album, *Rhythm of the Saints*, at the airport store. We danced together to songs on this album when she was very young, usually with me carrying her – dancing for both of us. She would hold tight to my neck and scream with delight. The airport store doesn't have that particular album, but they do have a Paul Simon double album.

We hug goodbye. I tell her I love her and I'll always be her dad, always want to be a part of her life. My door will always be open. She hugs me back and says she loves me and will stay in touch. Then she turns, walks through the departure door, and doesn't look back. I watch until she disappears from view. I hope she finds what she wants from life. She has a bright mind and a brave spirit. I really love that girl, my daughter, Elizabeth.

Thursday April 5, 2007

Niki's mood has shifted from elated to stressed. Today she asks for support in the middle of a panic attack. I hold her to help calm her. And help her move boxes.

Niki also talks for hours on the phone with Elizabeth, in Arkansas. There's a drama, which I'm not to know about. Elizabeth urgently needs Niki in Arkansas. Occasionally, when I pick up the phone to make a call, Niki's already on the line with Elizabeth, who weeps. Niki tells her, 'Yes, it is a tragedy for everyone that we have to move. But because your Dad doesn't love me, and doesn't believe me about your sexual abuse, yes, we have to return to Arkansas.' Elizabeth sounds homesick.

Wednesday April 11 – Saturday April 14, 2007

My sister has flown from Cape Town to spend time with me after Niki and Jenny leave. Suzanne suffers no fool lightly. Her lifetime of work as a journalist, politician and board member of a large public entity, as well as her natural courage and intellect, make for a formidable presence. Niki's not happy when she hears Suzanne's in Australia. 'Your sister cannot come to Margaret River while I'm here,' she insists.

So Sue stays with her old school friend, Jennie (Jenny's Grade 1 teacher), who now lives in the small country town of Harvey, halfway between Perth and Margaret River. Jenny wants to see Auntie Suzanne, so we plan a three-day visit. Niki's furious. 'Why such a long visit? Jenny doesn't want to hang around with a bunch of old people for three days.'

Hello? What did Jenny do for months on end when Niki returned with the girls to Arkansas over summer holidays? But I let it slide. We spend three wonderful days with Suzanne and Jennie. Jenny has long conversations with my sister, who tells me Jenny is very sad and very confused. She can't understand what happened to her family, to her wonderful life.

Tuesday April 17, 2007

Today I drive Niki and Jenny from Margaret River to Perth for their evening flight to America. Little is said. I distract myself listening to music. There's nothing I want to say. I can't talk privately with Jenny. At the departure gate, Niki kisses me goodbye, saying, 'Thanks for the adventure. Time to move on to the next adventure.'

I hug Jenny and tell her I love her. They leave. I don't remember much. I'm numb.

Jenny has an inner beauty of ageless grace and wisdom, integrity and intelligence, along with an almost otherworldly loving and kind spirit. Jenny is special. I know she loves me and she knows I love her. We will reconnect somehow, sometime, somewhere.

Tuesday May 1, 2007

After the storm comes the clean-up. In the process of deleting documents from our family computer, I discover an audio recording made by Niki and Elizabeth during their session with a local psychic, in early 2006. Listening to snippets of dialogue feels like the discovery of infidelity, with its shock of ignorance, naivety and betrayal.

The recording paints a stark picture of enmeshment. Niki's brainwashing of Elizabeth about her abuse as a child had matured into a mutual understanding and acknowledgement, between mother and daughter, that childhood sexual abuse had occurred. This 'extramarital relationship' was a secret between themselves, or maybe shared with a few friends – and with this psychic – but not with me; the father, the husband, the unbeliever.

Friday May 11, 2007

During the last half of 2006, Elizabeth had weekly therapy sessions with Michele. As an act of closure for me, I ask to speak with her. We meet today.

Michele compliments Elizabeth. 'Whatever the truth regarding sexual abuse when she was two years old, Elizabeth was not using it as a crutch. She desperately wanted to confront it and live a normal life. Elizabeth had no memories of abuse and wasn't sure what happened, but she was sure some sort of sexual abuse had happened.' Michele says she told Elizabeth that, no matter what happened, she could still live the life she wanted.

'I didn't identify her as someone exhibiting the typical symptoms of childhood sexual abuse,' Michele tells me. 'Teenage issues seemed her main concern.'

Michele thought Niki was obsessive in her need for Elizabeth to believe she was a victim of sexual abuse. She also told Michele, 'Unless Richard agrees Elizabeth was sexually abused, I'll divorce him and return to America.' Michele told Niki she thought that was an extreme position, given Elizabeth wasn't even sure what happened – and that differences of opinion are justified and acceptable. But Niki insisted, 'I absolutely know sexual abuse happened. If Richard doesn't agree, I'm divorcing him.'

That Elizabeth sat through these discussions with Niki and Michele mirrors the journey our marriage took over the last fifteen years; Niki's sexual abuse obsession colliding with my different opinion, and Niki and Elizabeth developing a bond of belief that excluded me.

Michele thinks Elizabeth will, eventually, have to separate from Niki to build her own life, a life beyond obsession. However, at the moment, they are locked together in a partnership to protect and support each other, especially over the question of childhood abuse.

Michele recommends I do not attempt to share my beliefs with Elizabeth until she's ready to hear them. 'Elizabeth's priority is to protect Niki against threats to her obsession,' she warns. 'Only much further down the road, when Elizabeth wonders, "what really happened?" and asks your opinion, should you share your beliefs.'

Which are that Elizabeth was brainwashed from three years of age about sexual abuse, and the only abuse she really suffered were her mother's obsession and her father's failure to protect her from it.

Last Contact And Loss

May 2007 – July 2008

After an eighteen-year smorgasbord of raising children, corporate life, farm life and then a final, frantic banquet, my table is bare. I held onto the false hope that, with time, Niki's obsession would dissipate, the girls would flourish into happy and independent young women, and our family would fulfil its bright, prosperous and happy potential. My wishful thinking was not rewarded.

On the bright side, the girls share with me their American lives: school, friends, horse riding, senior prom and band practice. And Jenny sends remarkable draft manuscripts. I send Margaret River news. The vibe's good. There's no talk of The Family Drama.

In early 2008, the girls talk about a trip back to Margaret River midyear. Then Elizabeth wonders about me coming to America, and the three of us doing a road trip from Alaska to Arkansas. 'Dad, like the road trips we used to do, remember!' Then we discuss a July road trip in Western Australia. Finally, they decide to come back to Margaret River, relax and just hang out with friends.

A week after they arrive, Elizabeth's relationship with her new boyfriend in America suddenly ends. She appears in my furniture workshop, distraught. 'I've just been dumped,' she says, then leans her head onto my chest and cries. I feel sad and anxious, not sure how to comfort her. So I just hold her.

Monday July 21, 2008

This morning, in the Perth airport departure lounge, they sit either side of me, Elizabeth's head on my right shoulder, Jenny's head on my left.

They surround and embrace me. We're connected. Then they disappear down the departure ramp – jeans, sweatshirts and backpacks.

Four hours later in Margaret River, I walk through the detritus of their visit: scattered belongings and unmade beds. The sadness of the silence overwhelms me. I can't breathe. I go outside and howl. Their bedroom doors stay closed for weeks.

August 2008 – October 2009

Young adults want to walk their own pathway. They look mostly ahead, into the future, and occasionally behind, to where parents stand, watching and waving. Even though Elizabeth and Jenny are on the other side of the planet, I watch and wave.

Elizabeth completes her freshman year in May 2009, then, in July 2009, moves into an apartment near her university. We talk by phone about furniture and not being lonely. 'Dad, it's time I moved out by myself,' she says. In September 2009, her second-year studies begin and she writes, 'Dad, my apartment, classes and professors are all awesome.' I'm so happy for Elizabeth.

Tuesday October 27, 2009

Then the wheels of her life fall off. I don't know why. Today, in a long phone conversation, she says she's withdrawn from university because of anxiety, and is in therapy with someone who tells her the manner in which she arranges protective barriers around play objects indicates childhood abuse. Soon after that, all communication ends. I call and email, but no response. Jenny suggests I leave Elizabeth alone while she works herself out.

March 2010 – April 2010

In March and April 2010, I travel to Nepal with a group of volunteers to build a high-altitude hothouse in Phortse village, and then trek on to Everest Base Camp. It's an arduous and remarkable experience. As we trek through the majestic landscape, we pass hundreds of cairns, constructed stacks of stones. To make a stack of stones is a Buddhist act of worship and an offer of prayer for loved ones. At Base Camp, on the barren glacial landscape, I make my own stack of stones.

Placing stone upon stone I think about my loved ones. I think about Elizabeth's sad and difficult life. About our loss of communication. My grief overwhelms me and I release torrents of tears and snot. As if in conversation, I talk to Elizabeth. I tell her I love her. That I wish her a happy life. That I miss her. That if my not being a part of her life helps her to be happy, well, then, I have to accept that. After this catharsis of snot, tears and acceptance, I feel at peace.

Tuesday April 20, 2010

Home again from Nepal, and I email pictures of the mountains and our hothouse construction to Elizabeth and Jenny. I'm stunned when Elizabeth immediately emails back. She praises my pictures and hothouse work and asks questions about the trek. She says she has a 'snail mail' letter to send to me, and that she's progressed in therapy and would like to see me in September, when I plan to visit her and Jenny, 'if that doesn't inconvenience you too much? I would just really love to see you and talk to you … I have a lot of things to share with you, but I don't want to trigger you. So you just let me know, okay? I miss you a lot and … I love you very much.'

I've just trekked to Mount Everest. Why, I wonder, would Elizabeth worry she'll inconvenience or trigger me? But mostly, I'm excited and happy she's communicated with me, and soak up her loving correspondence. I email back expressing love and gratitude.

Thursday April 22, 2010

Then Elizabeth sends 'the scariest email I've had to write ever'. The email states her terms for a future relationship with me. Her terms are that I must believe she was sexually abused when she was a child. And I must not believe that Niki contaminated her, 'because that undermines my relationship with the one person who has truly supported my sanity my whole life'. Elizabeth says she's been through months of therapy with a very professional analyst who has no doubt Niki is not a hysterical mother. 'I don't care what the therapists you talked to said when I was little. I was split already when I was little.'

Elizabeth tells me she's been diagnosed with 'dissociative disorder not otherwise specified', and slips into alternate people, 'meaning I am no longer myself'. She says having alternate people has always been her coping mechanism, 'especially living with you. I had to be functional around you. But they weren't there because of you, they were there because I suffered abuse when I was forming my identity. No-one disputes this except you.' Elizabeth says she initially wondered if that meant I was involved in her abuse, 'but I have completely dismissed that. I do know that part of you loves me and I also know that the rest of you would never want to see a child or animal hurt.'

Elizabeth's email says she doesn't yet know all of her alternate people, but the ones she does know, don't 'trust or like you at all. Poison would like to kill you. She wants me to tell you that. They are having me write this email to protect myself. Elizabeth loves you. But the rest of us know that you are capable of great manipulation to protect yourself, and that manipulation has huge mental consequences for us.'

Elizabeth says that if I'm ready to believe her, we can talk. But if I don't believe her, then her alternate people can't trust me, 'and they demand this boundary.' She tells me I must accept she was sexually abused as a child, 'if we are ever going to have any sort of relationship. Period.'

As I read her email I try to juggle conflicting beliefs, like a circus performer with spinning clubs. One belief is that Elizabeth is my intelligent, brave, beautiful daughter, and despite her crazy childhood, she can live her own, normal life. I believe that. Another spinning club is the belief that the vortex of powerful, irrational forces spiralling around her as a child have finally pulled her from, 'Dad, I wish I was normal,' into some Arkansas carnival of craziness, down some sideshow alley of multiple personality mirrors. Her email says that, so I have to believe it.

Then one more spinning club, one more belief, hurtles down. Elizabeth has become Niki. Now it's Elizabeth who'll bolt if I challenge her belief she was abused as a child. Now it's Elizabeth who'll flee if I challenge her alternate people diagnosis. Now it's Elizabeth who'll leave if I tell her what she wrote is nutty – a brainwashed fantasy built on a foundation of obsession. The only thing I'm allowed to say is, 'Yes, Elizabeth, I believe you,' instead of, 'Yes, Niki, you're right.'

In my reply, all I say is that I love her unconditionally and I want her to be happy. I avoid disagreement and try to be supportive. As with Niki, I feel helpless, or don't have the courage, to say what I really believe. It's a hollow response, devoid of the desperate sadness I feel for my precious daughter – but it seems all I can say within her set boundaries.

Saturday May 1, 2010

My low-key response elicits a tirade of resentment from Elizabeth. She tells me I'd been triggered, I'd fragmented, I was in denial. That my reply 'had about as much substance as a watermelon. Sweet and watery, with a bunch of seeds you need to spit out.' That my saying I love her unconditionally meant that I hadn't changed my beliefs. That I didn't believe her. That I am either 'some form of multiple personality, or just a simple bullshitter'.

Elizabeth again sets her boundary requirement. 'The only reasonable way to end the issue is to LISTEN to me when I tell you what MY experience tells ME. PLEASE. TRUST me that much.' Elizabeth says I'm just treating her as a pawn in my game against Niki.

After these instructions to believe her, I'm perplexed when she then asks that I be honest with her and say 'what you think and feel … Lying to me is not protecting me.' She then says she doesn't know who she's talking to, 'Liar or insane person. Hope you can come to terms with which it is and let me know.'

I'm devastated. Elizabeth fights the demons in both our pasts. She says I have to be honest – tell her what I think and feel – not lie to her. But at the same time, I must believe she was abused when she was two years old. She feels I haven't acknowledged her reaching out to me. I desperately want to reach back to her. But to reach back, I have to push my hand through this craziness.

Monday May 3, 2010

After much soul-searching, I write back. Mostly, I just want Elizabeth to know I love her. That I'm heartbroken not having her in my life. I try to be honest. I say I desperately want to be a part of her adult life. That I'm sorry if she thought my response lacked substance. 'I felt tired for you, how exhausting it's all been – and just said I love you … I felt sad, a sense of inevitability …'

I tell Elizabeth she thinks she knows me from living with me, 'but mostly you saw a father living through an 18-year, slow motion train wreck, with you as a ground-up passenger … I am not interested, nor have I ever been interested, in using you as a pawn against Niki … I was only ever interested in you, your wellbeing – and holding the family and myself (yes I have fragility) together as the wreckage tumbled around us …'

Tuesday May 4, 2010

The next day, Elizabeth's 'snail mail' handwritten letter arrives in my postbox. It's a most beautiful letter. She tells me how much she loves and misses me. And looks forward to seeing me when I visit in September. She shares fond memories of her grandfather, my father, when he visited Australia. And she shares fond memories of her childhood with me. 'What I admire and miss you most for is the way you taught us to walk and swim and live in the Australian landscape.' She says I made her feel safe as a kid, 'by knowing everything about the environment, telling us, and sharing it and experiencing it with us.'

Then Elizabeth says, 'you deserve an explanation for the … silence thing. For a while I had this feeling of huge anger towards you, and I had to figure out why … And I did, and the end result is I figured out that I love you very much. I appreciate what you did for us as kids even though there were mistakes…'

I sense I've been slammed in the guts by a sledgehammer. I hold the writing paper she once held and want to hold her, be close to her. She's tried so hard to reach out to me, but now she probably thinks I've slapped her hand away. Not reached back.

Wednesday May 19, 2010

Today Elizabeth turns twenty-one. I email an early morning greeting. Then call her mobile phone, to wish her 'Happy birthday!' She seems disinterested and reluctant to talk.

May 2010 – July 2010

After this, all communication ceases. I agonise that Elizabeth thinks I've rejected her, and so she's given up on me.

Then a larger worry plays out, like a stuck record, going around and around in my head. In one of her emails, Elizabeth told me, 'You just gave up on me.' I know I did not save her from Niki's obsession. I was beaten, for sure, because I didn't fight hard enough or fight properly. I felt helpless. I didn't want to break up the family. But did I give up on Elizabeth? Did I stop caring? I never stopped caring. Over and over, the stuck record asks, 'Are you giving up on Elizabeth now? Are you failing her again, like you did before? Why don't you explain her childhood of brainwashing? Why don't you tell her what happened?' I agonise over these questions for months.

Monday July 26, 2010

Today, I try to tell Elizabeth what happened:

> You believe you now understand what you experienced at 2 and 3. But I don't believe you do. It was very tragic and damaging and I wrote and forecast disastrous consequences.
> But I have felt helpless throughout your life, since you were 3, to do anything about it. Which is why I was often withdrawn – depressed. And why I broke down with you on the track, at the gate. It was a blubbering expression of helplessness. I had all this 'knowledge' but had taken no action to do anything. My options were appalling. I blubbered away about how 'I had never really spoken my mind, never really asserted myself, but boy-oh-boy if I wanted to I could unleash a tirade!'
> Your emails were honest and courageous and reaching out to me. I tried to answer them best I could – the most loving way I could. But I felt set up to fail. You set your boundaries quite strongly.
> Boundaries are good and necessary ... but in terms of our relationship it's the same old story. I remain silent about what I know and believe, while you make your statements about what you now believe you experienced when you were 2 years of age and the resulting mental health consequences ...
> So I remain sitting silently, as I've done most of your life. By my own choices and inactions. I'm doing with you what I did with Niki. I'm not to disagree with you, or you might shut me out (or Niki might leave and take you and Jenny away, same story line, same ending, always

unbearable, always avoided.)

... I am in many ways shut out of your life. We have lived and experienced lots of joy and adventure together – like the Australian environment! But I believe your inner life has mostly been determined by Niki's paradigm of sexual abuse and abduction, which I believe, based on what I observed, you were brainwashed to embrace from childhood. You and mom became partners and protectors / defenders of each other and this 'interpretation' of the world around you. And I was the outside sabotaging enemy ...

I never had and still don't have, any bitterness toward anyone. I never wanted to cause anyone hurt. But I soon learnt I couldn't say certain things! Silence and calm became my approach. I felt when you were 3, and I still feel now, an immense helplessness to say anything that rocks the boat. And no good outcome ever seemed a consequence of me screaming, 'this is bullshit and very damaging for Elizabeth!!!!' ...

So instead of screaming out my feelings, you saw my periods of silence and withdrawal and eventual depression. While I was pouring my dysfunction into a 450 page diary. Which tells my story of what I saw happening to you that I believed was very abusive.

I love you Elizabeth, profoundly! And I grieve and I weep about what happened to you, and then between us, and our 'separation'. I feel as stuck now as when you were 3! ...

I love you unconditionally. You can make negative comments about me and believe whatever you like – about me, you, your life. And you can even tell me one of you wants to kill me. But I accept YOU and never stop loving you as much as I always have and always will.

Thursday August 12, 2010

Elizabeth's answer is that I have again denied her reality. She says that since I continue to say her mother brainwashed her, 'it is beyond the point of reconciliation.' She tells me she doesn't care what I think happened to her when she was two years old. And that months of good therapy prove she was not manipulated by her mum, and that she did experience 'real sexual trauma. Do you think I can somehow manipulate a forensic psychologist?'

Elizabeth's shown my letter to her psychologist and they agree that if

I visit her, it would cause a major setback – so I'm not to see her in September. 'I asked you to believe me and my feelings,' Elizabeth concludes. 'You were unable to do anything but tell me YOUR feelings … I'm done talking to you … What matters is what I think and feel, since it happened to me … The absolute only way I would be willing to talk to you again is if you believe me. Other than that, Goodbye.'

Epilogue

The diary continues, but my story ends here.

After August 2010, grief is my companion. When I see children, I see Elizabeth at that age. When I see young adults, I see Elizabeth as a young adult. Images from the past and from an imagined future, arrive uninvited. These fleeting pictures haunt me. I would have loved to be a part of her life as she matures, studies, explores and spreads her wings into adulthood. I think Elizabeth would have liked the same thing. We challenged each other's thinking, at least until we reached a bridge too far on her journey toward the abyss.

After August 2010, I begin to research publications on the abuse hysteria of the 1980s and 1990s. I want to understand what happened to my family. The last time I'd read on this topic was seventeen years ago, in Bartlesville. What I discover is an abundance of material: personal accounts of individual tragedy and family breakdown; sociological treatises on hysteria and panic about ritual abuse; investigative exposés of flawed criminal prosecutions and unjust imprisonments; clinical accounts of psychiatric and therapeutic malpractice involving bizarre and unwarranted diagnoses; memory-science studies on the tragic consequence of brainwashing and the creation of false memories; and historical studies – worthy of detective novel status – that reveal the sinister side of the multiple personality disorder and satanic ritual abuse hoaxes.

In the material I research, the explanations given for the hysteria of the 1980s and 1990s often slant toward the perspective of the explainer. Sociologists, for example, talk about seismic shifts following the demise of the single-income nuclear family – mothers entering the workforce, the rise of feminism, and so on. These shifts created the day care boom, with parenting responsibilities moved partially outside the home. This, in turn, according to some social scientists, created the guilt that fuelled hysterical parental overreactions to child abuse claims. Psychiatrists and psychologists, on the other hand, talk about flawed psychotherapy and spectacular, unwarranted diagnoses, as well as poorly understood memory science, especially regarding false memories. Then there are the studies of flawed prosecutions, with sad tales of tainted evidence and fabricated stories generated by the leading, suggestive and coercive questioning of children and adults.

All of these explanations are reasonable, and address various aspects of the abuse hysteria. My family, however, was a nuclear family – we were not dependent on day care and Niki was a full-time mother. And the therapists who worked with Elizabeth did not reach spectacular diagnoses. Stepping away from the perspective of any particular discipline, I'm inclined to see a simpler explanation. I think the root cause of the abuse hysteria catastrophe is the inclination of humans, as is our right, to behave irrationally – to be delusional, to be gullible, to be eccentric, to be idiosyncratic, to meld fact and fiction, to believe in conspiracies, to believe in crazy stuff – and, yes, to be stupid. We are all only human. I think it was ultimately this unthinking abandonment of reason and sceptical investigation that created the debacle.

Hilary Evans and Robert Bartholomew, in their 2009 book, *Outbreak! The Encyclopedia of Extraordinary Social Behavior*, say this about delusions, usually generated by hysteria:

A delusion is a false belief that is held despite evidence to the contrary … Social delusion … describes the spontaneous, temporary spread of false beliefs … such as the delusion that hundreds of thousands of American children were being stolen for the purpose of satanic rituals. Some of the most difficult [delusions] to explain are those outbreaks that occur in developed countries, where people could be expected to know better. The Satanism scare in late 20th century America, for example, flourished in an educated and well-informed society possessing unequalled information technology. It seems that these advantages, far from blocking the spread of the delusion, actually facilitated it, demonstrating that no community, however sophisticated, is safe from such a tragic misconception ... This terrible delusion ... happened to real people, often to people like you and us.

Yes, it did. It happened to my family.

Niki was not alone in falling victim to the abuse delusions of the 1980s and 1990s. Whole communities lost their grip on reality. In California, parents dug under the grounds of a preschool in search of the secret tunnels their children claimed were used by Satanists for ritual sacrifice. A judge swore in six of a woman's multiple 'alter' personalities in a rape trial after the woman claimed that, even though the sex was consensual, the man should have realised he was making love to her child 'alter', who was incapable of consent. The man was convicted. In England, children were removed from their parents' custody when one child talked about seeing ghosts in his bedroom after watching a horror movie. The examples are numerous – the hysterical and delusional abuse narrative spread far and wide.

After years of study, my journey ends where it began. What I learnt happened to my family confirms what my sense of my experience was at the time. Which was that a fraud stole my family from me; that a fraud stole my daughter from me; that a fraud stole her young life from her. The 1980s and 1990s produced a wave of abuse craziness – a tsunami of irrational and delusional abuse hysteria which swept over the cultural landscape, leaving behind injustice and tragedy on a grand scale. Millions of lives were impacted – including those of my family.

How does a casualty of this era of abuse craziness recover and reconstruct? On January 7, 2001, The New York Times Magazine published an article by Margaret Talbot that noted the passing of Peggy McMartin Buckey, a principal protagonist in the most notorious child abuse case in American legal history: The McMartin preschool abuse trial. Following criminal investigations beginning in 1983, four members of the Buckey family and three teachers at the preschool were eventually indicted on hundreds of counts of child abuse at the nursery. Questioning of the children by parents, therapists, prosecutors, social workers and police investigators elicited bizarre tales of rape, sodomy, pornography, animal torture, human sacrifice, satanic ritual abuse and other implausible, if not impossible, acts.

The trial ran for seven years and was the longest and most expensive in the history of the American legal system. When it ended in 1990, no convictions were obtained and all charges were dropped. However, the media storm of publicity surrounding the trial unleashed the nationwide (and eventually worldwide) hysteria over child abuse. As with the Buckeys and their preschool teachers, hundreds of people prosecuted in similar trials spent long periods in prison before their innocence was established. Sadly, some victims remain in prison.

In hindsight, it may seem easy for us, today, to understand how this hysteria was unleashed. However, in her 2001 article, Talbot suggests that it's probably easier for people to simply forget – rather than try to explain – why they believed in things that are now patently absurd. Talbot then suggests it's probably impossible to explain the satanic ritual abuse fixation of the 1980s, the belief that Devil-worshippers had infiltrated American day care centres and were, 'raping and sodomising children, practicing ritual sacrifice, shedding their clothes, drinking blood and eating feces, all unnoticed by parents, neighbours and the authorities.' I think Talbot has dodged the issue. I think the simple explanation is that it's hard for us to admit to our irrational delusions, to admit to being conned by hoaxes and frauds.

Talbot goes on to say that forgetting wouldn't be an option if you were one of those unfortunate individuals falsely accused and prose-cuted. Especially if you were convicted and spent years in prison. Talbot eloquently makes the point that if you were one of those unlucky souls caught up in the hysteria, for the rest of your life you would wonder what hit you, 'what cleaved your life into the before and after, the daylight and the nightmare'.

I still wonder what hit me. My life still bifurcates between the 'before and after, the daylight and the nightmare'. I'm stuck with grief.

Since 2010, I've had no contact with Elizabeth. For a while I kept sending birthday and Christmas cards with cheques, which were not cashed. I wish her life works out the way she hopes. I hold out little hope for reconciliation, at least in the near term. I do hope that she might, in her later decades, reflect on her life and ask herself whether it's reason-able to believe her dreams of abuse represent what really happened to her, or that there might be another explanation. And one day, maybe, she'll be sceptical about her forensic psychologist's diagnosis of multiple personalities – one of whom was named Poison and wanted to kill her father. Maybe she'll even be open to the possibility that there was merit in her father's belief that all of this was delusional nonsense. A father can dream.

The lessons to learn from my cautionary tale are: be sceptical, search for evidence, do not make rash assumptions, do not jump to quick conclusions, try to uncover the truth. Ask yourself if what you believe is reasonable. Have the courage to take action if what you think is happening is wrong. Protect your children against craziness. And, if need be, seek the help of a competent child protection agency, and maybe a good lawyer as well.

Don't do what I did. Nothing. Even after my daughter pleaded with me for the chance to be normal, I did nothing – until I wrote this story about a fantasy, about an obsession, about losing my children, and about doing nothing.

Postscript: Jenny's Short Story

My diary is principally a story about Niki, Elizabeth and me. However, many ask, 'What about Jenny?' This is her short story, as I understand it. One day she may tell it in her own words.

Jenny was also a casualty of the craziness. As a child, while Elizabeth plummeted into the black hole of Niki's obsession, Jenny never quite crossed the event horizon. She came perilously close at times, but escaped the therapy and questioning about sexual abuse. However, there was collateral damage, so the therapy came later.

When Elizabeth was loud, Jenny was quiet. When Elizabeth wanted attention, Jenny wanted solitude. But she observed and processed. And commanded respect. Her inner compass points naturally toward high values. She also has uncanny wisdom; past events are analysed and summarised with almost perfect recall; precise opinions are articulated. Her assessments and insights are astounding.

On her first day of school, at Loreto Primary, I walked with her into her classroom. She chose her desk, sat down, pulled her shoulders back, looked ahead and asked for knowledge. She never stopped asking. By the end of her second year at Margaret River High School she was top student in many subjects, but felt a bit odd in a school where the student vibe was generally less than academic. Jenny craved a new school – Bunbury Cathedral Grammar.

Like a tale of two homes, for Jenny, 2006 was probably the best of times and the worst of times. Her life oscillated between friends and the joy of learning at boarding school during the week, and The Family Drama at home on weekends.

Since 2006 I've spoken a few times with Jenny about my beliefs regarding her mother's obsession. These conversations were fairly brief – it felt impossible for me to portray in all its gory detail the epic scope of our family tragedy. And I didn't want to sound bitter, pillorying her mother with short, malicious and unsubstantiated statements. I referred mainly to 'a hysterical overreaction'.

In 2010, when I visited Jenny at her university in Arkansas, I gave her a digital copy of my diary up to that time. Hundreds of pages of recorded dialogue and events, as well as therapists' reports. I wanted her to have this data file should anything ever happen to me. This information documented, albeit in a barely readable format, the crazy events that I believe led to the breakup of our family.

After I gave her these diary notes, we had some robust email conversations about The Family Drama. Jenny took a neutral stance. I sensed she strived to maintain an arms-length relationship when it came to discussion of our family issues – to be fair to both parents and maintain her own sanity. I admired her stance, and our conversation on the topic soon ended. We resumed our usual relaxed banter about her life and interests.

Jenny returned on holiday to Margaret River in June–July 2011, during her US university summer break. My sister Suzanne arrived just after Jenny and they spent lazy days together, watching videos and on walks – 'a stumble in the jungle', Suzanne called them – through the bushland on my farm.

Jenny relaxed and opened her emotional doors and windows. She said she loved being back in Australia, back in Margaret River, back on the farm. She also talked to Suzanne about the pressure she felt at home, in Arkansas, because of The Family Drama. I avoided discussion of that topic. I didn't want Jenny to think a visit with Dad meant a rehash of my opinions. I could not say more than what I'd already said in my journal – which she now had. I knew Jenny walked a tightrope, carrying her love for both parents. I didn't want a puff of breath from me to unbalance her. She deserved to be safe and stable on her tightrope.

During her stay, Suzanne and my partner, Elaine, told me they thought Jenny wanted to stay in Australia. I dismissed that notion. Surely Jenny was happy studying at her university in America? It felt wrong for her to walk away, halfway through her studies. And I feared Jenny might become isolated in Margaret River. I sensed she wanted to curl up in the sanctuary of my farm and shut out the world, and I did not want that to happen.

Jenny, if I was wrong, and you did want to stay, I made a terrible mistake. I failed you and I am so sorry. I did not appreciate your need for refuge. And I would have loved, more than anything, for you to make your life in Australia.

On the last night of her wonderful visit, we celebrated with a dinner party. There was music and dancing and laughter. As the night wrapped up, after we farewelled guests and walked together, back into the house – Jenny stopped me in the entranceway. With a worried look she said, 'Dad, I'm not looking forward to going back to the camps.'

The camps? Is Jenny held hostage in camps? My mind raced. I imagined open green fields with neat rows of white tents. What is she talking about? She's boarding at university. Maybe I've had too much wine. So I asked Jenny what she meant.

'You know, Dad,' she answered, 'Mom's camp versus Dad's camp.'

Jenny was under pressure in Arkansas to join 'Mom's camp'. I told Jenny I didn't want to engage in camp warfare. I asked if that's what happens in America. 'It's okay when I'm away at college,' she answered, 'but it's pretty bad when I'm at home.'

How naive I was to believe Jenny could cope with the camp warfare in Arkansas. Jenny held out her hand to me, but I slapped it away.

Later, at the airport, when she was about to leave, she began to cry. The thought she was afraid to return to America alarmed me. If that was true, I would not let her board the plane. Jenny assured me she was only crying because she'd had such a good time during her visit, and she was sad to leave.

In June–July 2012, Jenny and I holidayed together through parts of Europe and Scandinavia. I sensed something was wrong, that storm clouds had gathered over her spirit. She had undertaken a study-abroad program at St Andrews University in Scotland, beginning in January 2012, which had not gone well. I thought she was upset about that, or just didn't enjoy travelling with her older father. I tried to reassure her that I had no academic expectations. When we parted company in London,

Jenny guided me to the tube platform for Heathrow Airport, and helped load my bags into the carriage. She would spend an extra day in London with her cousin Roy. As we faced each other in the carriage, she seemed impatient to leave. I felt desperate for her to stay. I hugged her, and asked her to promise to visit me in Australia when she finished university in 2013. She said she would.

After her return to college in September, we resumed our relaxed emails, then switched to long Skype conversations. Jenny was happy and I was relieved. This was her last year of study and her classes, professors, friends, room and roommates – all sounded great.

Everything seemed to go well during her final year of study, although she complained of poor sleep. Then, on Friday evening May 10, 2013, my phone rang. It was Jenny. It was about five in the morning her time, on the day of her final exam, and she was walking the grounds of her university, in distress. She hadn't slept for two days. She needed to talk to someone.

We spoke for hours and I tried to settle her. Accumulated anxiety had overwhelmed her, but I couldn't pinpoint the source of her anxiety. Her exam was in the afternoon. I persuaded her to forget studying and go to bed. She calmed down. I told her how much I loved her and that I wanted her to come to Australia, after university, to catch her breath. Jenny said she had two papers to finish for one class, but could travel after that. She slept, and passed her afternoon exam.

In mid-May 2013, Jenny graduated cum laude with a Classics degree. After that, she returned home to Niki and sank into depression. Her confusion over The Family Drama, and the stress of camp warfare, finally took their toll. I tried calling and emailing but Jenny had switched off. I became desperately worried.

Finally, on Friday June 21, 2013, Jenny called my sister Suzanne at her home in Cape Town. The call arrived on the morning of a work day for Suzanne, and went on for nearly two hours.

Jenny told Suzanne that since she'd returned home she was constantly badgered by Niki and Elizabeth to agree that her father was wrong in his beliefs about Niki and Elizabeth and sexual abuse. She was followed around the house, room to room, day and night, being told, 'Your father is a sick and horrible man,' and, 'Don't you see it? Don't you realise your father caused us all misery and harm by not believing Elizabeth was abused? Why don't you see that? What's wrong with you?'

Camp warfare was raging again. Poor Jenny.

Jenny asked Suzanne, 'Is Dad okay? Is he really sick like Mom and Elizabeth say?'

Suzanne replied that, 'Yes your father became depressed.' That obviously I was distressed about what happened to the family and that I loved her and Elizabeth.

Suzanne says she became exhausted by Jenny's replay of comments by her mother and sister depicting me as evil, lost her patience, and told Jenny she must, 'Get away from such a toxic, unhealthy and bullying home environment.' That it was wrong for Niki and Elizabeth to try to alienate her from her father. Suzanne offered to find work for Jenny in Cape Town – in publishing, her dream job – and said she could live with her. She pleaded with Jenny to give this serious thought.

Suzanne says it was only afterwards she realised Jenny's call was a cry for help. She had expressed fear and confusion. She sounded trapped, cornered – and as if she wanted to escape. She needed a friend, a confidante. Someone she trusted.

Suzanne felt she'd failed Jenny, who'd wanted to continue talking. She regretted terminating their conversation, to go to work. She tried repeatedly to call Jenny over the next few days. Then sent email after email offering love and support, and work in Cape Town. Jenny did not respond.

After her long conversation with Jenny, Suzanne called to alert me to Jenny's distress. I also tried calling her. Then emailed, offering to fund her expenses if she wanted to travel to Cape Town. However, all communication from Jenny ceased. I felt lost in a fog of distress.

Why was Niki doing this to Jenny? The only answer I came up with was Niki's desperate need to be right about Elizabeth's sexual abuse. And for Niki to be right in Jenny's eyes, I had to be wrong.

Finally, in mid-July 2013, Jenny talked with me on Skype. She said she was okay, but that didn't jive with her other comments. Her life comprised driving Niki and her grandmother to various medical appointments, or staying holed up at home in her bedroom. 'I feel like I have a wall keeping me blocked,' she told me. 'And like I'm slowly being covered in leaves. I feel like it would be better if I could get the wall out of the way.'

Jenny was depressed. I asked if she had suicidal thoughts.

'No,' she said, 'but I want to see someone about my wall.'

I had tickets for her to travel to Australia, in December 2013, and Jenny said she still intended to come. I felt relieved, but she had four more months to survive in Arkansas. 'Why not travel to see friends in the US?' I suggested. 'Maybe consider seeing Suzanne in Cape Town? I'll pay for your travels.' I sensed Jenny would love to do that, but she would likely be made to feel a traitor to the cause – abandoning Niki and Elizabeth and joining forces with the devil. Jenny was in a world of stuck. And disappeared again. Months of silence went by. I went onto blood pressure medication, distraught with worry.

In late November 2013, I spent two weeks in Timor-Leste on a Rotary project, out of email contact. I landed in Darwin on December 5 and switched on my iPad. Jenny was supposed to arrive in Australia the following week. A mantra played in my mind, 'Please, no email from Jenny. Please, no email from Jenny.' I had received no emails from Jenny for about eight months. An email from Jenny would mean only one thing.

There was an email from Jenny. She could not come to Australia. Niki had gone through another round of surgery and Jenny needed to help out. 'I love you, Dad, and I really want to see you … God, I can hardly bring myself to send this.'

I replied to Jenny, 'I've never played tug of war with you about your decisions. Please, do what feels right for you … It's a loving thing for you to do for Mom …'

When I returned to Margaret River we spoke via Skype and Jenny said she was in counselling about her wall, had been diagnosed with severe depression, and was on medication. The depression was linked to The Family Drama, but we didn't dig into that pile of manure.

After this Skype talk, our only method of communication became occasional text messages. What a contrast to our previous long talks and rambling emails. It felt like Jenny's ship was sailing away, and I was on the dock, watching it head toward the horizon, not quite out of view.

I tried to rationalise Jenny's behaviour. The conversations I had with myself went something like: 'Jenny needs this separation so she can become her own person, declare her independence from The Family Drama. Maybe she should stay away from you? Not be reminded of what destroyed her life and happiness as a teenager? If that helps her live a happy life, then sail, Jenny, sail!'

But, of course, that was nonsense, and I knew it.

December 2013 and January 2014 were a blur of misery. Nothing made sense. There were occasional rays of sunshine from the odd text message. But even this silver lining was sucked up into storm clouds:

Richard: Hope you're ok Jenny. I'm worried about you. Thinking of flying over for a quick hello and hug. I presume no chance of a short break for you down here?

Jenny: Dad I'm still not sure when I can visit but I am certain that you visiting here would be a very bad idea. It would put me in the worst position imaginable.

The worst position imaginable? If I greet Jenny with a hello and a hug, it would put her in the worst position imaginable? Why? Because Jenny's boundaries were shattered. She couldn't navigate through The Family Drama in a way that allowed her freedom of contact with both parents. This spoke to the ripple effect, the storm effect, of hate in her life. Which flew in the face of Jenny's naturally loving instincts.

Jenny loves her mother and her father, as she should. But in her effort to sustain these loving relationships, I think she capsized into depression. She lost her grip on the tiller handle, navigating between the separate realities of her mother and her father, in the storm of The Family Drama.

This drama stole her life at fifteen years of age, when she lost her wonderful school life and friends in Australia. This intelligent girl suddenly woke up in Prairie Grove, Arkansas. And dumped her anger and despair into hundreds of pages of *Vertigo*, her novel about Claire, a teenage girl who blinks, then falls through the earth. In an instant, Claire vanishes from the joy, warmth and safety of friends on a school excursion in an Australian eucalypt forest, and wakes to a barren, unpleasant and incomprehensible life.

In February 2015, I felt so distressed by Jenny's silence, I flew to

Arkansas. When I walked, unannounced, into the bookshop where she now worked, her shocked and happy smile, her shout of 'Dad!' and her rush to hug me, was – and still is – the best moment of my life.

Jenny has since moved into her own apartment and loves her bookshop work, and helping edit a literary magazine. I try to connect with her weekly via WhatsApp. I sense Jenny's trying to find her own feet, follow her own drumbeat, after the trauma of the last eleven years. I hope that one day she will visit Australia; however, that seems a step too far for her, at the moment.

Jenny has good reason to set strong boundaries around how she builds her own independent life. However, I grieve at no longer being close to her. And agonise over how she must have suffered throughout her young life, and after leaving Australia. And I'm haunted by what may have been missed opportunities. Did I turn Jenny away in 2011 – did she want to stay in Australia? Should Suzanne and I have responded differently in 2013? My heart rips when I contemplate these possibilities. I physically buckle.

Jenny, I hope that before too long you can visit your home here in Margaret River, smell the eucalypts, marvel at the blue sky, savour the dry fresh air, watch the odd kangaroo hop by the kitchen window, and raise a glass of the 1991 cabernet sauvignon I've been saving all these years. In the meantime, I toast your independence and wish you love and happiness.

Further Reading

Following is a short list of selected titles for interested readers on the subject matters contained in my story:

- *The Memory Illusion, Remembering, Forgetting, and the Science of False Memory*, Julia Shaw, Random House, 2016
- *We Believe The Children, A Moral Panic In The 1980s*, Richard Beck, Public Affairs, 2015
- *Sybil Exposed, The Extraordinary Story Behind the Famous Multiple Personality Case*, Debbie Nathan, Free Press, 2011
- *My Lie, A True Story of False Memory*, Meredith Maran, Jossey-Bass, 2010
- *Outbreak! The Encyclopedia of Extraordinary Social Behavior*, Hilary Evans and Robert Bartholomew, Anomalist Books, 2009
- *Try To Remember, Psychiatry's Clash Over Meaning, Memory, and Mind*, Paul R. McHugh, Dana Press, 2008
- *The Day Care Ritual Abuse Moral Panic*, Mary de Young, McFarland & Company, 2004
- *Satan's Silence, Ritual Abuse and the Making of a Modern American Witch Hunt*, Debbie Nathan and Michael Snedeker, Authors Choice Press, 2001
- *Creating Hysteria*, Women and Multiple Personality Disorder, Joan Acocella, Jossey-Bass, 1999
- *Lost Daughters, Recovered Memory Therapy & the People It Hurts*, Reinder Van Til, William B. Eerdmans Publishing Company, 1997
- *Hoax and Reality: The Bizarre World of Multiple Personality Disorder*, August Piper, Jr, Jason Aronson Inc. 1997

- *Victims of Memory, Sex Abuse Accusations and Shattered Lives*, Mark Pendergrast, Upper Access, 1996
- *Diagnosis for Disaster, The Devastating Truth About False Memory Syndrome and Its Impact on Accusers and Families*, Claudette Wassil-Grimm, The Overlook Press, 1996
- *Remembering Satan, A Tragic Case of Recovered Memory*, Lawrence Wright, Vintage Books, 1995
- *The Myth Of Repressed Memory, False Memories And Allegations Of Sexual Abuse*, Elizabeth Loftus And Katherine Ketcham, St Martins Press, 1994
- *Making Monsters, False Memories, Psychotherapy and Sexual Hysteria*, Richard Ofshe and Ethan Watters, University Of California Press, 1994

Appendices

Following are five therapeutic assessments of Elizabeth prepared by a clinical psychologist, social workers and an occupational therapist, when she was three and four years old.

Appendix 1

Report by Dr Paul Schwartz,
clinical psychologist, Tulsa, Oklahoma:

<u>PAUL J. SCHWARTZ, Ph.D.</u>
LICENSED PSYCHOLOGIST / MARRIAGE AND FAMILY THERAPIST
CLINICAL MEMBER · AMERICAN ASSOCIATION FOR MARRIAGE AND FAMILY THERAPY

<u>SUMMARY OF PSYCHOLOGICAL EVALUATION/CONSULTATION</u>

NAME: Elizabeth Vos
DATE OF BIRTH: 5-19-89 (3 years, 3 months at
                                    time of consultation)
DATE OF EVALUATIONS/CONSULTATIONS: 7-17-92, 7-29-92, 8-5-92, 8-12-92
DATE OF DICTATION/REPORT: 3-7-93

<u>REFERRAL STATEMENT AND RELEVANT BACKGROUND INFORMATION:</u>

Elizabeth's parents, Richard and Nika Vos sought this examiner's
assistance in the late spring and summer of 1992 secondary to
concerns that their daughter may have been sexually abused or
molested. The intake which was initiated by Mrs. Vos on 7/14/92, and
written down by this examiner's office manager, Debra, Mrs. Vos
indicated that her daughter was possibly molested by another little
boy child. When the parents came in on 7/18/92 and completed the
application form they indicated that "Some of Elizabeth's reactions,
play, comments have made us concerned she may have been abused by one
or several caretakers in her past."

The parents had provided this examiner with about fifteen or sixteen
pages of typed notes based upon their observations of their
daughter's behavior which include some of the following behaviors:
masturbation, talking about monsters coming out of holes,
constructing of various play objects, discussing secrets, French-
kissing, talking about a blue man and a red man, changes in her
personality and mood involving hysterical crying and fits,
nightmares, regressive behaviors, playthings involving violence and
killing people, changes to a low pain threshold, etc. The mother
indicated to this examiner, and as so observed on these pages/notes
she continued to involve her daughter in frequent questioning periods
and sessions and the mother acknowledges in some instances she was
very frustrated and anxious because of her daughter's behavior and
responses to her questions.

The parents indicate that Elizabeth had related to them, in the past,
when she was attending a pre-school, that a boy poked her in the
genital area with a gun and that at another time, at home, a boy
poked her in the stomach and the genital area and that Elizabeth
tended to freak out and exhibit a major overreaction. While she was

Vos, Elizabeth
Page Two

out of this pre-school environment when this examiner saw her, the
mother and father continued to question where she learned some of
these behaviors from and whether she in fact learned from some boys
(▆▆▆ and ▆▆▆) or a baby-sitter named ▆▆▆▆▆   Elizabeth had
alluded to, at a previous time that one of the directors of the pre-
school was doing things to her and/or that ▆▆▆was doing things
to her like French-kissing and/or one of the boys, ▆▆▆ or ▆▆▆,
were doing things to her. The parents are uncertain as whether all
of these individuals had sexually abused their daughter. At a later
time the mother continued to be very concerned (and seemingly
somewhat obsessed) with the fact that she felt her daughter was being
ritually sexually abused and that there was occult activity and
possible child pornography also going on. The mother's observations
continued to reaffirm that her daughter's behavior fitted this
pattern and she provided data from a book (Out Of Darkness) regarding
signs and symptoms of ritualistic abuse in children.

I received a letter from the father a day or two after we had a
follow up conference in August and the father indicated that both he
and his wife had apparently come away from the conference with
different understandings about this examiner's opinion. The parents
also indicated that both he and his wife had sought counselling with
Dr. Thomas Dohne, Ph.D. a clinical psychologist in Bartlesville.

The parents also presented information indicating that there were
numerous family changes and stresses which had occurred over the past
several months and year and they were uncertain whether any one of
these were also affecting Elizabeth (difficult pregnancy with younger
sister, Jennifer, Elizabeth's ear surgery causing a frightening
experience with anesthesia "black mask"), inappropriate play with
older boys at day care center, etc.

OFFICE OBSERVATIONS:

This examiner had an opportunity to observe and interact with
Elizabeth over three separate occasions, 7/29/92, 8/5/92 and 8/10/92.
For the most part Elizabeth presented herself as a rather normal and
healthy young girl and there were no extreme signs of emotional
lability, or inhibition. No thought disorder was suspected and her
overall reality contact appeared intact as she was well oriented to
time, place and person. She was generally cooperative relative to
her age with normal and fluctuating degrees of interest and
motivation with regard to the questions and tasks presented to her.
She generally presented herself as a rather bright, verbal and

Vos, Elizabeth
Page Three

sociable young girl though there were normal degrees of shyness and
anxiousness noted during initial separation from the parent that
brought her.

Various free play time was afforded Elizabeth and she took advantage
of this in a rather normal and healthy way and no unusual play
patterns were observed in her interactions with the dolls or
dollhouse or its contents.

In response to questions, Elizabeth did indicate that she attended a
pre-school and the people there were named Ms. ▇▇▇▇ and Ms.▇▇▇▇
and that they were nice to her and she did not provide any data
suggesting they were mean or hurt her in any way. With additional
questioning Elizabeth denies that her mother or father were ever mean
to her or did anything nasty to her. She did indicate on one
occasion that she had a baby-sitter named ▇▇▇▇ and that she was not
nice though she did not clarify as to why. She stated that later
that ▇▇▇▇ poked her in the nose, eyes and arm in response to this
examiner's (intentional) leading questions again suggesting that
Elizabeth basically wanted to please this examiner and answered yes
to anything presented. However, when asked if ▇▇▇▇ ever touched
her or poked her in her vaginal area ("tee tee") she stated no.
There was some normal evasiveness and unresponsiveness noted in that
Elizabeth tended to become rather frustrated with all of the
questions presented.

At a later time and session Elizabeth did acknowledge that ▇▇▇▇ and
▇▇▇▇ two boys that she knows, touched her in her tee tee area with
their hands and some magic marker drawings indicated scribbling and
interpretations that ▇▇▇▇ and ▇▇▇▇ hurt her. When this examiner
asked her if one of her pre-school directors (Ms. ▇▇▇▇) chops off
heads she stated, "Yes." Then she talked about a "blue school."

In another session she brought in some of her Barbie dolls and play
objects. Several questions were directed to her over this session,
some involving specific questions such as asking her if anybody ever
touched her vaginal area or tee tee and she stated, "No." She did
indicate that she wouldn't go back to the pre-school because they are
mean over there and that "They poke me" though she did not provide
any more specific answers and tended to become distracted and
disinterested in further questioning. Some puppet play was initiated
and this did not yield anything significant.

There were several opportunities for this examiner to talk with the

Vos, Elizabeth
Page Four

parents at the beginning or end of one or more of these sessions and
this examiner's notes indicate that on several occasions this
examiner cautioned the parents, particularly the mother, not to
continue to ask their daughter ongoing questions or overreacting to
Elizabeth's behavior.

DIAGNOSTIC SUMMARY:

As this examiner had already indicated to the parents, I did not find
any significant clinical support to confirm that Elizabeth Vos was
sexually abused and molested by any adult. It seems Elizabeth had
told this examiner on one or more occasions and her parents that she
was touched around her genital area by two boys, ▬▬▬ and ▬▬▬
and this may be the most specific and consistent/reliable data this
examiner has though again considering the age of these young boys one
would not interpret this as being sexual abuse, but more in the line
of "inappropriate or excessive sexual play between children."
Whether this was a factor which initiated some overreaction and
anxiety with this young girl is uncertain though the parents confirm
that at home when a boy poked her in the stomach and genital area she
"freaked out" and had a major overreaction and this may further
confirm that some of Elizabeth's inappropriate behaviors secondary to
these experiences with one or more boys on one or more occasions,
whether at home or at pre-school.

I also indicated to the parents that realizing this young girl's age
that it is very difficult if not impossible to elicit consistent
information even if something inappropriate did occur. I also
indicated to the parents I felt there was possibly some degree of
contamination and continued to prompt the parents to monitor
Elizabeth's behavior and keep notes though refrain from asking her
questions which this examiner felt was over done by the mother. It
is uncertain as to what degree of Elizabeth's behavior and responses
were related to her "desire to please her mother" based upon the
mother's questioning. The father expressed some concerns as to
whether his wife was overreacting to what was going on and whether
she was convinced that their daughter was being involved in some type
of ritualistic sexual abuse or some occult activity.

I had indicated to both parents, in the follow up consultation
session that while I was not in a position to totally or 100% rule
out that Elizabeth was being sexually abused, on the other hand I was
not in a position to state that she was, in fact, being abused by
anyone other than, again, indications that one or two boys may have

Vos, Elizabeth
Page Five

been sexually inappropriate with Elizabeth. While many of the
behaviors described by the mother and father as being manifested by
Elizabeth were of a concern to this examiner there was nothing
specific which would lead this examiner to believe that anyone at her
pre-school had in fact clearly molested her or involved her in any
type of occult or pornographic situations. There were too many
inconsistencies and/or not enough specific information to warrant any
ongoing suspicions to whether her previous baby-sitter, ███████ had
molested her or engaged in some type of "French-kissing" with
Elizabeth.

I had indicated to the parents that they are, of course, free to
consult with any other therapist or professional if they wanted to
further determine whether their daughter was sexually abused. I had
also indicated that they need to be careful in questioning and
monitoring Elizabeth's behavior so as not to increase her fear and
anxiety and that the best therapy was to provide a safe and stable
and nurturing home environment.

Paul J. Schwartz, Ph.D.
Licensed Psychologist and
Family Therapist/LMFT

PJS:sj/A-1

Appendix 2
Report by Faye Hegburg,
Licensed Social Worker, Bartlesville, Oklahoma:

Faye R. Hegburg, L.S.W.

TO WHOM IT MAY CONCERN:

At the request of the parents of Elizabeth Vos, the
following is a summary of my contact with her.

Richard and Niki Vos first came to see me on 8-13-92.
Niki spoke of her concern that three-year-old Elizabeth
had been sexually abused. She seemed to have a growing
conviction that Elizabeth had been a victim of ritualized
abuse. Niki presented photographs and notes she had kept
regarding Elizabeth's behavior to support and demonstrate
as much as possible the sources of her concern.

Richard and Niki had recently taken Elizabeth to see Paul
Schwartz, Ph. D., in Tulsa. Reportedly, Dr. Schwartz
informed the parents that he could not confirm that
Elizabeth had been sexually abused. Niki stated that she
could not feel confident of his conclusions.

Richard appeared reluctant to endorse Niki's dismissal of
Dr. Schwartz's opinions or to completely agree with her
conclusions about ritual abuse. Richard described various
stressors and influences experienced by Elizabeth and the
family over the past year that he felt could account for
Elizabeth's behavior. Primary among those factors were:
Niki's pregnancy with younger sister Jennifer during which
she was often ill and unavailable to Elizabeth;
Elizabeth's frequent ear infections which led to surgery;
Niki's and Richard's health conditions which finally led
them to a diagnosis of Chronic Fatigue Syndrome;
Elizabeth's bad experience with two older boys in a day
care center; and Elizabeth's frequent use of videos for
entertainment.

Richard and Niki clearly wanted to do what is best for
Elizabeth, but did not necessarily agree what that may be.
In discussion, we agreed that I would begin to see
Elizabeth in play therapy, keeping in mind both parents'
concerns. I clearly stated my role with Elizabeth to be
that of therapist, not investigator.

I first met with Elizabeth on 9-4-92 when her mother
brought her in for a get-acquainted visit. Niki agreed
that she may never know with certainty what kind of trauma
Elizabeth may have experienced and, therefore, our guide
would be Elizabeth's progress.

My first session with Elizabeth was on 9-9-92. We read
the first part of *A Very Touching Book* and talked about

Faye R. Hegburg, L.S.W.

Page: 2

feelings and types of touching. Elizabeth then explored
the play room. She was comfortable, open and engaged. At
the end of the session, I spoke with Niki, cautioning her
that, at some point, Elizabeth would become confrontive in
therapy.

In the next session on 9-16-92, Elizabeth was agreeable to
her mother leaving the building for the therapy hour.
Elizabeth played with the doll house and family becoming
the "protector" of the baby. When it was time to leave,
she resisted leaving the "baby" doll. She ran to Niki,
crying about the "baby". Niki seemed to be upset,
thinking that Elizabeth's reaction was because she had
left her.

My next session with Elizabeth was on 9-23-92. Niki
stated that Elizabeth had no nightmares in the past week.
Elizabeth was agreeable to Niki's leaving again, which
became the pattern thereafter. She played almost
exclusively with the sand tray, hiding the doll house
family in the sand.

I borrowed anatomical dolls to have available for
Elizabeth's visit on 9-30-92. She went to the dolls
immediately upon seeing them. After undressing the adult
female and boy dolls, she inserted her finger in the
doll's vagina and talked about "wiggling her fingers in
her teetee." She stated that _____ and _____ (two 5 year
old boys at day care) showed her how to do this. She
named the two male dolls _____ and _____ and "put them in
jail" for the remainder of the session.

Elizabeth continued this theme in her next session on
10-7-92. She also used hand puppets play monsters, again
using the boys' names. Elizabeth used the gun and knife
to shoot and cut the necks of the monsters. She continued
to use the knife and gun in subsequent sessions, asking me
to pretend to be a monster and then "killing" me.

These themes continued in sessions on 10-14, 10-21 and
10-28-92. In our session on 11-4-92, Elizabeth's play did
not incorporate "killing the monsters." She began to
play with the kitchen toys, talked about "Elizabeth being
happy." In puppet play she did not use the shark, as
usual, but chose the lamb, butterfly and kitten. After a
similar session on 11-11-92, I suggested to Niki that we
may think about terminating around the end of December if
Elizabeth continued such progress. Niki's experience of
Elizabeth at home was to see her being more playful, less
guarded and preoccupied.

Faye R. Hegburg, L.S.W.

Page 3

Before entering the play room with Elizabeth on 11-18-92, Niki stated that Elizabeth had told her about "being hurt by the bad people" and encouraged Elizabeth to tell me. I asked Elizabeth if she wanted to tell me something and she gave an evasive answer. She resumed some of her "killing the monsters" play theme, threw toys around the room and refused to help pick-up at the end of the session. She also returned to an earlier play theme of burying things in the sand.

In subsequent sessions on 12-2, 12-9, 12-16, 12-23 and 12-29, Elizabeth resumed play with the kitchen toys, began to use other toys for the first time including games, puzzles and books. At the present, she most often chooses to play with the familiar games shouting "I win!" as she successfully completes the task. Her parents continue to report that her behavior at home is "happier, more loving and lovable, more trusting and less terrified."

Even so, Niki's concern has not abated as she continues to review possible scenarios about what might have happened to Elizabeth. This concern seems to be fueled by two factors: 1) Niki's desire to respond to Elizabeth's trauma in ways to promote healing, and 2) her observations about Elizabeth's behavior and statements that support one scenario or the other. Niki has researched various resources that may help her answer her questions. At different times, this effort has been more or less of a team effort for her and Richard. They continue to see and interpret Elizabeth's actions in different frameworks, but seem to be accepting of the validity of each other's motives and goals.

I have met with both Richard and Niki on a regular basis throughout the time I have seen Elizabeth in therapy. We have discussed their parenting concerns and kept each other informed about Elizabeth's progress. My concern for Elizabeth at this point is that we allow her to recover according to her needs and at her pace. If we burden her with our adult need to understand and "know", we may keep the trauma alive for her.

Please feel free to contact me if there is any way I may be of assistance.

Respectfully yours,

Faye Hegburg, LSW, LMFT

FW/db

Appendix 3

Report by Veronica Oliver-Bell, Licensed
Clinical Social Worker, Oklahoma City, Oklahoma:

July 7, 1993

I have consulted with Niki and Richard Vos regarding their four
year old daughter Elizabeth. I have met primarily with Ms. Vos.
I have reviewed her notes and Mr. Vos' note regarding their
observations of Elizabeth and have reviewed reports by other
professionals and talked with Elizabeth's current therapist
Barbara Tillman, L.C.S.W. I have also interviewed Elizabeth.
The evaluation process was still in progress when the Vos'
received word that they would be transferred to Australia. I
prepared this summary in order to provide information that
hopefully would be helpful to Elizabeth's therapist in Australia.

This case is very complex. At this point in time it difficult to
reach a clear understanding of what has happened to Elizabeth,
although her behavioral symptoms as reported by her parents and
therapist are consistent with significant emotional trauma. I
will briefly present information from the parents and the
conclusions of other professionals consulted before presenting my
observations.

Elizabeth has made many disclosures--direct and indirect--to her
mother about being hurt physically and sexually by bad people and
monsters. Elizabeth's disclosures to her mother over the past 9-
12 months are unusual and bizarre and reflect rage, confusion,
terror, obsessive themes, and poor self-esteem. Among the
statements recorded in Ms. Vos' journal are the following:
        animals and people being hurt and killed;
        Elizabeth being thrown into cold water
        Elizabeth being tied to a tree
        Elizabeth being "cooked" and "cut up"
        Elizabeth having her legs and arms cut off
        Elizabeth being forced to eat and drink urine, feces and
blood
        Elizabeth being given "bad medicine"
        Elizabeth being hurt in her tee-tee (vagina) and bottom
(rectum)
        Extreme fear of family and herself being killed.
        Confusion about who her family is
        Confusion about whether she is loved
        Confusion about what is real and what isn't
        Reference to multiple locations where these events occurred
such as the "blue house", "naughty school" and "jail."

Reference to multiple perpetrators and multiple victims. (With regard to perpetrators, she has named specific people who were baby sitters).

On occasion Elizabeth has stated that her father, her mother, and grandparents have done things, or she fears they will do things, to hurt her, which they deny and appear to be untrue. Although these are isolated statements, they suggest that there are some elements of fantasy and/or generalized fear woven into Elizabeth's disclosures. Because of this aspect and Elizabeth's confusion about her family and what is real and what isn't, one has to consider that Elizabeth has a long term problem with reality testing. Yet none of the professionals that interviewed Elizabeth noted there was any indication of poor reality testing. Due to Elizabeth's young age it is recommended that when she is six months to a year older that she be given a battery of psychological tests in order to more specifically explore the issue of her reality testing. From a child development point of view, it is unlikely that Elizabeth would fantasize the type of events she describes because children of her age rarely fantasize about being powerless and victimized. In addition, it's unlikely that she would have such complex and detailed fantasies over and over if they did not have psychological meaning for her in her current life situation. Children do not tend to fantasize outside of their experience. Her parents have noted that Elizabeth has spent a significant amount of time watching videos and may be preoccupied with themes that occur in some of the videos. Although exposure to some of the videos may contribute to her embellishing some of her memories, it would not in and of itself explain the significant behavioral and emotional changes in Elizabeth.

Another developmental issue that complicates this case is Elizabeth's age. It is likely that any abuse she suffered occurred before the age of three. Although research supports that children as young as 2 1/2 can accurately recall traumatic events, it is usually fragments that are recalled. Thus her ability to remember, accurately recall and verbalize is limited to some degree by her young age. It may never be possible to fit these fragments into a meaningful account.

Another issue is that the family has had several stresses over the past two years including Elizabeth having tubes placed in her ears under anesthesia, Ms. Vos' difficult pregnancy, and the birth of a younger sister. It would not appear that these kinds of stresses would explain the kinds of disclosures she has made. They might explain some of her obsessive themes such as stating that she is pregnant, having babies and being extremely concerned about protecting her "babies".

Dr. Paul Schwartz, Ph.D., who was the first to evaluate Elizabeth

2

thought Elizabeth might have been involved in excessive and
sexually inappropriate sex play with two older boys at preschool
but found no consistent evidence that any adult had physically or
sexually abused her.   Dr. Linda Doyle, Elizabeth's regular
pediatrician, concluded that although there was no evidence of
vaginal trauma, her multiple episodes of vaginal irritation and
vulvitis and geographic tongue, in conjunction with her history
of behavioral and emotional problems, led her to conclude she had
been sexually abused.   Faye Hegburg, L.S.W. saw Elizabeth for
weekly play therapy from 09/04/92 to 12/29/92.   She did not state
a definite opinion but implies that based on Elizabeth's
statements she was sexually traumatized by two boys at her
preschool.   Her current therapist, Barbara Tillman (February,
1993-June, 1993), indicated that Elizabeth's behaviors toward her
in early sessions were suggestive of sexual abuse.   Elizabeth
repeatedly tried to kiss her on the mouth, tried to undress in
front of her, wanted Ms. Tillman to undress, and tried to lick
Ms. Tillman.   Ms. Tillman felt Elizabeth had been influenced by
too much questioning and interaction with her mother and a lack
of consistent limit setting.   As a result of these factors, she
could not reach any conclusion about the nature of Elizabeth's
trauma.   She described Elizabeth's behavior in early sessions as
extremely destructive, agitated, out of control, and marked by
serious difficulties with boundaries.   Elizabeth did not disclose
any specific or clear information about physical or sexual abuse.
Ms. Tillman believed Elizabeth improved over the course of
therapy primarily because she set clear limits during therapy and
encouraged the parents to do so at home.   She believed that
Elizabeth had been allowed far too much freedom and lacked
appropriate limits at home.   Dr. Block, state child abuse medical
examiner, examined Elizabeth in April and found no physical
evidence of sexual abuse.

I saw Elizabeth on 04/06/93.   She separated easily and appeared
comfortable in interacting with me.   She was quite verbal.   She
introduced herself as Laura and maintained this throughout the
session.   She would correct me if I called her Elizabeth.   She
first played in the sand tray and showed more than normal
interest in the plastic spiders and snakes.   She insisted that
she was going to take one of the snakes home.   She did a lot of
burying of a "babysitter" and a child.   She said babysitters are
"yucky" and "mean."   She wanted to play with the puppets.   I
pretended to be a turtle who was hurt and scared and she was a
rabbit who befriended the turtle.   During this play she
spontaneously disclosed that monsters threw her in bad water,
tied her up and tried to cut her.   She said they hurt her tee tee
and bottom.   She said the monsters were in a blue house and they
wore costumes.   She said they also hurt others kids and some of
those kids went to heaven.   Then the judge sends everyone to
hell.   The monsters have knives and cut up bodies and cook them.
She said her mom helped her by "turning me back into myself."
When I said I didn't understand, she said she used to think she

3

wasn't real. Throughout these disclosures she said, "They don't believe me. They don't think I'm telling the truth." She seemed very worried that her story would not be believed. Elizabeth's disclosures did not occur in response to direct questioning from me but were spontaneous and emotionally congruent. It is surprising that she does not appear to have made similar disclosures to any of the other professionals involved although they all saw her for longer periods of time.

It is my opinion based on my contacts with the family and my review of the records that Elizabeth has been seriously traumatized. Due to her sexual acting out I believe the trauma was at least in part due to sexual abuse. It is highly unlikely that her story could have been maintained over time as vividly as it has if it was not based on personal experience. The bizarre nature of her disclosures are consistent with documented disclosures of alleged ritual or sadistic abuse cases involving multiple perpetrators and multiple victims. Thus, it is important to explore the possibility of ritual abuse and try to reach some determination regarding its validity. As a result of repeated questioning it may be that Elizabeth has embellished some of her story. Nonetheless her story cannot in my opinion be dismissed because her mother questioned her in an understandable attempt to learn why her daughter was behaving strangely. Elizabeth has improved as more structure and consistency has been provided both at home and in therapy. Clearly she would benefit from ongoing therapy aimed at understanding the nature of the trauma if possible and processing and integrating the trauma. It may also be helpful for her to be involved in a therapeutic preschool program if one is available in the town they live in in Australia.

Sincerely,

Licensed Clinical Social Worker
Board Certified Diplomate in Clinical Social Work

Appendix 4
Report by Barbara Tillman,
Licensed Social Worker, Bartlesville, Oklahoma:

Barbara A. Tillman
██████████████████████
██████████████████████

July 12, 1993

To Whom It May Concern:

I first met Niki and Richard Vos, the natural parents of Elizabeth, on January 6, 1993. The presenting concern was that Elizabeth, then 3 1/2, DOB 5/19/89, may have been a victim of ritualistic sexual abuse.

Both the mother and father kept extensive daily accounts of the child's behavior, responses, interactions. On the the second visit they presented me with hundreds of pages of this journaled, detail information dating to July, 1992.

Elizabeth had seen Paul Schwartz, PHD, in July and August, 1992; and had been in therapy with Faye Hegburg, LSW, from September to December, 1992. Dr. Schwartz wrote an evaluation in March, 1993, and indicated the behaviors described by Mrs. Vos were of "concern but there was nothing to lead that examiner to believe that anyone in pre-school had molested her or involved her in any occult or pornographic situation." He indicated that as early as July, 1992, he clearly cautioned the parents from questioning and monitoring her behavior so as not to add to her anxiety.

The second therapist, Faye Hegburg, saw both parents and Elizabeth on a weekly basis. Some themes were played out and abandoned by Elizabeth in lieu of more appropriate play. She did tell of two boys, five years old, at pre-school showing her how to wiggle her finger in her "tee-tee" (vagina).

By the time the parents came to me, the mother was convinced that her child was a victim of ritualistic abuse - possibly part of child pornography ring. She suspected one and all - baby-sitters, day care providers in and out of the home, even the natural father at times. The more she read the more symptomatic behavior she identified and was compelled to find out from the child and allowed the child behavior to go boundless and out of control.

I began to evaluate on the basis of real knowledge. This is a 41 year old mother, second marriage, 43 year old father, second marriage. Both, by their own admission, highly dysfunctional families of origin. They met in a chronic fatigue syndrome support group and were married four months later. Initially Niki believed she could not get pregnant, got pregnant shortly after the marriage. She had a difficult pregnancy with Elizabeth. The child was born and had an early history of ear problems and was repeatedly treated with antibiotics. At age 14 1/2 months experienced yeast infections. At age 21 months tubes were placed in her ears. While she was put under with a mask over her face. At 18 months old the mother got pregnant with second child and the pregnancy was even more difficult. Niki was often unavailable to Elizabeth who was often placed in day care. Jenny was born when Elizabeth was 2 years, 4 months. Mom's time was more in demand with the new baby. Elizabeth now demanded that Mom breast feed her as well as her sister. Mom was still breast feeding Elizabeth she came to see me when Elizabeth was 3 1/2 years old. It was a means of soothing the child.

Traumatized at 21 months, spending a great deal of time away from mother due to the complicated second pregnancy. Now the baby's demands, and her being 2 1/2 years old, Elizabeth entered the normal time of exploring and independence, assertiveness and aggression.

As I read and listened and saw that there were no boundaries set for this child, all behavior was considered interpretive of ritualistic abuse, she was allowed to be in the house in winter nude or came to the office twice a week in summer plastic shoes or barefoot even in the ice and snow in a summer dress. The writings spoke of being allowed to destroy her and families property such as figurines or Christmas balls as an expression of her anxieties. Mother was continuing to play the investigative role, overwhelmed by her conviction that her child was a victim of abuse.

The father's writings were more reflective of the same incidents in more normal explanation, outgrownths maybe of discussions with the child of videos that she had seen or experiences of the day or week.

I indicated to both Mr. and Mrs. Vos that information that Elizabeth could share would be highly contaminated by the questioning, investigative approach that the mother took. I would listen and be open to concerns that I would encounter. This was difficult for the mother who wanted desperately to have her theory supported and I could not do so.

Elizabeth came twice weekly starting with January 27, 1993, through the middle of May, 1993. Initially her behavior was difficult to control. She would bite, lick me, pull at my hair or clothes. I needed to remove my jewelry before she came in. I set limits for her in the room. She was more open and respectful and took pleasure from respecting those limits. We read books even on monsters like "Lemont, the Friendly Monster". I encouraged the parents strongly to cooperate to (1) set limits at home; (2) to follow them consistently; (3) if, in fact, Elizabeth had been abused, the mother had been sufficiently empathetic to her trauma and now needed to abstain from any further questionings and allow her to heal and grow. (4) That Mr. and Mrs. Vos needed to work as a team with a common goal visible to the children. (5) Spend some quality time as the days were non-ending the mother was now exhausted but they both still wrote in their daily journal. (6) I reinforced this message several times to Mrs. Vos who called a national abuse hot line and confirmed my approach to the child was therapeutic and correct. Later she still continued to seek confirmation for her belief, going to see Cecelia Owen Beckhams, MSW, in Oklahoma City, who was more supportive of her concerns.

In summary, my evaluation of Elizabeth is that she is a bright 4 year old who has experienced trauma: successive ear infections, yeast infections, being put to sleep to put her tubes in, experiencing the mother's difficult pregnancy and birth when she was 2 years 4 months. The traumas, compiled with being 2 1/2, caused agressive, demanding behavior. This was then interpreted by the mother more and more daily in light of ritualistic abuse, which fed her anxieties with no boundaries on her demands or actions her behavior became more and more out of control. With reinforcement of the boundaries first in the office and then at home, normalcy returned to this happy bright 4 year old who became a pleasure to both mother and father to deal with.

Barbara A. Tillman
ACSW, LSW

Appendix 5

Report by Helen Davidson, Senior Occupational
Therapist / Psychiatry, Perth, Australia:

OUTPATIENT SHEET
(INCLUDING ACCIDENT & EMERGENCY)

Med Rec. N°:	C5603457
Surname:	VOS
Forename:	Elizabeth
Sex:	F D.O.B. 19/5/89

AFFIX LABEL HERE

Date	NOTES: (All entries should be dated and signed)

Elizabeth has been seen for play therapy since October 1993, having been referred by Dr Geoff Dixon, Consultant Psychiatrist. The Vos family had been referred to Dr Dixon on their arrival in Perth, having had both psychiatric assessments and therapy for Elizabeth in the United States.

I have seen Elizabeth for weekly play sessions of 45 minutes, commencing the end of October, 1993 in blocks of 6 sessions, with a parental review at the conclusion of each block. The sessions are unstructured, where Elizabeth is free to direct the play herself, with my role being observer of themes and content of the play, her mood and emotions displayed throughout, and the process by which she chooses to engage myself in the various themes enacted. Emotions displayed are reflected back to Elizabeth along the lines of a humanistic client – centred model of acceptance of the child's cognitions and feelings, rather than in an interpretative way aimed at promoting insight.

Elizabeth presents as a very friendly, warm child who relates enthusiastically and confidently to adults. Her verbal skills reflect a capable child who is able to organize her thoughts and relate them with clarity in a mature manner.

Elizabeth is very organized in her play and has clear and definite ideas about the way she wishes anyone playing with her to be involved. She is very assertive with adults, but is also able to negotiate if she senses some resistance, rather than being bossy and commanding, treating the adult in an instrumental way, as is sometimes seen with very assertive children.

The themes of Elizabeth's play centre around children becoming sick, mother's giving birth, mother's nurturing, sibling competing for their mother's attention, father being at work or dead, and animals being lost or buried in snow or sand. Some of these themes do relate to some of Elizabeth's own experiences, particularly the illness and the birth of a sibling and the rivalry and sense of displacement she may have experienced at the time.

Initially, there was an intensity about the way some of the play themes were repetitively re-enacted, particularly the birth and the burying where the "playfulness" was lost, and I felt indicated some anxiety and conflict. However, latterly, Elizabeth's play has been less intense, with an easy flow between themes which have had a greater variety of imaginative scenes which reflect more variation in mood, feelings and outcomes.

Elizabeth has made reference on a couple of occasions to children being hurt or harmed by adults, but was not comfortable with any reflections I made concerning her anxiety around this and generally retracted the statements, claiming they were "just an expression". Elizabeth's mood and affect at the time gave me a sense that this represented more than the age appropriate capacity for reality orientation and separating out "make believe" from fact. However, I would not wish to overstate this, nor draw conclusions with reference to past experiences, but merely acknowledge that Elizabeth has seemed careful not to play out destructive themes whilst with me in contrast to her play at home which has had repetitive themes of death and violence with much dialogue concerning this.

OUTPATIENT SHEET

Date	NOTES: (All entries should be dated and signed)

When Elizabeth first presented she also steadfastly refused to do any drawing, painting or expressive work, which was a little unusual for someone of her age and also because she so willing played in a structured manner. When she did use some clay later on it was in a regressive, smearing style which was immature and not entirely age-appropriate, particularly when contrasted with her other well organised free play. However, recently she requested to do some clay work which was very age-appropriate and similarly, she has requested to draw and paint with good outcomes.

At times Elizabeth is hypervigilant around the content of adults' conversations and will anxiously attend to words such as "cut" or "hurt", although seemily occupied in play. I feel that reflecting her own safety both presently and in the future needs to be stressed in a non-intrusive way, and that movies or stories which have themes relating to children, adults or animals being harmed, should be avoided as much as possible.

In the near future, I feel it also could be appropriate to help Elizabeth bring a sense of closure to whatever she has experienced in the past, in some sort of symbolic age appropriate way, as discussed previously with her parents.

In summary, Elizabeth has presented throughout as a child who does not relate in a fearful or submissive way to adults, whose mood is predominantly happy, and whose play has been well organised and age appropriate, but with some intensity and themes which reflect some anxiety and conflict. Some of these themes are relevant to her own history of recurrent "strep" throat, and the birth of her younger sibling, Jenny, and the sibling rivalry and sense of displacement she may have experienced at this time. Her denial of themes of harm and hurt once expressed reflects some anxiety, and her responses to words in adults conversation have also indicated a hypervigilance which is based on anxiety.

Some review appointments will be offered to Mr & Mrs Vos with the opportunity for more regular contact if they have concerns about Elizabeth's emotional health.

Hm Davidson

Helen Davidson
SENIOR OCCUPATIONAL THERAPIST / PSYCHIATRY

cc: Parents
Dr Geoff Dixon, Consultant Psychiatrist
Dr Hansen, G.P.
Psychiatry Dept File

Richard Vos was born in Perth, Australia, where he completed high school. He received an honours degree in geology in South Africa and a doctorate in geology in the USA. After two years as a university lecturer and then two years as a geological consultant, he joined US oil giant Phillips Petroleum (now ConocoPhillips) and rose through the corporate hierarchy to become Exploration Manager of Phillips's Australian operations. He led the team that discovered the giant Bayu-Undan gas condensate field in the Timor Sea.

After retiring from corporate life to his farm in Margaret River, Richard pursued other interests, especially furniture making, reading history and work with local volunteer organizations.

Richard is the author of numerous scientific articles. This is his first book.

Email: richard@jarrahpress.com